A Definitive Study of Evidence Concerning John Wesley's Appropriation of the Thought of Clement of Alexandria

A DEFINITIVE STUDY OF EVIDENCE CONCERNING JOHN WESLEY'S APPROPRIATION OF THE THOUGHT OF CLEMENT OF ALEXANDRIA

Neil D. Anderson

Texts and Studies in Religion
Volume 102

The Edwin Mellen Press
Lewiston•Queenston•Lampeter

Library of Congress Cataloging-in-Publication Data

Anderson, Neil D., 1952-
  A definitive study of evidence concerning John Wesley's appropriation of the thought of
Clement of Alexandria / Neil D. Anderson.
    p. cm. -- (Texts and studies in religion ; v. 102)
  Includes bibliographical references and index.
  ISBN 0-7734-6559-6
    1. Wesley, John, 1703-1791. 2. Methodist Church--Doctrines--History. 3. Clement, of
Alexandria, Saint, ca. 150-ca. 215--Influence. I. Title. II. Series.

BX8331.3.A53 2004
287'.092--dc22

                             2003061519

This is volume 102 in the continuing series
Texts and Studies in Religion
Volume 102 ISBN 0-7734-6559-6
TSR Series ISBN 0-88946-976-8

A CIP catalog record for this book is available from the British Library

The Edwin Mellen Press   The Edwin Mellen Press
Box 450   Box 67
Lewiston, New York   Queenston, Ontario
USA 14092-0450   CANADA L0S 1L0

The Edwin Mellen Press, Ltd.
Lampeter, Ceredigion, Wales
UNITED KINGDOM SA48 8LT

Printed in the United States of America

For my parents
James W. and Betty M. Anderson

Table of Contents

Foreword

In the tradition of the extensive scholarly labors of Albert Cook Outler, considerable attention has been given to tracking some of the patristic sources of Wesley's teaching. But in one instance the evidence has been challenging to evaluate, namely, the question of Clement of Alexandria as a source for Wesley.

The specific contours of Wesley's actual use of Clement of Alexandria have remained an enigma. This alleged dependency or correlation is not merely a matter of curious interest, but a significant and intriguing question in contemporary Wesley scholarship, because Wesley himself according to his own attestation utilized Clement of Alexandria in his crucial discussion of Christian perfection.

Neil Anderson of the faculty of Asbury College has undertaken the analysis of this correlation with great skill and acumen, and with a vast knowledge of the relevant sources. The works of Ted Campbell, David Bundy, David C. Ford, and Randy Maddox have opened up various perspectives in the arena of this search, as well as the superb work of Frank Baker and Richard Heitzenrater. Aware of these arguments, Anderson has built his case with patience and diligence from primary sources — both patristic and early Church of England sources — in dialogue with contemporary scholarship. The explicit argumentation developed in chapter five is a tightly knit correlation of the major factors affecting the extent of Wesley's dependence of Wesley upon Clement and differences between them. But these conclusions could not be derived without the explicit grounding of the whole course of argument in the book.

This careful study shows the extent to which Clement's portrait of Christian character is a model for Wesley's writing on The Character of a Methodist, and other texts on Christian perfection. Professor Anderson shows how Wesley was closer to the holiness traditions of ancient Eastern and Alexandrian Christian writers than to Augustine and the West in some respects.

There can be no doubt that Wesley himself regarded Clement of Alexandria's work as very significant to him personally and worthy of adaptation for his audience. It is quite probable that Wesley had a working knowledge of Clement, and that he made his own distinctive applications of all that he considered relevant in Clement to the eighteenth century evangelical revival. There can be little doubt that John and Charles Wesley were profoundly influenced by the renowned Clemens Alexandrinus scholar Archbishop John Potter, whom they regarded as a significant mentor.

Professor Anderson is cautious not to overstate his case, and to set forth the arguable evidences both for and against the claim of a close relation between the substantive thought of Clement and Wesley. Any subsequent attempt to define the relationship between Wesley and the early Christian fathers must take into account this rigorous study by Neil Anderson. Students of Wesley and of the history of the evangelical revivals will revel in numerous unexpected insights concerning the sources of modern evangelical teaching on the holy life.

Thomas C. Oden, Ph.D.
Drew University
Madison, New Jersey

September 3, 2003

Acknowledgements

This book began initially as a Ph.D. dissertation prospectus approved by The Caspersen School of Graduate Studies at Drew University. The idea for it came in the spring semester of 1993 in the form of a term paper produced for Professor Tom Oden's Wesley Seminar. A revision of that paper was read in September of the same year at The Free Methodist Graduate Students Theological Seminar in Indianapolis, Indiana.

I am indebted to the members my doctoral committee at The Caspersen School of Graduate Studies: to Tom Oden for his patient supervision; to Jim Pain for inspiring a profound respect for the Eastern Church Fathers; and to Ken Rowe for responding to the draft of each chapter with corrections and suggestions. The staff of Drew's excellent libraries — The Rose Memorial Library and The Methodist Library and United Methodist Archives and History Center — provided invaluable assistance. The administrative staffs of the libraries at The General Theological Seminary in New York City and New Brunswick Theological Seminary in New Jersey provided access to some important and rare documents. Professor Richard P. Heitzenrater of The Divinity School at Duke University gave helpful information on Wesley's *Oxford Diaries*. Finally, and above all, I owe a debt too great to repay to my wife Darlene, for her loving support and sacrifice over many years.

Introduction

This is a study of the relationship between the thought of John Wesley, an eighteenth century British evangelical who founded the Methodist movement, and Clement of Alexandria, a second century Christian philosopher and catechetical school headmaster. In terms of historical and social location, the distance separating these two could not be greater; but considered in terms of the essence and meaning of the Christian life they hold remarkably similar perspectives.

The thesis argued here is that John Wesley read and drew upon the thought of the revered second century church father Clement of Alexandria in formulating his doctrine of Christian perfection and the experience of holiness of heart and life. The author does not claim that Clement was Wesley's sole or primary theological source, but rather that he was one of Wesley's inspiring repositories for ideas relating to faith, regeneration, perfection, and personal transformation.

The challenge taken up is threefold: (1) to research every possible avenue by which Wesley's self-avowed dependence upon Clement of Alexandria might be proven (or disproved); (2) to unravel some of the complexities of Clement's thought related to Christian experience; and, (3) to identify legitimate connections between Clement's second century Eastern soteriology and Wesley's eighteenth century Methodism.

Chapter 1
Anglicanism and Christian Antiquity

The question of John Wesley's confidence in Clement of Alexandria as a theological source is properly examined in the context of the Anglican Church's overall reliance upon the early church fathers. From its founding under Henry VIII, Anglicanism attempted to establish its authority upon both Scripture and the holy tradition. The appeal to the early church on matters of faith and practice became a pillar in the church's approach to theology. As we survey this aspect of Anglican theological method and identify some its leading representatives, we will attempt to discover a proper background for understanding John Wesley's appeal to the primitive church in general and his reliance upon Clement of Alexandria in particular.

A. The Via Media
Of The Church of England

When John Henry Newman set out in 1828 to investigate the foundations of Anglicanism in the writings of the patristic church, his inquiry led him from a narrow evangelical perspective into the mainstream of Anglican thought. The Anglicanism which Newman discovered (and eventually abandoned in order to embrace Roman Catholicism) had already thrived for three centuries. Newman found that Caroline divines such as James Ussher and John Pearson had established the collective wisdom of the church fathers as a fountainhead for informing the faith and practice in the Church of England.[1] But even prior to the reign of Charles I (1625-49), the Church of England had employed the ancient ecumenical tradition as a theological source for the proper interpretation of Holy Scripture. This move was accomplished under King Henry VIII in the *Ten Articles* of 1536.

Following the Church of England's break with Rome in 1534, Henry and his archbishop Thomas Cranmer sent a delegation of English clergy to Wittenberg to confer with Martin Luther. The purpose of this meeting was to see if any common ground might be found that would lend support for Henry's plan to take control of England's Church away from Rome and the papal magisterium. Edward Fox, Nicholas Heath, and Richard Barnes were sent to represent Henry's interests. The Wittenberg Articles were the result of the collaboration.[2] Though less Protestant than the Lutheran Augsburg Confession, Henry was dissatisfied with the Wittenberg document because it did not provide the balance between Protestant reforms and traditional catholic liturgy that he and Cranmer had hoped.

Upon the delegates' return, Henry had articles drafted that reflected his preference for traditional catholic liturgy and yet maintained his supremacy over the affairs of the church in England. The *Ten Articles*, which remained in effect until 1553, borrowed language from the Wittenberg statement. Lutheran influences are especially noticeable in the articles on justification and the number of the sacraments, but so also are a number of catholic practices that Lutherans clearly rejected.[3] Among its more notable features, the *Ten Articles* established

---

[1]   H. D. Weidner, introduction to *The Via Media of the Anglican Church by John Henry Cardinal Newman* (Oxford: Clarendon Press, 1990), xxiv-xxv.

[2]   See Gerald Bray, ed., *Documents of the English Reformation* (Minneapolis: Fortress Press, 1994), 119-61. Bray provides the original in Latin together with his own translation in a side-by-side format. The introductory notes and analysis (pp. 118-19) are especially good.

[3]   Ibid., 162-74. Cf. also S.L. Greenslade, *The English Reformation and The Fathers of the Church* (Oxford: Clarendon, 1960), 5. There apparently was disagreement over what constituted the

Holy Scripture as the primary source for Anglican faith and practice. The *Ten Articles* also established as a secondary and supporting repository three of Christianity's formative creeds (the Apostles', Nicaean, and Athanasian Creeds respectively), the first four ecumenical councils, and the consensually received teachings of the church fathers.[4]

By and large, the English Reformers viewed the *traditio quinquesecularis*, i.e., the consensually received catholic writers of the first five centuries, as decisive in establishing the true nature and authority of the church.[5] These centuries contained the development of the earliest, most 'primitive church', and therefore they are the most authoritative in determining the true apostolic faith and practices.[6] By limiting the scope of tradition's authority as a sourced for theology to the centuries preceding the rise of Roman authority, the *Ten Articles* not effectively overthrew papal control of England's church and its affairs. It also established a rubric for doing theology that was compatible with a *via media* that appealed to Henry, viz., the middle way between Roman Catholic liturgy and Protestant soteriology.

---

limits of Christian antiquity among English theologians. John Jewel regarded the first six centuries as crucial; the Westminster Conference (1559) set the limit at five centuries.

[4]   See Art. 1, Par. 1 in Bray, *Documents*, 164: "[A]ll bishops and preachers shall instruct and teach our people . . . [to] believe and defend all those things to be true, which be comprehended in the whole body and canon of the Bible, and also in the three creeds, or symbols, whereof one was made by the apostles, . . . the second was made by the holy council of Nicaea, . . . and the third was made by Athanasius, and is comprehended in the Psalm *Quicunque vult;* and that they ought and must take and interpret all the same things according to the selfsame sentence and interpretation, which the words of the selfsame creeds or symbols do purport, and the holy approved doctors of the Church do entreat and defend the same." In paragraph 5 clergy are admonished to condemn all opinions "which were of long time past condemned in the four holy councils, that is to say, in the Council of Nicaea, Constantinople, Ephesus, and Chalcedon, and all others since that time in any point consonant to the same."

[5]   Horton Davies, *From Cranmer to Hooker* (1534-1603), vol. 1, *Worship and Theology in England* (Princeton: Princeton University Press, 1970), 11.

[6]   Wesley often used the phrase 'primitive church' in sermons and debates. It is likely though that for him, the concept of 'primitive church' ended with the Council of Nicaea in 325 A.D.; but he also affirmed the importance of later 4th and 5th century writers such as John Chrysostom and Augustine.

4

The notion of a *via media* appeared as early as Thomas Crowell (1485-1540), who articulated a political version before Parliament.[7] Much later, others such as George Herbert (1593-1633), and Simon Patrick (1625-1707) would be found to follow suit. It was Thomas Cranmer (1489-1556) and the Caroline Divines, however, who made it the governing principle of Anglican theology. From the beginning, the *via media* served England's political interests by establishing the authority and independence of its Church — a move accomplished by appealing to Scripture and tradition.

It was important for the Reformers to build a solid case justifying ecclesiastical separation from the Roman See, while at the same time preserving the important doctrine of apostolic succession, which is the basis of ordination and authoritative teaching. The appeal to Scripture as the primary source of Christian teaching undermined Rome's magisterial power in political and theological matters. Indeed, (Thomas) Cromwell and Cranmer had seen to it that England's king was charged with articulating the Christian faith on the basis of Scripture and genuine apostolic teaching.[8] We find theological primers for literate laypersons ca. 1530 that defended these and other reforms instituted under Henry.[9] Such developments helped insure that future popes would find it no easy task to reassert theological and political influence in England.

The appeal to Christian antiquity established the catholicity of England's Church. The church fathers were employed as secondary sources of authority in matters of faith and practice. The Reformers argued that logically, primitive

---

[7] A. G. Dickens, *The English Reformation*, 2d ed. (London: BT Batsford, 1989), 135. For Cromwell, the *via media* consisted of "that middle road in affairs of Church and State which rejected both stiff reaction and presumptuous innovation."

[8] Ibid., 203: "In the view of Cranmer and Cromwell 'a pure and sincere doctrine of the Christian faith' should be formulated closely upon Scriptural authority, should be set forth by a Christian King in Parliament and accepted by the people without opinionated haggling over details."

[9] See Dickens, *The English Reformation,* 205: "The primer forms another characteristic manifesto of the Henrician *via media,* denouncing various [Roman Catholic] superstitions, yet condemning Zwinglian disbelief in real and corporeal presence."

Christianity was the purest, most pious of all subsequent ages because of its historical proximity to Jesus of Nazareth and the twelve apostles. The founders of Anglicanism relied upon the fathers as well as the creeds arising out of the ecumenical councils, for establishing theological continuity between the Church of England and the church of the earliest successors to the apostles.[10]

Rediscoveries of ancient texts during the late medieval and Renaissance era, coupled with the invention of the printing press, led to a quantitative and qualitative increase in scholarship of all kinds.[11] New editions of primitive church writings became widely available in their original Latin and Greek versions. Though there was interest in patristic scholarship on the Continent, study of the fathers thrived in England. Thomas Cranmer, John Jewel (1522-71), John Whitgift (1530-1604) and Richard Hooker (1554-1600) all made extensive use of a broad range of patristic texts.[12]

The Anglican Reformers looked to the church fathers as authorities on matters of faith and practice that, though not equal to Scripture, certainly followed close in rank. S. L. Greenslade notes:

> The Fathers are not in themselves an absolute standard, but they are
> positively important as a guide to the meaning of scripture, as an

---

[10] See Henry R. McAdoo, *The Spirit of Anglicanism* (Charles Scribner's Sons, 1965), 321. McAdoo comments on the writings of Bishop Lancelot Andrewes (1555-1626): "The whole theme of [Andrewes' work] . . . was that Anglicanism had no specific teaching other than that of Scripture interpreted by the Primitive Church with which it had a continuity historical and doctrinal."

[11] William P. Haaugaard, "Renaissance Patristic Scholarship and Theology in Sixteenth-Century England," *Sixteenth Century Journal* 10.3 (1979): 37 f.

[12] Ibid., 41, n. 14. Most editions of the fathers were in their original languages, Latin or Greek; but, by the middle of the sixteenth century English translations of certain authors and works had begun to appear. Most of these, however, consisted of smaller works such as sermons. By the beginning of the seventeenth century, Haaugaard notes that England "had emerged as a center for patristic studies. . . ." See Ted Campbell, "John Wesley's Conceptions and Uses of Christian Antiquity" (Ph.D. diss., Southern Methodist University, 1984), 317-320 for a list editions and translations of the ante-Nicene fathers.

6

indication of a scriptural way of life for the Church; they have *auctoritas*, weight, they are to be esteemed.[13]

Although they held a high view of Scripture, Anglican theologians were not biblical literalists. Neither did they overlook the role of subjective religious experience in the hermeneutical task; rather, they subjected experience to the scrutiny of reason.[14] When Anglicans lined up their authorities in support of one of their arguments or to refute an argument being made by the Roman See, they appealed first to Scripture, then to the fathers. This method imparted to Anglicanism a distinctively evangelical zeal on the one hand, and catholic piety on the other. The result was a religion that incorporated the Reformed doctrines of Protestantism with the traditional piety of old catholicism. Scripture and tradition, Protestantism and Catholicism — these formed the heart of the Anglican *via media*.

B. The Fathers and Church Authority

As we have seen, Anglicanism preserved the catholic piety of primitive Christianity. When the political situation forced Henry to act in his own best self-interest, none doubted that he wanted to remain catholic; but neither did anyone doubt that in order to fulfill his ambitions he needed to challenge the Roman magisterium. Since the only catholicism England had ever known was Roman, it

---

[13] Greenslade, *The English Reformation and the Fathers of the Church*, 6. See *Cassell's Latin Dictionary*, 5th ed., s.v. *auctoritas*. The term conveys the idea of "support, sanction." The notion that the fathers provide 'sanctioning' authority for Anglican doctrine is apt.

[14] The Anglican divines rejected the speculative logic that characterized the thought of John Calvin. They believed that Calvin's system failed to make proper use of reason. For them, Calvin's views on the divine decrees — election and reprobation — were irrational because of their unrelenting logic resulting in the loss of any real human freedom (McAdoo, *The Sprit of Anglicanism*, 25-26). Bishop Robert Sanderson, although at first a moderate Calvinist who held a sublapsarian view of election, soon recognized the irrationality of the Calvinist system. Its reliance upon the utter transcendence of God and the logic of predestination from which it derives was in error, according to Sanderson. He therefore argued for "the rule of right reason." Scripture is decisive in determining the truth, but reason in the form of "sound judgment" determines the meaning of Scripture by viewing how its meaning was received and applied in history, especially by the ancient church (ibid., 48).

was necessary for Henry to separate faith and practice from the authority of the pope. Among those Henry called upon to design a distinctively Anglican style of catholicism was Thomas Cranmer, arguably the chief architect of the Anglican Church.

1. Thomas Cranmer

As one of the founders of the Anglicanism's confessional faith, Cranmer (1489-1556) drew heavily upon the church fathers.[15] Among things, he either authored himself or helped write the *Ten Articles,* the *Prayer Books* of 1549 and 1552, and the *Forty-Two Articles.* Geoffrey Bromiley notes that Cranmer had "a very high respect for the catholic authority of the fathers and the early creeds and councils."[16] Although he had a particular affinity for the "old Fathers" — e.g., Irenaeus, Tertullian, and Cyprian — Cranmer also employed the theolical insights of writers from the Nicene and post-Nicene periods such as Athanasius, Basil the Great, Cyril of Jerusalem, John Chrysostom, and John of Damascus in the East, as well as Jerome, Ambrose, and Augustine in the West.[17] Such a breadth of sources inevitably contributed to the *via media* that that characterized the later church.

Although the appeal to the consensually received writers and doctrines of early Christianity was crucial, it is important to note that Cranmer based his confidence in the fathers in Scripture, insisting that it must always remain the authority by which the fathers and councils are judged. In the tract *A Written*

---

[15] The following studies and biographies are recommended: C. H. Smyth, *Cranmer and the Reformation Under Edward VI* (London: SPCK, 1973); Peter Newman Brooks, *Thomas Cranmer's Doctrine of the Eucharist,* 2nd ed. (Houndmills, G.B.: Macmillan Academic and Professional, Ltd., 1965, 1981); Jasper Ridley, *Thomas Cranmer* (Oxford: Clarendon Press, 1962).

[16] G.W. Bromiley, *Thomas Cranmer Theologian* (London: Lutterworth Press, 1956), 13.

[17] "A Written Confutation of Unwritten Verities," John Edmund Cox, ed., *Miscellaneous Writings and Letters of Thomas Cranmer* 2 vols. (Cambridge: The University Press, 1846), 2: 22-36 *passim.* See also Bromiley, 16: "The argument [set forth in *Confutation*] is an interesting one and typical of the method of Cranmer as a well-versed patristic scholar."

Confutation of Unwritten Verities Cranmer declares that "the writings of the old Fathers, without the written Word of God, are not able to prove any doctrine in religion."[18] He points to a number of patristic writers who support the tenet that Scripture alone is the foundation of true Christian doctrine. *Confutation* provides an important example of early Anglican theological method — Scripture first, interpreted and supported by the consensually approved primitive tradition. If for no other reason, the tradition must be valued simply because the fathers were closer historically to the apostles; it is essential in critiquing doctrines and protecting for future generations the correct interpretation and application of Scripture.

Cranmer understood that the fathers themselves held a high view of Scripture; this in turn assisted him in establishing content and preserving the catholicity of England's faith. G. Bromiley observes:

> The self-subjection of the fathers to Scripture was of particular importance to Cranmer's own thinking. On the one hand, it preserved him from an uncritical enthusiasm for the fathers, as though any issue could be settled by a patristic tag irrespective of the Bible. On the other hand, it gave catholic authority to his primary contention, that the church and individual Christians are always under the judgment of Scripture, and therefore constantly under the possibility and indeed the necessity of reformation.[19]

Cranmer rejected the concept of an ecclesiastical magisterium that spoke with an authority equal to or greater than Scripture. In this respect, he and his English contemporaries were in step with their counterparts on the continent, who also claimed that the catholic faith articulated by the fathers had been grounded in Scripture.[20] However, in contrast to the Continental Reformers, Cranmer

---

[18] "A Written Confutation of Unwritten Verities," 2: 22.

[19] Bromiley, *Thomas Cranmer Theologian*, 24.

[20] See Greenslade, *The English Reformation and the Fathers of the Church*, 7. Both Luther and Erasmus recognized that the church fathers had generally acknowledged their limitations.

envisioned a church decidedly more catholic in its practices, especially in terms of its liturgy. This had been Henry's desire all along, a genuinely catholic church minus papal authority.

The Roman Church had always laid exclusive claim to the proper understanding and use of Christian antiquity. Cranmer is arguably the first of the British divines to employ the fathers against longstanding Roman dogmas and practices. Rome's authority was based on the power of the keys, which Matthew's gospel records were given to Peter.[21] Since Peter was the chief apostle and first bishop of the church at Rome, the Roman See argued that its authority lay in an unbroken succession of bishops.

Cranmer questioned this claim, contending that the Lord never intended to create a succession based in ecclesiastical offices, but rather apostolic succession is grounded in teaching the true gospel faith. Cranmer and his contemporaries found in the ancient fathers evidence that supported this view and employed them against what they believed had been a misuse of tradition by the Roman Church, in part by arguing for the primacy of Scripture supported by the consensual patristic witness.

There is no denying that in part they, like Henry, desired a uniquely British church that would never be subject to the demands or whims of Rome. However, ecclesiastical politics was not the sole, nor would many argue, primary factor motivating their reliance on Christian antiquity. There were also some serious theological differences. British Reformers, Cranmer being the forerunner, could not subscribe to the complicated and highly speculative dogmas concerning salvation that had emerged from high medieval scholasticism. In his *Notes on Justification* Cranmer doest not directly attack the Roman Church or pope.[22] Instead, he seeks to discover the essence of justification by returning to a plain

---

[21] Matthew 16:18.

[22] Cox, *Miscellaneous Writings and Letters of Thomas Cranmer*, 2: 203-211.

reading of Scripture and a careful accounting for the insights of the primitive fathers. Cranmer opposes the "unwritten verities" of Roman Catholic theology. There is no question that Cranmer's scholarship and critically held theological concerns drove him to the positions he took.

At least five of the *Homilies* of the Church of England (which were produced during the reign of Henry but were not published until the ascendancy of Edward VI) are thought to have been authored by Cranmer.[23] Of the five that have been generally thought to be his, Cranmer is not reticent to employ evidence from the church fathers in support of his argument. In the third homily *Of the Salvation of All Mankind,* he mentions a bevy of patristic writers representing both East and West, including Basil, Ambrose, Hilary, Origen, John Chrysostom, Cyprian, and Augustine. All, according to Cranmer, support a Protestant understanding of justification.[24]

Horton Davies is surely correct in observing that Cranmer was guided by a certain nostalgia for a return to biblical religion, one unencumbered by superstition.[25] However, it was more than nostalgia that led the Archbishop to a dual reliance upon Scripture and tradition. He was interested in a truly

---

[23] Davies, *From Cranmer to Hooker* (1534-1603), 229: "It is generally agreed that of the 12 homilies in the first book, Cranmer wrote 5: *A fruitful Exhortation to the Reading of Holy Scripture; Of the Salvation of all Mankind; Of the true and lively Faith; Of Good Works;* and, probably, *An Exhortation against the Fear of Death.* Bishop Bonner is the reputed author of the homily, *Of Christian Love and Charity,* while Archdeacon John Harpsfield is believed to have written the homily, *Of the Misery of all Mankind.* With less confidence the homilies, *Against Whoredom and Adultery* and *Against Swearing and Perjury* have been attributed to Cranmer's chaplain, Thomas Becon."

[24] *Certain Sermons or Homilies Appointed to Be Read in The Time of Queen Elizabeth; and Reprinted By Authority From King James I., A.D. 1623* (1822; reprint, Philadelphia: Edward C. Biddle, 1844), 21. The author (assuming Cranmer) quotes St. Ambrose but does not provide the locus from which the citation is drawn. He mentions the other writers by name as supporting the argument. Since this was a sermon, not a theological disputation, the argumentation is not as tight as the latter would have demanded. See also the fourth homily, *Of The True, Lively, and Christian Faith,* where the writer cites liberally the fathers (ibid., 30, 33-34).

[25] Davies, *From Cranmer to Hooker* (1534-1603), 230.

theological reformation in England; and he realized that the only way to achieve it was by grounding it in Scripture and the best interpreters from Christian antiquity. Bromiley points out that Cranmer's work was "dominated by a theological aim and interest. He had no primary interest in the practical reformation of the church, which he was content for the most part to leave to the civil authorities."[26] Cranmer was not an innovator of theological thought; rather, he was a traditional scholar who sought to inspire a truly religious reformation. By amassing evidence from Scripture and the church fathers, Cranmer began a tradition that, because of its eclecticism, would produce no single seminal figure quite like an Augustine, a Thomas Aquinas, a Luther, or a Calvin. Yet as the church entered into a rediscovery of the holy tradition with its prolific writers and momentous councils, England's church would produce a son like John Wesley. Together, Scripture and tradition would form the basis of a reasonable religion that was institutionalized by Cranmer and others in the church's confessional faith.

2. John Jewel

There were other thinkers whose work affected the whole of the English Reformation. Bishop John Jewel (1522-71) was a younger contemporary of Cranmer and staunch defender of Anglicanism. Jewel also established the authority of Anglican doctrine upon the teachings of the church fathers. He shared Cranmer's penchant for employing patristic authorities in polemics against various Roman practices.

At one point, Jewel's criticism of Roman Catholicism earned him the ire of one Thomas Harding, who responded in kind. In the preface of his reply, Jewel attacks Harding's position in an almost ad hominem fashion:

> It misliketh you much, M. Harding, that, in so many and sundry cases by me moved, wherein standeth the greatest force of your religion, I should say you and other of that part are *utterly void, not*

---

[26] Bromiley, *Thomas Cranmer Theologian*, 8.

*only of the scriptures, but also of the old councils and ancient fathers; .
. . .*[27]

Then, in twenty-seven articles Jewel refutes Harding's argument by citing the church fathers.[28]

The most notable evidence of Jewel's use of patristic sources is his treatise *Apologia Ecclesiae Anglicanae.* Herein, Jewel justifies the existence of an independent Church of England by challenging Rome's claim to sovereignty concerning of the meaning and use of Christian antiquity. Jewel writes:

> [I]f we do shew it plain, that God's holy gospel, the ancient bishops, and the primitive church do make on our side, and that we have not without just cause left these men [i.e., Trent and the Counter-Reformers], and rather have returned to the apostles and old catholic fathers; and if we shall be found to the same not colourabley, or craftily, but in good faith before God, truly, honestly, clearly, and plainly; and if they themselves which fly our doctrine, and would be called catholics, shall manifestly see how all those titles of antiquity, whereof they boast so much, are quite shaken out of their hands, and that there is more pith in this our cause than they thought for; we then hope and trust, that none of them will be so negligent and careless of his own salvation, but he will at length study and bethink himself, to whether part he were best to join him.[29]

Frequently citing patristic writers, Jewel argues for a Protestant view of ministerial authority, marriage, Scripture, the sacraments, justification, the intermediate state, the Virgin Mary, and liturgy in the vernacular of the people.[30] In his discussion of the sacraments, Jewel claims to base his opinions broadly on

---

[27] John Ayre, ed., *The Works of John Jewel, Bishop of Salisbury,* 4 vols. (Cambridge: The University Press, 1845), 1: 93. Italics mine.

[28] Ibid., 1: 104-2: 811. An interesting feature of this dispute is that both Harding and Jewel cite patristic sources in support of their arguments — Harding in support of the Roman Catholic view, Jewel in support of the English Reformers.

[29] Ibid., 3: 56.

[30] Ibid., 3: 61-66.

the thought of such writers such as Tertullian, Origen, Ambrose, Augustine, Jerome, Chrysostom, Basil, and Dionysius. He argues that these and "other catholic fathers" regarded the sacraments as "figures, signs, marks or badges, prints, copies, forms, seals, signets, similitudes, patterns, representations, remembrances, and memories."[31] On the Eucharist, Jewel appeals the concept of 'real presence' which characterized the patristic church while eschewing the speculative logic of Roman 'transubstantiation'.[32]

In Part III of *Apologia,* Jewel argues against Rome's charge of heresy that Anglican teaching is commensurate with the doctrinal theology of the church fathers. For such a charge of heresy to stick, Jewel asserts that Origen, Ambrose, John Chrysostom, and Augustine must be judged heretics as well.[33] Even as the apostolic fathers were persecuted for the faith, England's Reformers are maligned for their devotion to the living God.[34] Furthermore, the utter inability of Rome to demonstrate convincingly that it has always conformed to the teaching of the primitive church constitutes glaring evidence of its departure from the religion of the apostles. Jewel states:

---

[31] Ibid., 3: 62. See the Latin original included in this same edition (p. 12). The following terms define the sacraments: *figuras, signa, symbola, typos, antitypa, formas, sigilla, signacula, similitudines, exemplaria, imagines, recordationes, memorias.*

[32] Ibid., 3: 63: "We affirm that bread and wine are holy and heavenly mysteries of the body and blood of Christ, and that by them Christ himself, being that true bread of eternal life, is so presently given unto us, as that by faith we verily receive his body and his blood. Yet say we not this so, as though we thought that the nature of bread and wine is clearly changed, and goeth to nothing; as many have dreamed in these later times, which yet could never agree among themself of this their dream."

[33] Ibid., 3: 67; "Were then Origen, Ambrose, Augustine, Chrysostom, Gelasius, Theodoret forsakers of the catholic faith? Was so notable a consent of so many ancient bishops and learned men nothing else but a conspiracy of heretics? Or is that now condemned in us which was then condemned in them?"

[34] Ibid., 3: 70: "But this is the most grievous and heavy case, that they call us wicked and ungodly men, and say we have thrown away all care of religion. Though this ought not to trouble us much, while they themselves that thus have charged us know full well how spiteful and false a saying it is: for Justin the martyr is a witness, how that all Christians were called *[atheoi]* . . . , that is, godless, as soon as the gospel first began to be published, and the name of Christ to be openly declared."

> As for . . . [the Roman Church's practice of their] religion, if it be of
> so long continuance as they have men ween [think, suppose] it is,
> why do they not prove it so by the examples of the primitive church,
> and by the fathers and councils of old times? Why lieth so ancient a
> cause thus long in the dust destitute of an advocate?[35]

Roman Catholicism, according to Jewel, had departed from the foundation laid by the apostles.

Like Cranmer, Jewel seeks a true *via media*. On the one hand, he sees England's Reformation as laboring on the same side with the Continental Reformers, especially when it comes to preaching. He writes:

> Forty years agone, and upward, was it an easy thing for them to
> devise against us these accursed speeches, and other sorer than
> these; when, in the midst of the darkness of that age, first began to
> spring and to give shine some one glimmering beam of truth,
> unknown at that time and unheard of; when also Martin Luther and
> Hulderic Zuinglius, being most excellent men, even sent of God to
> give light to the whole world, first came unto the knowledge and
> preaching of the gospel; . . . [36]

As we have already seen, on the other hand Jewel affirms the piety of the ancient catholics.

Jewel gives an exhaustive defense against the charge that England's Reformers created a schism in the church of Jesus Christ. Though acknowledging that England's church indeed effectively divorced itself from Roman Catholicism, Jewel agues that the move was necessary. "We have truly renounced that church," he states, "wherein we could neither have the word of God sincerely taught, nor the sacraments rightly administered, ..."[37] No sentiment better sums up his position, nor sets forth a better case for seeking guidance from the early church fathers in creating a new branch of Christendom.

---

[35]   Ibid., 3: 85-86.

[36]   Ibid., 3: 74.

[37]   Ibid., 3: 92.

3. Martin Bucer and Peter Martyr Vermigli

The Reformation in Europe, though different from England's, had a significant impact upon the thinking of the Anglican Reformers. Haaugaard observes the close association between Thomas Cranmer and two important Continental theologians, Martin Bucer (1491-1551) and Peter Martyr Vermigli (1500-1562).[38] Both men deeply influenced Cranmer's thinking and played roles in helping to advance the reformation on the continent.

Bucer had been a Dominican monk, but through a series of letters exchanged with Martin Luther, became convinced of Luther's views and in 1521 renounced his monastic vows. He eventually went to England where in 1549 he assumed the Regius Chair of Divinity at Cambridge. Bucer informally served as a consultant to Thomas Cranmer and is believed to have had a hand in developing the rite of ordination in the Anglican Church.

In 1547 Cranmer invited Peter Martyr Vermigli to England. Vermigli responded positively and a year later assumed Oxford's Regius Chair of Divinity. Later, he served as Cranmer's consultant on the 1552 *Book of Common Prayer.* Vermigli became a close associate by Bishop John Jewel with whom he carried on correspondence for many years.[39]

Bucer and Vermigli brought the influence of the Continental Reformation to bear in the Church of England's articles of faith and liturgy, but that was about as far as it went. Instead of an ecclesiastical unity established by explicit adherence to a confessional document, as was usually the case among the Protestant churches in on the Continent, the unity of England's Church was

---

[38] Haaugaard, "From the Reformation to the Eighteenth Century," *Study of Anglicanism,* S. Sykes and J. Booty, eds. (London: SPCK, 1988), 12.

[39] For a more detailed synopsis of the careers of Martin Bucer and Peter Martyr Vermigli see F. L. Cross and E. A. Livingston, eds., *The Oxford Dictionary of the Christian Church,* 3rd edition (Oxford: Oxford University Press, 1997), s.v. Hereafter, this resource will be abbreviated *ODCC.*

founded in a tolerance for differing opinions. It was a unity within diversity, as Haaugaard notes, grounded in:

> (1) the supremacy of Scripture, allowing for *varying interpretations of its application* to contemporary morals and church life, and (2) an agreed liturgy which, with many implicit theological perspectives, contained as explicit doctrinal standards, only the ancient creeds, and a brief children's catechism.[40]

The Church of England permitted latitude on non-essentials, which in turn gave rise to variations of opinion on how Scripture should be interpreted and applied. Confessional adherence to a common document was not required. England's Reformers believed that it was more important to conform to an established liturgy, which the *Book of Common Prayer* provided. This did not mean, however, that they disregarded the importance of theological agreement. Rather, they understood (much better than their continental counterparts) that all theology is in truth doxology — praise directed to God. The common liturgy contained in the *BCP* guaranteed unity of worship, which in turn would overcome disagreements on lesser matters.

4. Richard Hooker

While Cranmer and Jewel had led the English Reformation in reverencing the church fathers, Richard Hooker (1554-1660) added a third formal source for theology — reason.[41] Hooker arranged Scripture and tradition hierarchically and made both in a sense, subject to the scrutiny of natural reason. Henry McAdoo observes:

---

[40] Haaugaard, "From the Reformation to the Eighteenth Century," *Study of Anglicanism,* 14. Italics mine.

[41] See W. Speed Hill, ed., *Studies in Richard Hooker: Essays Preliminary to An Edition of His Works* (Cleveland and London: The Press of Case Western Reserve University, 1972) for assessments of Hooker's work and a helpful annotated bibliography.

> Hooker's work . . . [was] in one sense a defence of reason, an attempt to establish a liberal method which holds reason to be competent to deal with questions of ecclesiastical polity, and to be in itself an ultimate factor in theology.[42]

By arguing for the validity of natural reason as a source for theology, Hooker distinguished the Anglican way from Roman Catholicism on the one hand, and the continental Reformers on the other. Rome of course had extrapolated from its reading of the fathers a large magisterial authority that in the eyes of many had become overweening and intolerable. The continental Reformers, Hooker felt, had underestimated the capability of natural reason, subordinating it as it were to revelation minus critical examination.

From the close of the apostolic age through the seventeenth century, theology had been carried out on the basis of the church's written authorities, which by definition are the faithful record of divine revelatory acts. Scripture interpreted through the holy tradition served as the foundation for theological reflection. However, consensual opinion from the fathers to the Scholastics had been that natural reason is a useful methodological resource for evaluating Scripture and holy tradition. Hooker picked up this standard and incorporated it formally into Anglican methodology. Reason based in natural law, he argued, is antithetical neither to Scripture nor faith. All knowledge pertaining to salvation, which alone is contained in Scripture, demands reason as a means of appropriation.[43] Scripture and natural law serve together toward the same end; together they provide all that is necessary for life and salvation.[44]

---

[42]   McAdoo, *Spirit of Anglicanism*, 5.

[43]   John Keble, ed., *The Works of that Learned and Judicious Divine Mr. Richard Hooker: With An Account of His Life and Death by Isaac Walton* (Oxford: University Press, 1836), 1: 334-36: "If we define that [which is] necessary unto salvation, whereby the way to salvation is in any sort made more plain, apparent, and easy to be known; then is there no part of true philosophy, no art of account, no kind of science rightly so called, but the Scripture must contain it."

[44]   Ibid., 1: 339-40: "It sufficeth therefore that Nature [i.e., natural reason] and Scripture do serve in such full sort, that they both jointly and not severally either of them be so complete, that

Hooker's dual emphasis on Scripture and reason did not reduce in the least his regard for the church fathers. Like Jewel and Cranmer, Hooker found the primitive church to be a critical source for the establishment of dogma. He was sufficiently reformed to view the tradition, the source of doctrine, as less than divinely inspired; therefore, he insisted that every doctrine must subjected to the light of reason in order to confirm or deny its authority. Reason alone is able to discover whether church doctrines, which are essentially truth claims, can find support in Scripture and the fathers. Hooker opposed many of the ecclesiastical rites and practices of the Roman Catholic Church on the ground that they are neither found in Scripture "nor can otherwise sufficiently by any reason be proved to be of God."[45] He affirmed the practices commended by holy tradition so long as the tradition did not refute Scripture, nor claim certain practices to be immutable. He states:

> Those rites and customs being known to be apostolical, and having the nature of things changeable, were no less to be accounted of in the Church than other things of like degree; that is to say, capable in like sort of alteration, although set down in the Apostles' writings. For both being known to be apostolical, it is not the manner of delivering them unto the Church, but the author from whom they proceed, which doth give them their force and credit.[46]

Hooker's move to formalize reason as a theological source made tradition an important though subordinate source to Scripture, which in turn helped distinguish Anglicanism from both Roman Catholicism and Continental Protestantism. Tradition could not be viewed as equal in authority to Scripture (as in the Roman church), nor could it be discarded altogether (as in some forms of Protestantism). He asks:

---

unto everlasting felicity we need not the knowledge of any thing more than these two may easily furnish our minds with on all sides; . . . ."

[45]   Ibid., 1: 340.

[46]   Ibid., 1: 341.

[Are not certain customs of the contemporary church] . . . much more convenient and fit for the Church of Christ, than if the same should be taken away for conformity's sake with the ancientest [*sic*] and first times? . . . . The orders therefore, which were observed in the Apostles' times, are not to be urged as a rule universally either sufficient or necessary."[47]

Hooker consistently argued that the church fathers supported the authorities of Scripture and reason.[48] Yet he understood quite well the limitations of the ancient tradition. In his polemic against Puritanism, he writes:

St. Augustine was resolute in points of Christianity to credit none, how godly and learned soever he were, unless he confirmed his sentence by Scriptures, or by some reason not contrary to them. Let them [the Puritans] therefore with St. Augustine reject and condemn that which is not grounded either on the Scripture, or on some reason not contrary to Scripture, and we are ready to give them our hands in token of friendly consent with them.[49]

Hooker valued the contribution the church fathers had made in interpreting Scripture, but when it came to issues of authority, he rejected the approach of those whom he believed had misappropriated the fathers. Puritan thinkers fell into this category. They argued against Anglican ecclesiology on the grounds that the church fathers had largely been silent on the question of ecclesiology. Hooker

---

[47] Ibid., 1: 198-99.

[48] Ibid., 1: 326-28. Hooker believed that the fathers provided a kind of *via media* between faith and reason. On the one hand, they taught salvation by faith, not by reason. Though reason is good and useful in showing humankind the eternal blessedness of doing good works, the fact is it has been damaged by original sin. While human beings know what is good, they cannot achieve the good by reason alone. Persons cannot be saved by reason because their reason is flawed. The solution, as St. Ambrose once observed, is for God himself to instruct us in the way to heaven. The way to God, according to Hooker, is supernatural and therefore superior to human reason. Salvation can only be secured by faith. On the other hand, Hooker says that faith and reason should never be divorced from one another. When through faith salvation has come, reason shows that good works must necessarily follow.

[49] Ibid., 1: 376.

20

responded that such arguments were narrow-minded, methodologically questionable, and insufficiently catholic.[50]

Hooker plainly saw the danger on both sides in approaching the question of authority based on either *sola scriptura* or *sola ecclesia*. He recalls the Arian challenge of the third and fourth centuries, and the Donatist controversies of the fourth and fifth. In each case, both catholics and *heterodoxoi* claimed the high ground based upon what each believed to be the meaning of Scripture. Such an either/or approach, Hooker argues, can only result in entrenchment and self-delusion. Just because one thinks one's interpretation of Scripture is correct does not make it so.[51]

Though in the present day Hooker's approach might seem to beg the question, it is unfair to think that he has merely evaded the issue. Quite the contrary, Hooker believed that the function of reason in religious matters is to evaluate the veracity of faith claims that are grounded in revelation. Because divine revelation ultimately affects the doctrine of salvation, he rejects as fundamentally flawed any theological system that subordinates Scripture to the

---

[50] Ibid., 1: 376-90. By grounding their argument that Anglican ecclesiastical structure and liturgy are invalid because they are not explicitly taught in Scripture, Hooker contends that the Puritan Divines had taken a too narrow and literal approach. Such a *via negativa* approach to evidence would in itself have proven inadequate had not the Divines cited the church fathers who at times seemed to argue similarly! It would have seemed that Hooker had backed himself into a corner; but, in a carefully reasoned statement, he contends that his Puritan critics had totally disregarded the context in which the fathers had stated their *via negativa* arguments. The fathers, he asserts, never intended to disallow ecclesiastical practices and beliefs that could be reasoned out of Scripture, even though they may not be found explicitly therein. He concludes that it is wrong to disallow knowledge or belief on the basis that it is not definitively commended in Scripture. The church fathers would never have taken a *via negativa* argument to such an extent as to deny ecclesiastical structures and practices that are discerned by reason, especially reason that has been enlightened by faith.

[51] Ibid., 1: 411-12.

authority of the Church, which in his view was precisely the predicament of Roman Catholicism.[52]

While reason itself shows that Scripture must be primary, one must recognize that even Scripture does stand alone; it must always be interpreted. Hooker observes:

> For whatsoever we believe concerning salvation by Christ, although the Scripture be therein the ground of our belief; yet the authority of man is, if we mark it, the key which openeth the door of entrance into the knowledge of the Scripture. The Scripture could not teach us the things that are of God, unless we credit men who have taught us that the words of Scripture do signify those things. Some way therefore, notwithstanding man's infirmity, yet his authority may enforce assent.[53]

Hooker validated a common sense approach to doctrinal issues that was based in reason not all unlike the approach taken by the primitive church fathers. Though he did not play as vital a role as Cranmer and Jewel had in establishing the fathers as a source for Anglican thought, his work ultimately helped to insure the place of patristic scholarship for Anglicans down to Wesley's day. To the traditional triad of Anglican theological sources – Scripture, the fathers, and reason – Wesley would introduce evangelical awakening.

5. Lancelot Andrewes

Lancelot Andrewes (1555-1626) is an important figure in this survey for several reasons.[54] He was a competent biblical scholar who, under James I, was

---

[52] Ibid., 1: 423: "The schools of Rome teach Scripture to be so unsufficient [sic], as if, except traditions were added, it did not contain all revealed and supernatural truth, which absolutely is necessary for the children of men in this life to know that they may in the next be saved."

[53] Ibid., 1: 404.

[54] The following biographies and studies are especially recommended: Nicholas Lossky, *Lancelot Andrewes The Preacher (1555-1626): The Origins of the Mystical Theology of the Church of England,* trans. Andrew Louth (Oxford: Clarendon Press, 1991); Trevor A. Owen, *Lancelot Andrewes,* vol. 325, Twayne English Authors Series (Boston: Twayne Publishers, Div. of G.K. Hall & Co., 1981); Maurice F. Reidy, *Bishop Lancelot Andrewes, Jacobean Court Preacher*

responsible for the translation of a significant portion of the Authorized Version of the Old Testament Authorized Version. He also was an accomplished patristics scholar who gave Anglicanism a sacramental awareness and sense of the 'old catholicism' found in the writings of the church fathers. These sensibilities of the older catholic faith led him to oppose the predestinarian Lambeth Articles in particular and Calvinism in general. More than anyone else, with the possible exception of Bishop Laud, Lancelot Andrewes gave the Church of England its appreciation for high-church worship.

In the introduction to his translation of Andrewes' Latin *Preces Privatae*, F. E. Brightman observes the catholic character of the Bishop's personal devotion:

> But as the most notable preacher of his day, [Andrewes] . . . uses his opportunity to rebuke and counteract the 'auricular profession,' as he calls it, of an age which exaggerated the importance of preaching, and to insist that the hearing of sermons is not the chief part of religious observance, and that the Word is the stimulus to devotion and is useless unless it issue [*sic*] in this and in its central highest act, the communion of the Eucharist.[55]

Like John Jewel, Andrewes argued that Anglicanism is the best representative of the catholic faith that was founded in Scripture and promoted by the early councils, and fathers of the first five centuries. Brightman observes: "For [Andrewes] one Canon given of God, two testaments, three symbols, the four first councils, five centuries and the series of fathers therein, fix the rule of religion."[56]

Brightman lists among the ancient writers in Andrewes' repertoire Irenaeus, Tertullian, Cyprian, Arnobius, Lactantius, Jerome, Ambrose, Gregory of Nazianzus, Gregory of Nyssa, John Chrysostom, John Cassian, Augustine, and

---

(Chicago: Loyola University Press, 1955); Paul A. Welsby, *Lancelot Andrewes 1555-1626* (London: SPCK, 1958).

[55] F. E. Brightman, trans. and ed., *The Preces Privatae of Lancelot Andrewes, Bishop of Winchester* (London: Methuen & Co., 1903), xxxii.

[56] Ibid., xxxv.

Cyril of Alexandria.[57] As Brightman shows in his marginal notes, the *Preces* itself is thoroughly grounded in Scripture and the liturgies of the ancient church. Andrewes especially favored the Eastern church and was drawn to the liturgies of St. James, St. Basil, and St. John Chrysostom. As a result, the *Preces Privatae* exudes a profound sense of mystery and wonder at the sacramental nature of the Christian faith.

6. Jeremy Taylor

Seventeenth century England witnessed a continuation of the theological method advanced by Cranmer, Jewel and Hooker, but with greater stress upon recovering the holy living aspects of primitive Christianity. One of the exemplars of this emphasis is Jeremy Taylor (1613-67). Taylor is known for his devotional writings; but, he also was a careful reader of patristic sources, which he regarded as essential to the task of the practical theologian.[58] Commenting on Taylor's methodology, McAdoo writes:

> [Taylor] . . . embraced the full extent of the Anglican appeal to Scripture and to antiquity, expressing this with a liberality of view-point and a sensitive understanding of the nature and function of reason.[59]

---

[57] Ibid., xlvii: "Besides Holy Scripture and the directly devotional inheritance of the Church, Andrewes draws more or less on a long list of writers. . . . His sources include the Rabbinical writings; 'the ancient Fathers and light of the Church in whom the scent of this ointment,' of the Holy Ghost, 'was fresh and the temper true: on whose writings it lieth thick, and we thence slice it off and gather it safely.'" The citation is from Sermon 10 on the subject of Pentecost in *The Works of Lancelot Andrewes* 11 vols. (Oxford: J.H. Parker, 1841-54), 3: 287.

[58] The best overview of Taylor's work is by H. R. McAdoo, *The Eucharistic Theology of Jeremy Taylor Today* (Norwich: The Canterbury Press, 1988). Recommended is an older but also helpful work by H. Trevor Hughes, *The Piety of Jeremy Taylor* (New York: Macmillan & Co. Ltd., 1960). A modern critical edition of one of Taylor's most important treatises has been produced by P. G. Stanwood, ed., *Jeremy Taylor: Holy Living and Holy Dying*, 2 vols. (Oxford: Clarendon, 1989).

[59] McAdoo, *Spirit of Anglicanism*, 55.

Taylor's affinity for a 'reasonable' theology shows that he followed the
methodology of Richard Hooker, who appealed to the fathers as a reasonable
means of establishing the true meaning of Scripture. However, he is far less
interested in substantiating doctrine than he is in recovering the ethical piety of
the church fathers. Like Lancelot Andrewes Taylor revered the ancient Christian
writers for their profoundly sacramental view of reality and the Christian life.
The large volume of devotional literature he authored attests to his spiritual and
pastoral concerns; and his reliance upon the patristic witness in his sermons and
treatises distinguishes him among the Reformers of his day. Thomas K. Carroll
writes:

> Few if any, of Taylor's contemporaries, Anglican and Catholic, or
> his sixteenth-century predecessors, Roman or Reformed, had his
> sacramental grasp of patristic reality — the fullness of its totus
> Christus vision and the clarity of its poetic language.[60]

Carroll further notes that from the beginning of Taylor's tenure at Oxford "he read
widely in the symbolic language of the Greek and Latin Fathers . . . ."[61] The fact
is the good bishop valued the body of consensually received writers and works
that stretched well into the seventh century in the West and the eighth century in
the East.[62]

If there was a distinctive contribution which Taylor made to Anglicanism's
appreciation of Christian antiquity, it is his nuanced discussion of tradition found
in *A Discourse of the Liberty of Prophesying* (1647). Therein, he clarifies the
authority of the tradition vis-à-vis its fallibility. He makes several key

---

[60] Thomas K. Carroll, ed., *Selected Works/Jeremy Taylor,* The Classics of Western Spirituality
Series, ed. Bernard McGinn (Mahwah: Paulist Press, 1990), 59.

[61] Ibid., 17.

[62] Ibid., 7: "Like Newman two hundred years later, Taylor, too, could boast that he *followed the
Fathers,* a term reserved for Christian writers distinguished by orthodoxy of doctrine, holiness
of life, ecclesiastical approval and antiquity. In this context, antiquity is generally understood
to include writers down to Gregory the Great (ca. 600) or Isidore of Seville (ca. 630) in the
West, and John Damascene (ca. 750) in the East."

observations. First, Scripture is the sole repository of the church's faith, not the fallible tradition:

> I first consider that *tradition is no repository of articles of faith,* and therefore the not following it is no argument of heresy; for besides that I have shewed Scripture in its plain expresses to be an abundant rule of faith and manners, *tradition is a topic as fallible as any other:* so fallible that it cannot be sufficient evidence to any man in a matter of faith or questions of heresy.[63]

The issue of which he is speaking is the oral tradition, which is believed to have been passed down from the apostles to their successors. Taylor contends that claiming the authority of the tradition is insufficient grounds upon which to establish the apostolicity of authentic Christianity. The church fathers, he argues, were at times deceived and, occasionally even deceptive, in certain matters of faith and practice that they upheld as apostolic in origin.

On the other hand against this rather sharp assessment, Taylor maintains that the holy tradition is an extremely valuable source and guide in doctrinal and ecclesiastical controversies, but only when the following objective criteria are met. There must be: (1) evidence of Scriptural origin; and, (2) a clear demonstration of the belief or practice of having received universal consent. The subjection of doctrines and practices to these tests will not only serve as a correction to those who may misuse the holy tradition, but it will help the church-at-large arrive at a proper understanding of the role of Scripture in relation to the tradition. He writes:

> We are acquitted, by the testimony of the primitive fathers, from any other necessity of believing, than of such articles as are recorded in Scripture: and this is done by them, whose authority is pretended the greatest argument for tradition, ...[64]

---

[63] Jeremy Taylor, *The Whole Works of the Right Rev. Jeremy Taylor, D.D.,* ed. Reginald Heber, 15 vols. (London: C. and J. Rivington *et al.,* 1828), 8: 11. Italics mine.

[64] Ibid., 8: 24-25.

For Taylor and other holy living Anglicans, it is more important *how* one employs the tradition than whether one regards it all. Reading out of it doctrines that cannot be established in Scripture is a misuse.

Taylor therefore always took a cautious approach. Since he had long been an ardent critic of later church councils upon which the Roman magisterium depended, Taylor directed his appeal to tradition based on what was in effect the notion of consensus — that is, unity of opinion on doctrines essential to the faith. This meant significantly limiting historically the authoritative scope of the tradition to the centuries that were crucial in formulating the consensually held interpretations of Scripture and doctrines. This period of time took in the first four ecumenical councils – Nicaea I, 325 AD; Constantinople I, 381; Ephesus, 431; and Chalcedon, 451. Taylor was at least willing to acknowledge the value of the next three – Constantinople II, 553; Constantinople III, 680; and Nicaea II, 787. The authoritative tradition ended for him with the seventh council.[65]

In a carefully written conclusion to a discussion of the councils, Taylor cites (in Latin) Gregory Nazianzus. A profoundly intellectual and reflective man, St. Gregory expresses in a letter to one named Procopius his skepticism about church councils. Taylor cites the following from that letter:

> If one should tell the truth, I have been so disturbed that I flee all the bishop's councils, because I have seen of no council a glad and favorable end, because it will not have been a driving out rather than an increase and growth of evils.[66]

Although aware of Gregory's reservations, Taylor recognizes that we now see these events from much longer perspective. As he writes:

---

[65] Ibid., 8: 30. For a helpful introduction to these councils and the issues they addressed see Leo Donald Davis, *The First Seven Ecumenical Councils (325-787): Their History and Theology* (Collegeville, MN: The Liturgical Press, 1990). See also Karl J. Hefele, *A History of the Christian Councils*, W. Clark, trans., 4 vols. (Edinburgh: T&T Clark, 1872-95). Hefele curiously does not include the seventh council.

[66] Ibid., 8: 49. Cit. Latin. Translation mine.

> But I will not be so severe and dogmatical against them [viz., the councils]: for I believe many councils have been called with sufficient authority, to have been managed with singular piety and prudence, and to have been finished with admirable success and truth. And where we find such councils, he that will not with all veneration believe their decrees, and receive their sanctions, understands not that great duty he owes to them *who have the care of our souls,* whose "faith we are bound to follow," saith St. Paul; that is, so long as they follow Christ: and certainly many councils have done so. But this was then when the public interest of Christendom was better conserved in determining a true article [of faith], than in finding a discreet temper or a wise expedient to satisfy disagreeing persons.[67]

Taylor assents to the findings of the early councils because the fathers had acted in a time when truth, not accommodation, was the primary concern.

Bishop Taylor was not the least bit naive about how the church fathers could be misappropriated to support a skewed or heretical opinion. Therefore, he always looked for evidence of consensus – proof that a belief or practice had been universally accepted. Taylor well understood that that defenders of Roman Catholicism claimed to hold the high ground on consensual Christianity. Taylor's response often was to show that agreement among the father is not always demonstrable and that one or two statements scattered throughout a large number of writing and writers does not form a true consensus.[68]

A very good example of Taylor's method of refuting Roman Catholic doctrines has to do with one of the most significant theologians of the ancient church, St. Augustine. Taylor observes that during the first four centuries the fathers had taught human liberty with respect to sin and salvation. Then, St. Augustine came along and trying to understand the depth of human depravity and

---

[67]   Ibid. Italics mine. Taylor, like the church fathers, believes that disagreements over doctrine are rarely benign, that they ultimately impact pastoral theology and care.

[68]   Ibid., 8: 78: "There are some that think they can determine all questions in the world by two or three sayings of the fathers, or by the consent of so many as they will please to call a concurrent testimony: but this consideration will soon be at an end."

the overwhelming gracious of God changed everything (in the West, at least) with his teaching on absolute predestination.[69] Taylor attributes this shift in thinking to the excellence of Augustine's skill as a rhetorician among his peers and successors rather than a received consensus of thought. But in fact, Augustine's ideas conflicted, Taylor observes, with the testimony of earlier writers on the matter.

Taylor's larger point, however, is that such disagreements were not all that uncommon. The tradition did not speak with one voice on all matters. It is important to keep in perspective the relationship between the fathers and councils by examining the evidence for what is most reasonable to believe. As he states:

> Scripture, tradition, councils, and fathers, are the evidence in question, but reason is the judge: that is, we being the persons that are to be persuaded, we must see that we be persuaded reasonably: and it is unreasonable to assent to a lesser evidence, when a greater and clearer is propounded.[70]

The church fathers take their place alongside the church's councils and Scripture as evidence presented to human reason. Taylor shows that the *consensus patrum* is a nuanced concept that should always be employed with care. Where there is a true consensus on a given matter, Anglicans may rely upon it. Where there is not, the church does well to tread lightly. All of the evidence must be weighed; but always the primary source of right teaching is Scripture.[71]

---

[69] Ibid., 8: 78-79.

[70] Ibid., 8: 97-98. Here in section VIII entitled "Of the Disability of Fathers, or Writers Ecclesiastical, to determine our Questions with Certainty and Truth" Taylor is not arguing against the value of the church fathers in setting forth Christian doctrine. Rather, he has sought to keep in view their fallibility and to preserve the role of reason in settling controversies within the church. Cf. section X, "Of the Authority of Reason; and that it, proceeding upon best Grounds, is the best Judge [of Controversies]."

[71] Ibid., 8: 19. Taylor discusses how the patristic writers defended the church against heretical ideas on the basis of the apostolic tradition: "And the fathers, in these ages, confute heretics by ecclesiastical tradition; that is, they confront against the impious and blasphemous doctrines that religion, which the apostles having taught to the church where they did preside, their successors did still preach, and, for a long while together, suffered not the enemy to sow tares amongst their wheat. And yet these doctrines, which they called traditions, were nothing but such fundamental truths which were in Scripture . . . ."

Taylor fleshes out his argument further in the introduction to part two of *A Dissuasive from Popery*, when he rhetorically asks: "What use are the fathers to protestants in their writings?"[72] Protestants, he says, should "expound Scriptures according to the sense of the ancient fathers. . . . For the fathers were good men and learned; and interest, and partiality, and error had not then invaded the world so much, as they have since done."[73] In addition to their exemplary character, Taylor argues that their authority is also based on their historical proximity to the apostles. He writes: "We know the fountains were pure; and the current, by how much the nearer it is to the spring, is the less likely to be corrupted."[74]

To be fair, the Continental Reformers esteemed the primitive church as well and for similar reasons.[75] The English Reformers, however, generally held a higher view of the patristic tradition. Taylor himself explains how this is so:

> [The fathers] . . . speak reason and religion in their writings; and when they do so, we have reason to make use of the good things, which by their labours God intended to convey to us. *They were better than other men, and wiser than most men, and their authority is not at all contemptible, but in most things highly to be valued:* . . . Are not the books of the canonists and casuists, in a manner, little else than a heap of quotations out of their predecessors' writing? Certainly we have much more reason to value the authority of the ancient fathers.[76]

---

[72] Ibid., 10: 322.

[73] Ibid.

[74] Ibid., 10: 448.

[75] Indeed, John Calvin employed his familiarity with patristic writings in his polemicizing Catholicism and the Roman See. Calvin clearly distinguished between the authority of the apostles and later writers. He states: "The [apostles] . . . were sure and genuine scribes of the Holy Spirit, and their writings are therefore to be considered oracles of God; but the sole office of others [implying the apostles' successors as well as us] is to teach what is provided and sealed in the Holy Scriptures" (*Institutes of the Christian Religion*, IV.8.9).

[76] Taylor, *Whole Works*, 10: 323. Italics mine.

Taylor simply recognized that the fathers were the first and best sources of apostolic Christianity, and that all subsequent (viz., Roman Catholic) sources have tried to make their case by quoting the fathers.

Taylor's belief that the fathers were superior sources of Christian faith and practice seems to reinforce the Roman Church's claim that the tradition is divinely inspired. Calvin and the Protestant Scholastics who followed in his stead of course did not share this notion. Taylor himself never claimed unequivocally that the fathers were inspired texts; but what he does say is interesting:

> We do not admit [the fathers] . . . as infallible, but yet of admirable use; so in the testimony which they give of the doctrines of their forefathers concerning the way of salvation, we give as great credit as can be due to any relator [sic], except him that is infallible.[77]

For Taylor and later Anglicans, Scripture alone is the infallible rule of faith and practice; yet the interpretation of Scripture by the fathers, especially concerning doctrines central to salvation, is to be greatly esteemed. The fathers therefore are to valued as texts of great importance, even exceptional, certainly not inspired as Scripture is considered to inspired, but more *in-spirated* that the writings of later Christian thinkers.

Jeremy Taylor exemplifies the high regard for patristic thought in the Anglican tradition, and his influence upon pastors and theologians shaped the Church in a profound way. He made a strong case for appealing to apostolic authority, which is derived from Scripture and interpreted through the consensual tradition. Taylor's influence extended long after his death, even shaping the thought of young John Wesley, who in many ways shared some of Taylor's intellectual and pastoral gifts.

---

[77] Ibid.

7. John Pearson

Taylor's contemporary John Pearson (1613-86) was renowned for his scholarship in patristics. Pearson's work is laden with references to the church fathers, which he regards as essential and primary interpreters of Scripture. His most significant treatise, *An Exposition of the Creed,* showcases the breadth of his learning as it exegetes and supports with material from the fathers the Apostles Creed. The text is heavily footnote with excerpts from the Hebrew and Greek Scriptures along citations from the fathers in Greek and Latin. *An Exposition of the Creed* is truly a remarkable work.

In the dedicatory portion Pearson writes: "My design aimeth at nothing else but that the primitive faith may be revived."[78] Like the Divines whom we have already discussed, Pearson viewed the early Christian communities as the purest of all subsequent centuries. He seems to have regarded himself to be living in a polemical context similar to the ancient church, especially when he laments a growing skepticism toward faith in his day, which, as history would disclose, proved to be the pre-dawn of the Enlightenment. He writes:

> The principles of Christianity are now as freely questioned as the most doubtful and controverted points; the grounds of faith are as safely denied as the most unnecessary superstructions; that religion hath the greatest advantage which appeareth in the newest dress, as if we looked for another faith to be delivered to the saints: *whereas in Christianity there can be no concerning truth which is not ancient; and whatsoever is truly new, is certainly false.*"[79]

For Pearson, the old is the best; the new is to be regarded with suspicion.

---

[78] John Pearson, *An Exposition of the Creed* (1659; reprint, London: J.F. Dove, 1832), unnumbered dedication page. Pearson's pastoral side comes into view here with the opening lines: "To the Right Worshipful and Well-Beloved, The Parishioners of St. Clements, East-Cheap."

[79] Ibid. Italics mine.

32

It would be a mistake to dismiss the bishop's interest in ancient Christianity as merely a fascination with antiquarian ideas. Pearson was a pastor-scholar who delighted in the living, consensual tradition of Christian thought. His tribute to ancient, proven truth over and against contemporary, untried conjecture suggests the method that has come to be associated with Vincent of Lerins (d. 450). The theological method associated with Vincent, often called Vincent's canon, is simply: *quod ubique, quod semper, et quod ab omnibus creditum est,* "that which has been believed everywhere, always, and by all."[80] It is in this light that we can better understand Bishop Pearson's directive: "Look then for purity in the fountain, and strive to embrace the first faith, to which you cannot have a more probable guide than the Creed, received in all ages of the Church; . . ."[81]

Among Pearson's other treatises is a series of lectures on the attributes of God collected under the title *Lectiones de Deo et Attributis.* In his opening statement on theological method, Pearson identifies the Roman Church's sources of authority — Scripture, the councils, the consensus of the fathers, and the various pontifical decrees.[82] He moves on to compare and contrast these with the authoritative sources for the Reformers. Like the Roman church, the Anglican Reformers also depend upon Scripture, the councils, and the consensus of the fathers. Anglicans, however, give priority to Scripture; and, unlike the Roman Church they do not place the Apocrypha before the canonical New Testament. Anglicans also grant weight to the councils, but only those whose opinions were received by the ancient churches.[83] The Reformers receive the consensual fathers,

---

[80] In English translation see George E. McCracken, ed., *Early Medieval Theology, vol. 9, The Library of Christian Classics* (London: SCM Press, 1957), 38. The translator also notes briefly the importance of Vincent for the Church of England, especially Richard Baxter (p. 31).

[81] Pearson, *Exposition,* dedication page.

[82] Edward Churton, ed. *The Minor Theological Works of John Pearson, D.D.,* 2 vols. (Oxford: The University Press, 1844), 1: 3-4.

[83] Ibid., 1:5: "sed illa quae ecclesiae veteris sententiam referunt; . . . "

but only those who recognized and approved the Scriptures and rejected superstition. The pontifical decrees Anglicans do not accept.

John Pearson will become an important model for John Wesley in terms of scholarship and theological method. Pearson's appreciation for the 'old catholic' sources of the faith, i.e., the fathers, coupled with his reformed perspective on authority will play into Wesley chief concerns.

8. William Beveridge

Another figure that should be mentioned in the succession of Anglican divines is William Beveridge (1637-1708). Beveridge received his education at St. John's College, Cambridge in Scripture and patristics. His *Ecclesia Anglicana Ecclesia Catholica* is a commentary on the *Thirty-Nine Articles*. Extensive citations from the Greek and Latin fathers demonstrate that the Church of England's doctrines derive from the ancient ecumenical tradition. Describing his approach Beveridge writes:

> The method I propounded in this Discourse, was first to shew that each Article for the sum and substance of it is grounded upon the scriptures, so that if it be not expressly contained in them, howsoever it may by good and undeniable consequence to be deduced from them. Having shown it to be grounded upon the scriptures, I usually prove it to be consonant to right reason too, ... And lastly, for the further confirmation of it, I still shew each Article to be believed and acknowledge for a truth by the Fathers of the primitive church, ...[84]

Well into the treatise he declares: "For all our Articles are, as we may see, agreeable to scripture, reason, and Fathers: . . . ."[85]

---

[84] William Beveridge, "Ecclesia Anglican Ecclesia Catholica; or, The Doctrine of the Church of England Consonant to Scripture, Reason, and Fathers," *The Theological Works of William Beveridge, D.D.,* 12 vols. (Oxford: J. H. Parker, 1843), 7:x.

[85] Ibid., 7: 366.

Like those before him, Beveridge held the church fathers in their proper place to the primary source of authority, Scripture. The tradition is of inestimable worth wherever it casts light on the teaching of Scripture. Where is obscures or casts doubt however, it cannot provide grounds for the rule of faith. Reason also is a necessary source of authority in order to rightly apply Scripture and tradition to the needs of the contemporary church. In Beveridge's view, to overvalue the tradition of the fathers and the canons of the councils, making them the equal in authority with Scripture, would be to lapse into Roman Catholicism.

9. John Potter

John Potter (1674-1747) was arguably the most accomplished patristics scholar of his day in terms of lasting contribution to the field. Potter ascended from rather humble beginnings to become Archbishop of Canterbury. His education at University College and Lincoln College, Oxford prepared him for scholarly work in the classics and patristics, evidenced in works he produced on ecclesiology and church history. One of his most significant projects was to edit the works of Clement of Alexandria, which he published in 1715.[86] Potter was more of a seventeenth than eighteenth century style scholar, especially with respect to the church fathers. Like Beveridge and Pearson, Potter upheld the Anglican appeal to Scripture, reason, and tradition as the methodological foundation of faith. This latitudinarian response to those who were either more modern or more antiquated in their approach to religious authority is discussed by L.W. Barnard in his biography of Potter:

> Potter, against the Erastian views prevalent in his time, was certain that episcopacy and the apostolic succession was of the esse of the Church. A Church based on the presbyterian model never had any appeal for him, generous though he was to dissenters. The appeal to

---

[86] John Potter, ed., *Clementis Alexandrini opera, quae extant recognita and illustrata par Johannem Potterum, Episcopum Oxoniensen* (Oxford, 1715).

tradition in support of Anglican polity was as natural to him as to the seventeenth century Caroline divines.[87]

Although overall interest in patrology began to recede before the middle of the eighteenth century, Potter as well as any practiced and preserved Anglicanism's threefold appeal to Scripture, tradition and reason.[88]

C. Summary

This chapter has been designed to set the background for a proper understanding of John Wesley's interest in Clement of Alexandria. We have attempted to establish that the Anglican way of doing theology involved the use of the consensually received holy tradition, thereby making Wesley's appropriation of tradition a matter of course rather than a stroke of ingenuity. It is only by viewing Wesley through the lens of Anglicanism that we may understand his appeal to the early church in general, and to Clement of Alexandria in particular.

---

[87] L. W. Barnard, *John Potter, An Eighteenth Century Archbishop* (Elms Court, G.B.: Arthur H. Stockwell Ltd., 1989), 35.

[88] Ibid.: "After c. 1730 the appeal to Christian antiquity began to wain [*sic*] in England. Potter's work, together with that of Joseph Bingham and Daniel Waterland, is however a reminder that in the earlier decades of the eighteenth century the threefold appeal to Scripture, Christian antiquity and Reason continued to be force. It was this appeal which Potter embodies in his life and teaching . . . ."

Chapter 2
Wesley, The Fathers,
&
The Anglican Holiness Tradition

Scholars have long recognized that John Wesley revered the early fathers of the church. What has not been sufficiently explored is the precise use Wesley made of these sources.[89] This chapter is developed on the proposal that one of Wesley's primary uses of the fathers was to inspire and advance his vision of Christian holiness. This was not an original concept for Wesley; we know that there were precedents in the Anglican tradition with which he was acquainted. As an Anglican churchman, Wesley came naturally to incorporate patristic teaching and insights into the tasks of homiletics and theology. He was drawn to the church fathers because he, like his predecessors generally believed that they were a reliable source for what a living faith and holy witness should be.

A. Wesley's Affinity for the Church Fathers

Like many of the leading lights of Anglican thought in prior generations, Wesley's interest in the church fathers was neither antiquarian nor eccentric. His

---

[89] This is the question that drove Ted Campbell's exploration of Wesley and the fathers. See Ted Campbell, *John Wesley and Christian Antiquity: Religious Vision and Cultural Change* (Nashville: Abingdon Press, 1991).

reliance upon the patristic tradition as a way of doing theology was congruent with mainstream Anglicanism for the most part. While the evidence is not always as unambiguous or complete as one might wish, there can be little doubt that Wesley had read the church fathers and that he had regarded them as the principal sources to be consulted for the proper interpretation of Scripture.

Although he seems to have been broadly acquainted with the larger patristic tradition, Wesley generally did not hold as authoritative sources beyond the fourth century, and among these he favored the earliest. He avoided sources that could be linked historically to the genesis of the Roman magisterium. Much of his criticism centered upon the Church's claim to ecclesiastical dominance based upon an assumed unbroken line of bishops — i.e., apostolic succession.[90] Wesley adopted what he regarded to be the best of the primitive, consensually received writers in order to support his interpretation of Scripture and Christian doctrine. In spite of his differences with the Roman Church, Wesley nonetheless recognized the common ground upon which Anglicans (as well as Methodists) and Roman Catholics stood when it came to ancient orthodoxy and the foundational practices of Christianity.[91]

It has been regarded almost as axiomatic that Wesley's interest in patristic Christianity favored the early Eastern church. Although this is open to debate, the Anglican Church has generally had a greater affinity for the Eastern Greek Church than for the Latin West.[92] It is therefore not unusual that Wesley should find the Eastern writers to be a rich theological resource, especially concerning the issues that interest him most such as personal transformation and holy living.

---

[90] See "A Roman Catechism, Faithfully Drawn Out of the Allowed Writings of the Church of Rome, " Jackson, *Works,* 10: 87-128.

[91] See "A Letter to a Roman Catholic," Jackson, *Works,* 10: 79-86, esp. pp. 84-85.

[92] Obviously, this preference is premised to some extent on the fact that Henry founded England's Church based upon a breech with Rome.

In spite of a preference for the East, Wesley also cites Western writers, including Cyprian and to a lesser extent St. Augustine.

By his own testimony, John Wesley had learned to respect the authority of the church fathers when he was quite young. Near the end of his life he recalled: "From a child I was taught to love and reverence the Scripture, the oracles of God, and next to esteem the primitive fathers, the writers of the first three centuries."[93] At the age of twenty-two in 1725 Wesley found himself in anguish over whether to pursue ordination.[94] Obviously, no one can assess with certainty his state of mind at that time; but the evidence suggests that his decision to seek ordination came as the culmination of a struggle over the ultimate direction his life should take. His father, Samuel Wesley Sr. (1662-1735) , seems to have played a decisive role in helping John resolve the matter – quite unusual given what has always been thought to be the stronger influence of his mother. Wesley Sr. seized this tender moment in his son's life as an opportunity to impart guidance, which came in the form of reading. In 1725 he twice admonished John to read and carefully assimilate St. John Chrysostom's classical treatise on pastoral calling *De sacerdotio*.[95] Not just Samuel but the church everywhere viewed *De sacerdotio* as essential preparation for holy orders. Samuel wisely recognized that it would lead John to a place of clarity and decision concerning his call; and he knew it would

---

[93] "Farther Thoughts on Separation from the Church" in Rupert E. Davies, ed., *The Methodist Societies: History, Nature and Design* (Nashville: Abingdon, 1989), vol. 9, *The Works of John Wesley*, 538.

[94] Ordination was not the only issue troubling him during 1725. See Henry D. Rack, *Reasonable Enthusiast* (Philadelphia: Trinity Press International, 1989), 70-72.

[95] See Frank Baker, ed., *Letters, I*, vol. 25, *The Works of John Wesley* (Oxford: Clarendon Press, 1980), 157-59; 176-77 for the text of the two letters. *De sacerdotio* is the best known of John Chrysostom's extant works. See W. R. W. Stephens, trans., A Select Library of Nicene and Post-Nicene Fathers, ed. P. Schaff and H. Wace, First Series (Buffalo: n.p., 1886-90; reprint, Grand Rapids: Eerdmans, 1952, 1989), 9: 33-83. See also Graham Neville, trans., *Six Books on the Priesthood [De Sacerdotio]* (Crestwood, NY: St. Vladimir's Seminary Press, 1964, 1977). Much more than just a ministry manual, *De Sacerdotio* probes the intentions and motivations of the potential ordinand.

40

do so without any outside coercion. This bit of wisdom had its desired effect, for that year young John did indeed obtain clarity with respect to his calling to the priesthood, and he went on to receive deacons orders.

John Wesley's decision to enter ordained ministry marked the beginning of an intense decade of reading and reflection. From 1725 and continuing throughout his years at Lincoln College until departing for Georgia in 1735, he read an impressive number of books. These works included the classics of the ancient world, poetry, drama, philosophy, theology (Roman Catholic and Protestant, especially Anglican), and the natural sciences. R. P. Heitzenrater has prepared a bibliography of Wesley's reading during the crucial years of 1725-1735 compiled from Wesley's *Oxford Diaries* and financial records, all arranged chronologically by month and year.[96] Though the *Diaries* do not contain the whole of Wesley's reading over the decade, they do provide a window into the types of literature he found most interesting and useful.

Included in his reading were a number of Anglican theologians. Wesley gleaned from these sources an appreciation for the distinctive way Anglican thinkers had marshaled the church fathers in support of disputed points of Christian doctrine and practice. It was typical of the Anglican divines to cite excerpts from the fathers, sometimes extensively. As a result, Wesley's appreciation for the primitive church grew. We learn in the *Diaries* that he read Clement of Rome, Ignatius, Polycarp, Justin Martyr and Clement of Alexandria. Notably, he read the Clement of Alexandria in December 1734; but it is likely that this was not his only foray into this particular writer's thought given the evidence we shall present later.[97]

---

[96] Richard P. Heitzenrater, "John Wesley and The Oxford Methodists, 1732-35" (Ph.D. diss., Duke University, 1972), 493-526.

[97] Ibid., 500. V. H. H. Green in *The Young Mr. Wesley* (London: E. Arnold, 1961; reprint, London: Wyvern, 1963), Appendix I, 289-302 compiled a list similar (though less detailed) to the one produced later by Heitzenrater. As the first one to really grapple with this issue, Green cautioned against assuming that Wesley recorded everything in the *Diaries* he had read during the nine or ten year period in question.

It was during the latter part of the decade that Wesley's association with the Oxford Methodists provided him the opportunity to read the church fathers in a more disciplined way. Long afterward, he reminisced that the Oxford Methodists had desired only "to be downright Bible-Christians," a designation he understood as "taking the Bible as interpreted by the *primitive Church* and our own for their whole and sole rule."[98]

Wesley was not alone in his pursuit of primitive Christianity. John Clayton (1709-73), a fellow Holy Club member, led Wesley to a particular consideration of early Eastern writers as a richer theological resource. Clayton's interests reflected an earlier resurgence in patristic scholarship that had arisen during the seventeenth century.[99] As a result of Clayton's influence, Wesley was drawn into a more deliberate and serious study of the fathers.

Even as Clayton had once commended the fathers to Wesley, Wesley would commend the fathers to his readers, most of who were literate but formally untutored laypersons. The first volume of his series *A Christian Library* included many of Wesley's favorites in English translation such as Clement of Rome, Ignatius and Polycarp. The *Spiritual Homilies* of Macarius the Egyptian, which had earlier captured his imagination, he included as well.[100] In his introductory comments to the set, Wesley writes:

> The authors of the following collection were contemporaries of the holy apostles: one of them bred [*sic*] under our Lord himself, and the others well instructed by those great men, whom he commissioned to go forth and teach all nations. We cannot therefore doubt but what they deliver to us is the pure doctrine of the

---

[98]   "A Short History of Methodism," Jackson, *Works*, 8: 348. Italics mine.

[99]   See Albert C. Outler, *John Wesley* (New York: Oxford University Press, 1964), 9 and Rack, *Reasonable Enthusiast*, 90.

[100]   John Wesley, ed., *A Christian Library*, 30 vols. (Bristol: Farley, 1749-55; reprint, London: T. Blanshard, 1819) 1: 7-131.

gospel; what Christ and his apostles taught, and what these holy men
had themselves received from their own mouths.[101]

By granting authority to these texts, Wesley recognized that he would have to
address two questions: (1) the personal qualifications of the authors; and, (2) the
relation of their writings to Scripture. On the first, he declares that these "men . . .
[were] instructed in common by the apostles," that they were "particularly bred
and instituted by them" and that these are "the writings of men who had attained
to so perfect a knowledge of the mystery of godliness, as to be judged worthy by
the apostles themselves to be overseers of the great churches of Rome, Antioch,
and Smyrna."[102] Wesley believed that the personal piety of these early writers
authenticated what they taught.

On the second question concerning the degree of authority one ought to
grant these writers, Wesley states:

> We cannot, with any reason, doubt of what they deliver to us as the
> gospel of Christ: but ought to receive it, though not with equal
> veneration, yet with only *little less regard* than we do the sacred
> writings of those who were their masters and instructors.[103]

In other words, these writings ought to be received with only a little less weight
than canonical Scripture. Although such comments place Wesley theologically
on the side of old catholic church, he also was truly Protestant; for he parted ways
with Roman Catholic theologians who granted tradition the same authoritative
weight as Scripture. Howeverr, Wesley could never be considered altogether
Protestant on this issue when in fact he affirmed some degree of inspiration for
the tradition, especially when it came to interpreting accurately the meaning of
Scripture. He explains:

---

[101]   Ibid., 1: B2, i.

[102]   Ibid., 1: B2, iv.

[103]   Ibid., 1: iv. Italics mine.

The plain inference is, not only that they [i.e., Clement, Ignatius, and Polycarp] were not mistaken in their interpretations of the gospel of Christ, but that in all the necessary parts of it they were so assisted by the Holy Ghost, as to be scarce capable of mistaking. Consequently, we are to look on their writings though not with equal authority with the Holy Scriptures, (because neither were the authors of them called in so extraordinary a way to the writing them, nor endued with so large a portion of the blessed Spirit,) yet as worthy of a much greater respect than any composures which have been made since; . . . ."[104]

It seemed as though Wesley wanted to put to rest any doubt concerning his views of church tradition and its value for instructing believers in matters of faith and practice.

One occasion however stands out as vivid example of Wesley grappling in public with the issue of tradition and authority. Conyers Middleton of Trinity College Cambridge published a treatise in 1748 that called into question the authority of early Christian writings based on skepticism toward miracles purported to have occurred in the apostolic church.[105] Wesley was so troubled by Middleton that he delayed a trip to Rotterdam January 1749 for the sole purpose of composing a response.[106] It is hardly conceivable that Middleton's polemic, which was aimed at an educated audience, could have had much overall effect upon the Methodist revival. Yet in his open reply *Letter to Conyers Middleton* Wesley shows just how seriously he regarded the fathers and how important it

[104] Ibid., 1: vi. Obviously, this does not include Macarius (ca. 300-390) the desert father who came much later.

[105] Conyers Middleton, *A Free Enquiry into the Miraculous Powers, which are Supposed to have Existed in the Christian Church, from the Earliest Ages, through Several Successive Centuries. By which it is shown that we have no sufficient reason to believe, upon the authority of the Primitive Fathers, that any such powers were continued to the church after the days of the Apostles* (London, 1747).

[106] Ward and Heitzenrater, *Journals and Diaries, III*, 20: 262: "I had designed to set out with a friend for Rotterdam. But being much pressed to answer Dr. Middleton's book against the Fathers, I postponed my voyage and spent almost twenty days in that unpleasant employment."

was for him to establish the relationship between the piety of Methodists and that of the early church.[107]

Wesley's response to Middleton betrays a knowledge of the church fathers that would easily have escaped his biographers had this incident not occurred. For example, Wesley charges that Middleton's attack upon Christian antiquity must be regarded as spurious, since it gives evidence that the Cambridge librarian was insufficiently read in patristics. He writes:

> I do not find, indeed, that you make any objection to any part of the Epistles of Ignatius; no, nor of the Catholic Epistle as it is called, which is inscribed with the name of Barnabas. This clearly convinces me, you have not read it; I am apt to think, not one page of it; seeing, if you had, you would never have let slip such an opportunity of exposing one that was called an apostolic Father.[108]

Middleton apparently had been unaware of the disputed authorship of an epistle attributed to Ignatius and the doubtful provenance of the *Epistle of St. Barnabas*. Wesley rightly inferred that Middleton was not really familiar with patristic literature.

Wesley of course had read the fathers at Oxford, where he was afforded access to some of the latest and best critical editions of the day.[109] His facility with Greek and Latin, the languages of the Eastern and Western churches respectively, added even more weight to his argument. We see this demonstrated

---

[107] For an analysis of the larger issues at stake at the time see E. G. Rupp, *Religion in England 1688-1791* (Oxford: Clarendon Press, 1986), 275 f. Rupp links Middleton's polemic to Scottish philosopher David Hume and the emerging skepticism of Enlightenment thought. Rupp suggests that Wesley was moved to write "a not insignificant reply" by the devastating implications of Middleton's attack upon Christian antiquity, which, if left to stand, could have damaged the authority of the apostles and the New Testament itself. See also Ted Campbell, "John Wesley and Conyers Middleton on Divine Intervention in History," *Church History* 55 (March 1986): 39-49.

[108] "Letter to the Rev. Dr. Conyers Middleton," Jackson, *Works*, 10: 19-20.

[109] The few English translations that existed generally consisted of sermons and short devotional tracts rather than significant doctrinal treatises.

when he accuses Middleton of misinterpreting a passage by the ante-Nicene writer Athenagoras (fl. 177 AD):

> From Athenagoras you cite only part of a sentence, which, translated as literally as it will well bear, runs thus: "Who in ecstasy of their own thoughts, being moved by the Divine Spirit, spoke the things with which they were inspired, even as a piper breathes into a pipe." Does Athenagoras *expressly affirm* in these words, that the Prophets were 'transported out of their senses?' I hope, Sir, *you do not understand Greek.* If so, you show here only a little harmless ignorance.[110]

Wesley translates the text in question, noting where Middleton has drawn inferences that may not properly be taken.

In spite of evidence which shows that Wesley held the fathers in high esteem, he never taught that they were infallible, nor did he regard individual writers to be above and beyond reproach. He writes:

> I allow that some [of the Fathers] . . . had not strong natural sense, that few of them had much learning, and none the assistances which our age enjoys in some respects above all that went before.[111]

Wesley did not accept unquestioningly what the fathers wrote. In an offhanded comment in a sermon he blames St. Cyprian (ca. 200/10-258) and his immediate successors for perpetuating discord in the church. Probably, he was referring to a Cyprian's refusal to readmit Spanish clergy who had lapsed during the persecution of Christians under Decius ca. 250 A.D.[112] Wesley is also a harsh critic of St. Augustine. Still he writes:

---

[110] "Letter to the Rev. Dr. Conyers Middleton," Jackson, *Works,* 10: 51. Italics mine.

[111] "Letter to the Rev. Dr. Conyers Middleton," Jackson, *Works,* 10: 79. Middleton's translation suggests that the prophets were possessed by the Spirit to such a degree that their reason was overcome as they wrote. Wesley not only finds the translation in error, but he would find the very premise absurd and contrary to the text and meaning of Scripture.

[112] See W. Reginald Ward and Richard P. Heitzenrater, eds., *Journals and Diaries, III,* vol. 20 of *The Works of John Wesley,* (Nashville: Abingdon, 1991), 489. Similar concerns about Cyprian are echoed in the sermons. See "The Mystery of Iniquity," Albert Outler, ed., *Sermons II,* vol. 2 of 4 in *The Works of John Wesley* (Nashville: Abingdon, 1984-1987), 2: 461-62; "Of Former

> And yet I exceedingly reverence them, as well as their writings, and
> esteem them very highly in love. I reverence them, because they
> were Christians, . . . And I reverence their writings, because they
> describe true, genuine Christianity, and direct us to the strongest
> evidence of the Christian doctrine.[113]

Wesley was well read in a range of primary sources representing early Latin and

Greek Christianity; he gave considerable attention to the historical and social

context in which these writers lived. As a student of history, Wesley was able to

criticize the idiosyncrasies of the early church without losing sight of its authority

and worth.

No examination of John Wesley's use of the fathers would be complete

without noting how it influenced his calling and work as a pastor. *An Address to*

the Clergy (1756) is a particularly good example of the importance Wesley placed

upon pastors gaining some measure of familiarity with the primitive church. In

one place he poses a series of rhetorical questions concerning the qualifications

and training of a shepherd of souls:

> Can any who spend several years in those seats of learning [i.e., the
> university], be excused, if they do not add to that of the languages
> and sciences, the knowledge of the Fathers? the [*sic*] most authentic
> commentators on Scripture, as being both nearest the fountain, and
> eminently endued with that Spirit by whom all Scripture was given?
> It will be easily perceived, I speak chiefly of those who wrote before
> the Council of Nice [Nicaea]. But who would not likewise desire to
> have some acquaintance with those that followed them? with [*sic*]
> St. Chrysostom, Basil, Jerome, Austin [Augustine]; and, above all,
> the man of a broken heart, Ephraim Syrus?[114]

Times," *Sermons, III,* 3: 450; and "What is Man?," *Sermons, III,* 3: 458. Wesley offers a more
charitable view of the third century North African church in *Sermons, III,* 3: 586 ("On Laying
the Foundation of The New Chapel"). Here, Wesley lauds "the religion of the primitive
church, of the whole church, in the purest ages."

[113] "Letter to the Rev. Dr. Conyers Middleton," Jackson, *Works,* 10: 79.

[114] "An Address to the Clergy," Jackson, *Works,* 10: 484.

Though he may have had reservations about the ecumenical councils held in later centuries, his general regard for the fourth century writers following the Council of Nicaea was not lessened by the accession of Emperor Constantine and the rise of Christendom.

Because Wesley did not employ footnoting as modern scholars do, some mistakenly assume that he was carelessly eclectic in his use of sources. To the contrary, there is every indication that he had been highly selective in choosing the best of the consensual writers. Contemporary scholar Ted Campbell has produced a list of Wesley's references to patristic writers and writings.[115] Of the twenty-nine church fathers Campbell has identified in Wesley's repertoire, nineteen wrote prior to the Council of Nicaea. Twenty wrote in Greek, eight in Latin, and one in Syriac. Wesley had his favorites among the fathers. For instance, he cites more frequently Augustine, Cyprian, John Chrysostom, Justin Martyr, Origen, and Tertullian. Less frequently does he cite Arnobius, Athanasius, Basil, Dionysius of Alexandria, Macarius, and Theophilus of Antioch. Some authors — such as Athenagoras, Dionysius the Areopagite, Gregory of Nazianzus, Lactantius, and Minucius Felix — he appears to have cited only once. Though it is wise not to infer too much from these statistics, one cannot help but be impressed with the breadth of Wesley's acquaintance with the patristic tradition.

As we have already observed, Wesley's appreciation for the primitive church and its theological emphases must be viewed from the perspective his Anglican context. He learned reliance on the fathers through reading the Caroline Divines and the Anglican Reformers. Ultimately however, the roots of his method are found in the high medieval Scholastics. Though he never employed the medieval catena style of citing the fathers to support his arguments (as Pearson had in *An Exposition on the Creed*) Wesley did follow the traditional

---

[115] Campbell, *John Wesley and Christian Antiquity,* 125-134.

Anglican method of doing theology, viz., Scripture interpreted by the ancient consensual tradition.[116]

This theological method was reinforced for Wesley by the general religious malaise of Wesley's day. Anglicanism was spiritually ill. Since a return to Roman Catholicism no longer posed a real threat, the Church's problems had migrated inward. Anglicanism was engulfed in a spiritual battle against its own lethargy, ineffectiveness, and moral turpitude. Wesley to the end of his life believed that Methodism had been a movement raised up by God to reform the Anglican Church. For him, the road to a healthier Church of England lay in a recovery of the past – beyond the Reformers, high medieval Catholicism, and even the ecumenical councils of the fourth and fifth centuries. Wesley idealized the future of the Church through the mirror of the apostles and their successors, those primitive ante-Nicene fathers, whom he believed to be the purest interpreters of Scripture and best models of Christian practice. His was a romantic vision, to be sure. It captured his imagination during the halcyon days of Oxford Methodism; and, though it eventually mellowed with the passage of time, it was a vision that he never really lost. Wesley and the early Methodists endeavored to model their lives after the teaching of the apostles and their nearest successors, the early fathers In so doing, they were sometimes ridiculed and often derided; but they believed they were doing God's work, bringing revival to the established Church. They wanted to effect change, not only in their own lives, but in the life of every person in England. Wesley's appeal to the fathers was a tool he used to unpack the meaning of the gospel and its call for personal righteousness. Holiness was the goal; drawing upon the insights of the ancient

---

[116] Horton Davies, *From Cranmer to Hooker (1534-1603)*, 15-17 discusses the role the patristic church was accorded in Anglican hermeneutics and liturgy. The catena style of reference involved citing line upon line, or in a series or chain. Pearson used this quite effectively in *Exposition*, but because he made no attempt to translate his sources from Greek and Latin, his notes were accessible only to the well educated.

fathers was just one of the means he used to support his argument that personal holiness is both the gospel demand and attainable in this life.

B. Wesley's Anglican Mentors in Holy Living

Although it is well understood that John Wesley and the Methodists held as their special calling "to spread scriptural holiness over the land," what is not well known is that they were preceded in fact, if not in spirit, by leading Anglican thinkers in previous generations. Our present task is to survey this evidence as it appears in Wesley's works. Our goal is to establish that in appropriating holiness of heart and life as the theme of his ministry, Wesley was following some key Anglican thinkers and their use of the fathers. These theologians were part of the English branch of what has been called the 'holy living' tradition. Wesley himself was the epitome of that lineage in the Church of England.

1. Thomas Cranmer: Personal Transformation

The emphasis upon holy living in the Anglican Church is found at least as early as Archbishop Thomas Cranmer. The collected Church of England *Homilies*, for which Cranmer is largely responsible, is a good example of the typical Anglican concern for faith-motivated piety and holy living expressed through good works. The *Homilies* demonstrate that Anglicanism was never just a religion of the Cross, but that it held dear the sacramental, spiritual presence of Christ evidenced by a transformed way of life.

Wesley found in Thomas Cranmer an ardent ally of holiness teaching, an enthusiast, if you will, for holy living. For example, in *A Farther Appeal to Men of Reason and Religion*, Wesley defends Methodists against the charge of religious enthusiasm using Cranmer as an archetype. He declares that Cranmer had been a member of an entire generation of "enthusiasts" who believed that ordinary Christians should expect to pray for and receive the vital presence of the Holy Spirit for everyday living. Moreover, these "modern enthusiasts" are to be numbered no less among such ancient fathers as Origen, John Chrysostom, and Athanasius.[117] Wesley's point in the larger context is to link together the witness of the apostles, the testimony of the Eastern fathers, and the piety of the Anglican Reformers. Collectively, these sources attest with one voice that the chief product of the inward, living presence of the Holy Spirit is holiness of heart and life.[118] The pericope demonstrates that in Wesley's mind, the founders of Anglicanism had based their idea of sanctification on early church sources.

2. Jeremy Taylor: Holy Living

Jeremy Taylor (1613-67) is remembered for his emphasis upon inward and outward holiness. As we saw in our earlier discussion, his interests lay primarily in the area of pastoral theology and care. Wesley was well acquainted with Taylor's thought. Between 1729 and 1733 he read a number of Taylor's works including *Discourse on the Nature, Offices and Measures of Friendship; Ductor Dubitantum; The Golden Grove; Opuscula; The Worthy Communicant;* and *The Rule and Exercises of Holy Living and Dying.*[119] Wesley was most impressed with Taylor's *Rule and Exercises of Holy Living and Dying,* which he not only owned himself but also later published in his multivolume *Christian Library.*[120]

---

[117] "A Farther Appeal to Men of Reason and Religion, Part I," *The Appeals to Men of Reason and Religion and Certain Open Related Open Letters,* Gerald R. Cragg, ed., vol. 11 of *The Works of John Wesley* (Nashville: Abingdon, 1989), 175. Enthusiasm was a perennial charge leveled at Methodists. Generally, enthusiasm was defined as any religious manifestation outside of what Christians ordinarily experience. Those who made such accusations understood enthusiasm to encompass a variety of things including visions, miraculous healings, and behaviors such as intense weeping, moaning, or shouting. For an overview of the enthusiasm controversy involving Methodists, see Rack, *Reasonable Enthusiast,* 207, 275-78.

[118] "A Farther Appeal . . . Part I," Cragg, *Works,* 11: 155-62. The thrust of Wesley's argument is that believers throughout history have experienced the testimony and unction of the Holy Spirit, that these blessings were not confined to the age of the apostles.

[119] See R. Heitzenrater, "John Wesley and The Oxford Methodists, 1732-35," 521. As with the rest of Wesley's reading, we cannot assume that this was the whole of his acquaintance with Taylor.

[120] *A Christian Library,* 9: 133-297.

Taylor based *Holy Living and Dying* on three sources: Scripture, the church fathers, and the classics of the ancient world.[121] Numerous references to patristic writers are found, including Augustine, Jerome, Gregory the Great, Basil, John Chrysostom, and Cyprian. By 1700, *Holy Living and Dying* had become a classic in its own right. Wesley first encountered it shortly after taking his B.A. from Christ Church before he became a Fellow at Lincoln College. He recalls having learned from Taylor the importance of keeping a daily journal.[122] Later, he writes: "In 1725, I met with Bishop Taylor's *Rule of Holy Living and Dying*. I was struck particularly with the chapter upon *intention*, and felt a fixed intention to give myself up to God."[123] Indeed, self-abnegation in the pursuit of holiness characterized Wesley's spiritual pilgrimage during those years.

3. John Pearson: Sanctification and

The Spirit-Filled Life

Among the Anglican Divines most admired by Wesley was Bishop John Pearson (1613-86), whom he mentions at least a dozen times. In most of these instances, Wesley is found citing Pearson's *Exposition of the Creed* (1659). As we saw earlier, Pearson was regarded as one of the leading doctrinal theologians of his time. Pearson especially revered the primitive Christian ideal of Holy Spirit-enabled holy living, which drew Wesley into Pearson literary circle.

In *A Farther Appeal to Men of Reason and Religion Part I* Wesley numbers Pearson among the venerable Spirit-empowered "enthusiasts" who stand

---

[121] P. G. Stanwood, *Jeremy Taylor: Holy Living and Holy Dying*, 1: xliv-li.

[122] Ward and Heitzenrater, *Journals and Diaries, I*, 18: 121.

[123] Ward and Heitzenrater, *Journals and Diaries, IV*, 21: 510. For other witnesses of Taylor's influence, see *On Laying the Foundation of the New Chapel*, Outler, *Sermons, III*, 3: 580; *A Plain Account of Christian Perfection*, Jackson, *Works*, 11: 366.

alongside Origen, Athanasius, and Chrysostom.[124] Although one might dismiss this remark as hyperbole, Pearson's description of the patristic doctrine of holiness is indeed compelling, so much so that Wesley cites several pages from *Exposition* on the subject.[125] One finds that Pearson gives a detailed description of the Holy Spirit's work of sanctification. The portions of *Exposition* Wesley includes indicate that he agrees with the bishop's views, the major lines of which are: (1) saving faith as "an internal illumination of the soul" that is initiated and imparted by the Holy Spirit; (2) the sanctifying and regenerating work of the Spirit that brings about "the renewing of man in all the parts and faculties of his soul"; (3) Spirit-empowered obedience to God; and (4) the assurance of God's love through the inner witness of the Holy Spirit.[126] Pearson argues throughout that inward and outward sanctification are the purpose and end of salvation. He declares: "Whatsoever is wanting in our nature of . . . holiness and perfection must be supplied by the Spirit of God."[127] Wesley could not have agreed more.[128]

---

[124] "A Farther Appeal to Men of Reason and Religion Part I," Cragg, *The Appeals to Men of Reason and Religion*, 11: 175.

[125] Ibid., 11: 163-165. The complete passage from which Wesley cited *passim* is found in John Pearson, *Exposition,* 489-95. Pearson's footnotes in the original are primarily of patristic sources.

[126] "A Farther Appeal to Men of Reason and Religion Part I," Cragg, *The Appeals to Men of Reason and Religion*, 1: 163-65 *passim.*

[127] Pearson, *Exposition,* 489.

[128] It is curious that twelve years later Wesley wrote somewhat critically of Bishop Pearson's treatment of the doctrine of faith. In a letter to Richard Tompson dated March 16, 1756, Wesley wrote: "Bishop Pearson's definition [of faith] is abundantly too wide for the faith of which we are speaking . . . . Neither does he give that definition either of justifying or saving faith"(Telford, *Letters,* 3: 174). Pearson had defined faith primarily as *assent* leading to confession (*Exposition,* 1-20 et seq.). Although he cites numerous patristic writers (including Clement of Alexandria) and early medieval sources, Pearson is primarily dependent upon Thomas Aquinas. See esp. Aquinas' arguments concerning the object of faith and faith as an intellectual act in *Summa Theologiae,* Pt. II-II, q. 1, a. 1 and q. 2, a. 2 respectively. Wesley apparently regarded Pearson's formal definition of faith, which was based upon the philosophical question of truth, as inadequate for the circumstances that occasioned his exchange with Tompson. The *experience* of faith, which Pearson classified appropriately under

4. William Beveridge: Eastern Sacramentalism

Bishop William Beveridge (1637-1708) was a historical theologian whose interests had lain primarily in the Church of England's *Thirty-Nine Articles* and the liturgical practices of early Eastern Christianity. Though he wrote primarily for scholars, Beveridge's works nonetheless enjoyed a wide audience.

Wesley began an intense study of Beveridge in September of 1736 during the midst of his mostly unfruitful sojourn in Georgia colony. Recalling the time, he writes:

> Mon. 13 [Sept., 1736]. I began reading with Mr. [Charles] Delamotte, Bishop Beveridge's *Pandectæ canonum conciliorum.* Nothing could so effectually have convinced us, that both particular and general Councils may err, and have erred; and that things ordained by them as necessary to salvation, have neither strength nor authority, unless they be taken out of holy Scripture.

> Mon. 20 [Sept., 1736]. We ended (of which also I must confess I once thought more highly than I ought to think) the Apostolical Canons; so called, as Bishop Beveridge observes, "because [they are] partly grounded upon, [and] partly agree . . . with, the traditions delivered down from the Apostles." But he observes farther, (in the 159th page of his *Codex canonum ecclesiæ primitivæ.* And why did he not observe it in the first page of the book?) "They contain the discipline used in the Church at the time when they were collected: Not when the Council of Nice met; for then many parts of it were useless and obsolete."[129]

This may not have been Wesley's first encounter with Beveridge, but it certainly was the most significant.[130] The treatise that Wesley read is entitled *SUNODIKON, sive Pandectae Canonum SS. Apostolorum, et Conciliorum ab*

---

his doctrine of the Holy Spirit, Wesley never contested. Pearson clearly was a better systematic theologian than Wesley.

[129] Ward and Heitzenrater, *Journals and Diaries, I,* 18: 171-72.

[130] Beveridge's works were collected in *The Theological Works of William Beveridge, D.D.,* 12 vols., Library of Anglo-Catholic Theology (Oxford: J. H. Parker, 1842-1848).

Ecclesia Graeca receptorum nec non Canonicarium SS. Patrum Epistolarum.[131] The *Synodikon,* as it is usually called, contains among other ancient documents a compilation of eighty-five canons which originated in the Eastern Church known as the *Apostolic Canons.*[132] These consist of the disciplinary (as opposed to dogmatic) canons of the Eastern Church; their emphasis is upon ecclesiastical practice and priestly ethics. The dating and authorship of this document has been a subject of debate since ancient times.[133] Beveridge believed that the *Apostolic Canons,* though not written by the apostles themselves, nonetheless reflected the teachings of the Twelve and had been collected soon after their death by their immediate successors.[134]

Wesley held the *Apostolic Canons* in high regard when he began to read Beveridge, probably because he believed that the *Canons* reflected the actual liturgical practices of the apostles. Somewhat naively, he had hoped that in the pristine environment of Georgia he might evangelize the native American Indians

---

[131] Beveridge, *Codex canonum ecclesiae primitivae,* vols. 1 and 2 in *The Library of Anglo-Catholic Thought,* appearing as vols. 11 and 12. The significance of Beveridge's work on the *Apostolic Canons* is discussed by Henry R. Percival, ed., *The Seven Ecumenical Councils of the Undivided Church, vol. 14, A Select Library of Nicene and Post-Nicene Fathers,* Second Series, P. Schaff and H. Wace, eds. (Grand Rapids: Wm. B. Eerdmans Publishing Co., 1991; reprint; New York: New York, C. Scribner's Sons, 1900), xvii-xix; 591-93. Hereafter, this set is abbreviated NPNF 2.

[132] For a synopsis of their contents see Percival, *NPNF 2,* 14: xvii-xix.

[133] The history of this debate is complex. The best source is Hefele, *A History of the Christian Councils,* 1: 449-57. The *Canons* themselves may have been distilled from the larger *Apostolic Constitutions,* as Hefele points out. The *Apostolic Canons* appear in English translation in *NPNF 2,* 14: 594-600. They also appear with the *Apostolic Constitutions* and an introduction in A. Roberts and J. Donaldson, eds., *The Ante-Nicene Fathers,* 10 vols. (Grand Rapids: Eerdmans, 1950-53, 1980-83), 7: 387-505. (Hereafter, references to this set will be designated by the abbreviation *ANF.*) Some scholars have argued that the *Apostolic Constitutions* and *Canons* can be dated no earlier than the fourth century (ca. 350-375 A.D.). See a series of articles by C.H. Turner in the *Journal of Theological Studies (JTS)* beginning with "A Primitive Edition of the Apostolic Constitutions and Canons: An Early List of Apostles and Disciples," *JTS* 15 (1914): 53-65; "Notes on the Apostolic Constitutions," *JTS* 16 (1915): 54-61; "Notes on the Apostolic Constitutions," *JTS* 21 (1920): 160-68; "Notes on the Apostolic Constitutions," *JTS* 31 (1930): 128-41.

[134] See Percival, *NPNF 2,* 14: 593.

and establish them as a Christian community reminiscent of the apostolic age. His reading in Beveridge did not overthrow his belief in the origin of the *Canons*, but it certainly tempered it. Beveridge restored balance to the way Wesley would view the church fathers from then on. It convinced him that the tradition's authority derives solely from how accurately it reflects the teaching and implications of Scripture. Tradition must always be subordinated to the canon of Holy Scripture.

Beveridge's grasp of the history and thought of the Eastern Church, with its profound sacramental view of salvation made a deep impression upon young John Wesley living in the remote Georgia colony. The bishop's comments on the nature of the early church and the character of primitive Christianity supported Wesley's concern for disciplined, holy living.

C. Critical Assessments
Of Wesley's Use of Patristic Sources

Although scholars have generally acknowledged the similarities between Wesley and the church fathers, there have been relatively few attempts to assess the way he used patristic sources. Wesley himself was not forthcoming in this regard. As a result, it has been easy in subsequent generations to dismiss his references to the fathers as rhetoric designed to gain authority for his arguments rather than claims having real substance. In our view, Wesley's use of the fathers was more sophisticated than has generally been thought. In this section we shall examine the better analyses of Wesley on this issue.

One of the earliest writers to explore Wesley's grounding in patristic thought was R. Denny Urlin (1830-1907). Urlin is to be credited with undertaking the first critical study of Wesley's sources. His *John Wesley's Place in Church History* (1870) marks the beginning of the kind of objective analysis that was sorely needed after Wesley's death almost eighty years before. Urlin argued that throughout his career Wesley took the ancient consensual tradition as his primary source for the correct interpretation of Scripture.[135]   Urlin was convinced that Wesley had used the Eastern church fathers as a source for many Methodist practices such as the class meeting, lay preaching, the love feast, the watch night vigil, visitation of the sick, and extemporary prayer. According to Urlin, all were analogues of practices that Wesley had discovered by reading the fathers of the East, and that he was attempting to recover for Methodism.[136]

Urlin substantiates Wesley's fondness for the primitive church by bringing to light some previously unpublished manuscripts.[137] These writings produced in Wesley's hand had been in the possession of Rev. Richard Reece (d. 1850), who had been a member of the Wesleyan Conference. Reece received them from John Pawson (1737-1806), one of Wesley's younger contemporaries and a lay Methodist preacher. In spite of his the high esteem Wesley had for him and the credit due him for preserving these documents, Pawson unfortunately is responsible for having lost more of Wesley' private papers than the few he saved.[138]

---

[135]   R. Denny Urlin, *John Wesley's Place in Church History* (London: Rivingtons, 1870), 23. Urlin states that this book is not a biography; rather, its purpose is to correct the lack of critical analysis by Wesley's early biographers due to a lack of documentary evidence. As a trained barrister, Urlin's writing was mainly in the field of English law. However, he produced two additional volumes on John Wesley and Methodism, including *The Churchman's Life of Wesley* (London: S.P.C.K., 1880), an attempt at a balanced and objective biography, and *Father Reece: The Old Methodist Minister, Twice President of the Conference* (London: Elliot Stock, 1901).

[136]   Urlin, *John Wesley's Place in Church History,* 62-68.

[137]   Ibid., 69-74. See Appendix 1 "The Unpublished Manuscripts."

[138]   One of the most ironic and tragic events following Wesley's death is attributed to John Pawson.   In the years immediately after Wesley's demise in 1790 several biographies appeared, two of which were essentially hagiographic in character. A third was produced John Whitehead that was more balanced because it had taken into account the private papers and diaries from Wesley's middle years that had never been published. Upon returning these papers to the house at City Road Chapel where Pawson was now living, Pawson took it upon himself for some unknown reason to burn the majority of these papers, never telling anyone until after the deed was done. For a complete recounting of this matter and the events leading up to it see Richard P. Heitzenrater, *The Elusive Mr. Wesley* 2 vols. (Nashville, Abingdon, 1984), 2: 168-73. Apparently Pawson did not burn all Wesley's papers; again, why he did not is unclear. The unpublished papers that I refer to above and that are reproduced in Appendix 1 are the papers that Pawson did not burn.

Nevertheless, the manuscripts provide compelling evidence of Wesley's fascination with the ancient Eastern church. Though the Pawson/Reece manuscripts leave open certain questions concerning Wesley's observance of Eastern practices, they nonetheless prove decisively that he had studied and reflected upon early Eastern Christianity at some length. His motivation probably originated in his immersing himself in Beveridge during his sojourn in Georgia.[139] Furthermore, the manuscripts demonstrate that Wesley's knowledge of the fathers was more comprehensive than many of his biographers have recognized. One can only imagine what additional insights were lost with the destruction of his private papers.

In the early twentieth century, John S. Simon focused on the Wesley brothers' relationship with John Clayton and the Manchester Nonjurors.[140] The Wesleys first met Clayton in 1732, even though Clayton had been at Oxford since 1726. Their meeting blossomed into a friendship, which in turn resulted in Clayton deciding to associate himself with the Holy Club.[141] One of the more significant aspects of the friendship lay in Clayton's introduction of Wesley to Thomas Deacon, who was the leader of the Manchester Nonjurors. The Manchester sect had been the most separatist of the three Nonjuring groups. Deacon, who was a practicing physician, was their bishop. Simon observes that

---

[139] See discussion above.

[140] John S. Simon, *John Wesley and the Religious Societies* (London: Epworth, 1921), 96. The most comprehensive treatment of the Nonjurors is still Thomas Lathbury's *A History of the Nonjurors* (London: William Pickering, 1845).

[141] Clayton would remain an important friend throughout the years that were decisive in Wesley's theological formation. Wesley first mentions Clayton in the "Introductory Letter" to his *Journal*. There, he recounts their initial meeting on April 20, 1732 (Ward and Heitzenrater, *Journals and Diaries, I,* 18:131, esp. n. 45). Clayton is mentioned again upon Wesley's arrival at Manchester, March 17, 1738 (*Journals and Diaries, I,* 18: 230). Finally, Clayton appears once more in the entry for October 30, 1743 (*Journals and Diaries, III,* 20: 2, esp. n. 2). For comprehensive accounts of the relationship between Clayton and the Wesleys see Luke Tyerman, *The Oxford Methodists* (New York: Harper & Brothers, 1873), 24-56 and Heitzenrater, "John Wesley and The Oxford Methodists, 1732-35," 158-70.

58

under Deacon's tutelage Wesley "began to study the *Apostolical Constitutions* and *Ecclesiastical Canons*" and that as result "his lively imagination was excited by the visions of Church life in primitive times."[142] This of course occurred prior to his reading of Beveridge, which we noted above, making Wesley's ongoing interest in these documents are the more noteworthy.

Simon points out that in spite of his close association with the Manchester sect and his appreciation for their emphasis upon liturgical worship, Wesley never accepted, as the Nonjurors had, the high medieval Roman Catholic doctrine of transubstantiation. While Anglicans had always held St. Thomas and the Schoolmen in high regard, they did not care for the Aristotelian metaphysics governing the concept of the transformed substance of the elements. Wesley followed the 'real presence' language of classical Anglicanism and the primitive church.[143]

Other scholars in the early to mid-twentieth century noticed Wesley's affinity for the patristic church, but none gave the kind of scrutiny it deserved. Maximin Piette, for example, mentions the friendship between Wesley and Clayton in conjunction with their study of the primitive church. Piette also discussed Wesley's desire to institute the practices of the early church among the Native Americans of Georgia.[144] However, he fails to probe beyond the surface issues and deal with the difficult question of the fathers' influence on Wesley's thought.

---

[142] Simon, *Wesley and the Religious Societies,* 103. See also Lathbury, *History of the Nonjurors,* 496-52 for a treatment of Deacon's prayer book and the Separatists.

[143] It is beyond the scope of this study to delve further into Wesley's views on the sacraments and their relation to early Anglicanism. See Ole Borgen, *John Wesley on the Sacraments* (Grand Rapids: Francis Asbury Press, 1985), 68 for a brief analysis of the similarities between Wesley and Cranmer. Horton Davies in *From Cranmer to Hooker (1534-1603),* 111-20 summarizes Cranmer's views on the Eucharist.

[144] Maximin Piette, *John Wesley in the Evolution of Protestantism* (New York: Sheed and Ward, 1937), 289-94.

Harold Lindström explored Wesley's doctrine of Christian perfection and speculated concerning Wesley's testimony that he had used Clemens Alexandrinus as a theological source for the doctrine. Although Lindström recognized the similarity between Wesley's doctrine of sanctification and the "ideal of perfection" held by Clement and the Eastern Church, he did not elaborate.[145]

It wasn't until the 1960's renewed interest in John Wesley's use of the church fathers emerged. Albert Outler served as the catalyst for this movement.[146] As a patristics scholar in his own right, Outler endeavored to better understand the connection between Wesley and the ancient Eastern Church. His 1961 address to the American Theological Society, *John Wesley's Interests in the Early Fathers of the Church,* set the stage for reopening the question. Outler argued that the Eastern Church with its distinctive understanding of salvation was crucial in Wesley's theology:

> All of Wesley's heroes from Christian Antiquity are Eastern, and this helps to explain the emphases in his soteriology and spirituality that never were so prominent in Latin Christianity, and did not always stand in the Anglican tradition in quite the same nuances as in Wesley; few of them were as eager to hold the two traditions of *sola fide* and "holy living" in paradoxical balance as Wesley was. It was from the Eastern Fathers that Wesley learned to conceive of salvation as a process, and of the *ordo salutis* as an articulated continuum of stages, both of "moments" and also of process.[147]

---

[145] Harold Lindström, *Wesley and Sanctification: A Study in the Doctrine of Salvation* (London: Epworth Press, 1946), 159-60.

[146] See Outler, *John Wesley,* 9-10. See also Thomas C. Oden, Leicester R. Longden, eds., *The Wesleyan Theological Heritage: Essays of Albert C. Outler* (Grand Rapids: Zondervan, 1991). In this collection essays, note especially "Towards a Re-Appraisal of John Wesley as a Theologian," " The Place of Wesley in the Christian Tradition," and "John Wesley's Interests in the Early Fathers of the Church."

[147] "John Wesley's Interests in the Early Fathers of the Church," Oden and Longden, *The Wesleyan Theological Heritage,* 107-08.

60

Outler's work was ground breaking in that he proposed a series of analogies between Wesley's theology and ancient Eastern Christianity:

> John Wesley's reflection of early and Eastern motifs of Christian spirituality [is as follows] — (1) a therapeutic view of the *ordo salutis* as contrasted with any forensic one; (2) the *telos* of human life in God; (3) the person and primal agency of the Holy Spirit in Christian existence; (4) prevenient grace; (5) the concordance of grace and free will; (6) the inspiration of Scripture and its pneumatological interpretation; (7) salvation as the restoration of the image of God in humanity; (8) ascesis and discipline in Christian living and, above all; (9) the distinctions between the "moments" of justification and sanctification and, therefore, a doctrine of open-ended perfection in this life . . . .[148]

Outler eventually narrowed the scope of his research to an investigation of Wesley's appreciation for three Eastern church theologians — Macarius the Egyptian, Ephraem Syrus and Gregory of Nyssa.[149] Outler was convinced that Wesley's thought bore some similarity to the Eastern traditionrepresented by the above thinkers.

Other scholars picked up Outler's insights took the question further in an attempt to gain greater clarification. John Merritt, for example, attempted to show the similarity between Wesley and Macarius (Gregory of Nyssa) on the doctrine

---

[148] Ibid., 102-03.

[149] Ibid., 106. See also *John Wesley*, 9, n. 26 where Outler describes the well-known problems associated with the Macarian authorship. There, he seeks to correct Wesley's belief that the fourth century desert monk Macarius had actually authored the works attributed to him. Citing Werner Jaegar's seminal study, *Two Rediscovered Works of Ancient Christian Literature: Gregory of Nyssa and Macarius* (Leiden: E.J. Brill, 1954), Outler sought to establish a reasonable link between Wesley and Gregory of Nyssa, whom he regarded as the true author of the Macarian *Spiritual Homilies*. On the problems associated with the authenticity of the Macarian corpus, see Johannes Quasten, *Patrology*, 4 vols. (Westminster, MD: Christian Classics, 1950, 1986), 3: 162-66.

of Christian perfection.[150] David Ford, however, argued that Wesley's view of sanctification was not entirely congruent with the view held by Macarius.[151]

The most comprehensive study to date of John Wesley's employment of the fathers has been carried out by Ted Campbell. Campbell's survey of Anglican faith and practice in relation to that of the primitive church is useful in understanding Wesley's desire to recover the piety of Christianity's formative centuries. Campbell argues that there were three distinct ways in which Christian antiquity was appropriated in Anglicanism. Wesley, he proposes, combined all three.[152] This would tend to support the conclusion that Wesley's reverence for Christian antiquity was grounded in a three-fold desire to be part loyal churchman, part reformer of the status quo, and part polemicist against the Roman Church. In spite of his argument for a rather sophisticated appropriation of patristic sources, Campbell remains curiously skeptical that Wesley had been influenced by the substance and content of what he read in the church fathers. Campbell's skepticism is largely based upon the absence of asceticism in Wesley, which characterizes the Eastern church's life of faith, and which he reckons would need to be in evidence if one were to posit a substantial relationship between Wesley's theology and early Eastern Christian thought.[153]

---

[150] John G. Merritt, "Dialogue Within a Tradition: John Wesley and Gregory of Nyssa Discuss Christian Perfection," *Wesleyan Theological Journal* 22, no. 2 (Fall 1987): 92-116.

[151] David C. Ford, "Saint Makarios of Egypt and John Wesley: Variations on the Theme of Sanctification," *Greek Orthodox Theological Review* 33, no. 3 (1988): 285-312. Ford's analysis raises an appropriate caution for Wesley scholars.

[152] See Campbell, *John Wesley and Christian Antiquity,* 20-21; 52-53. Campbell attributes to Wesley a combination of conservative, programmatic, and polemical uses of Christian antiquity.

[153] Commenting on his research vis-a-vis Albert Outler, Campbell writes: "I fear that my research disappointed him [Outler] in some ways: he had hoped, in particular, that it would confirm his suspicion that Wesley's doctrine of sanctification was in essence that of ancient Eastern Christian asceticism, which came to Wesley from Gregory of Nyssa by way of the so-called 'Macarian' homilies. Although my researches have indeed shown that Wesley was attracted to Macarius, they also show that Wesley consistently omitted references to ascetic life and to the

62

Professor Campbell points out that Wesley's use of patristic sources, while generally in accord with conservative Anglican usages, departs from them as well. For instance, he notes that Wesley was undecided whether ancient catholics had made correct decisions in condemning Pelagianism, Nestorianism, and Eutychanism. He also points out that Wesley viewed certain heresies — e.g., Montanism, Donatism, and Novatianism — as better representing "scriptural Christianity" than the positions eventually upheld as orthodox.[154] While it may seem, as Campbell suggests, that Wesley departed from a conservative Anglican appropriation of the church fathers in these instances, it may be that this supposed departure simply represents a more nuanced understanding of the issues on Wesley's part. Perhaps, Wesley was not so much rejecting fourth and fifth century conciliar decisions as he was grappling with his own, and what he viewed as the primitive church's, commitment to holy living as the ordinary expression of authentic Christianity.[155] If such was the case, then Wesley's affinity for the fathers becomes all the more understandable and clear.

notion of *theosis* — 'divinization' or 'deification' — perhaps the most distinctively Eastern note of the Macarian literature" (*John Wesley and Christian Antiquity*, x).

[154] Campbell, *John Wesley and Christian Antiquity*, 77-78.

[155] See Appendix 2: John Wesley On Early Church Heresies.

Chapter 3
John Wesley's Adaptation
Of Clement Of Alexandria

In the previous chapter we attempted to demonstrate that Wesley's method of citing the fathers as secondary sources of theology had its precedent in classical Anglicanism. We discussed some of the evidence in which he cites the early writers and reviewed recent scholarly opinion on the question. Now, we want to examine specifically the evidence surrounding Wesley's references to Clement of Alexandria (ca. 150-215 A.D.). At the outset however, it is crucial to remember one incontrovertible fact: of all the church fathers Wesley names, none is cited with more specificity concerning his theological formation than Clement of Alexandria. Furthermore, there are none who Wesley seems to have spent more time contemplating that Clemens Alexandrinus so far as Wesley's surviving works are concerned. On the basis of the written evidence alone, even though not overwhelming, there are grounds for a careful examination and comparison of the John Wesley and Clemens Alexandrinus on the topic that seems to have most occupied both, the doctrine of Christian perfection.

A. "On Clemems Alexandrinus'
Description of a Perfect Christian"

The earliest reference to Clement of Alexandria among the published works of John Wesley is an anonymous poem, *On Clemems Alexandrinus' Description of a Perfect Christian.*[156] The poem first appeared in Wesley's edited volume of *Hymns and Sacred Poems* published in 1739.[157] Designed to capture the essence of Clement's thought, the poem combines a lofty vision of holiness with an optimistic view of human nature. The writer believes that Christians transformed by mystical love for God can overcome the harsh vicissitudes of life. It is a poem about faith and character. The theme is simple: the soul that aspires to holiness must thoroughly rest in God. Wesley published the poem again in 1744, including it in *A Collection of Moral and Sacred Poems from the Most Celebrated English Authors.*[158]

It is fairly certain that the poem, whoever its author may be (though it could easily have been Wesley himself), was composed during the days of the Oxford Holy Club. Its inclusion among the early literature of the revival signifies Wesley's approval of Clement's idea of holiness. In a broader sense, the poem attests to primitive Methodism's preference for the Eastern Church's notion of sanctification as moral transformation. This observation is borne out in the preface to *A Collection of Moral and Sacred Poems*, which Wesley dedicated to Lady Huntingdon. Lamenting the state of English culture at the time, he writes:

> It has been a common remark for many years, that poetry which might answer the noblest purposes, has been prostituted to the vilest, even to confound the distinctions between virtue and vice, good and evil. And that to such degree, that among the numerous poems now

---

[156] See Appendix 3 for a discussion of authorship and the text.

[157] John Wesley, *Hymns and Sacred Poems* (London: W. Strahan, 1739), 37-38.

[158] John Wesley, ed., *A Collection of Moral and Sacred Poems from the Most Celebrated English Authors,* 3. vols. (Bristol: Farley, 1744), 3: 196-97.

extant in our own language, there is an exceeding small proportion which does not more or less fall under this heavy censure. So that a great difficulty lies on those who are not willing, on the one hand, to be deprived of an elegant amusement, nor on the other to purchase it at the hazard of innocence or virtue.[159]

Not all of the poems included in the three volume 1744 edition of *Moral and Sacred Poems* were specifically Christian in origin or content. A few derive from the Greek and Latin classics.[160] Wesley remarks further to Lady Huntingdon that because of England's present moral state "many have placed a chaste collection of *English* poems, among the chief desiderata of this age."[161] Almost apologetically he writes:

There is nothing therein [i.e., in the collection] contrary to virtue, nothing that can any way offend the chastest ear, or give pain to the tenderest heart. And perhaps whatever is really essential to the most sublime divinity, as to the purest and most refined morality, will be found therein. Nor is it a small circumstance, that the most just and important sentiments, are here represented with the utmost advantage, with all the ornaments both of wit and language, and in the clearest, fullest, strongest light.[162]

Wesley held closely the connection between faith, personal virtue, and the transformation of society. Though these things had been of perennial concern, they were especially relevant in Wesley's day.

From the late seventeenth century until the middle of the eighteenth (ca. 1688-1750) English society had been regarded by many political and religious leaders to be in a state of moral deterioration.[163] By their vocation and status

---

[159] Wesley, *Moral and Sacred Poems,* 1: iii-iv.

[160] See Samuel Wesley's "Eupolis' Hymn to the Creator," *Moral and Sacred Poems,* 3: 3-8.

[161] Ibid., 1: iv.

[162] Ibid., 1: v-vi.

[163] See E. G. Rupp, *Religion in England 1688-1791,* 278-79.

within society, the clergy were on the front lines of the battle to stem the tide of moral decline. A renewed interest in moral theology arose, along with a trend toward moralistic preaching. At the heart of these developments was a strong desire on the part of the church to connect personal faith with holy living. This movement extended across ecclesiastical boundaries to engage Anglicans, Puritan Dissenters, and Roman Catholics. Numerous moralistic works were produced during the period — all directed toward the reforming of society through an appeal to personal virtue. This literature captured the imagination of common folks from around the middle of the seventeenth century and beyond for many decades. These were people who desired not only an improvement in society at large, but they recognized that the way to accomplish this end was for individuals themselves to contribute by living ethical lives.

Throughout the restoration period, moralistic literature was produced by such writers as Richard Allestree (*The Whole Duty of Man* [1657], *The Gentlemen's Calling* [1659], *The Causes of the Decay of Christian Piety* [1667]), Edward Calamy (*The Godly Man's Ark, or the City of Refuge in the day of his Distress* [1657]), Thomas Doolittle (*Treatise Concerning the Lord's Supper* [1665]), Edward Pearse (*The Great Concern: or A Serious Warning to a Timely and Thorough Preparation for Death* [1671]), Joseph Alleine (*An Alarm to Unconverted Sinners* [1665]), John Bunyan (*The Pilgrim's Progress from This World to That Which is to Come* [1678]), Thomas Ken (*A Manual of Prayers for the Use of the Scholars of Winchester College* [1675]), Simon Patrick (*A Book for Beginners: or, An Help to Young Communicants* [1679]), William Beveridge (*The Excellence and Usefulness of the Common-Prayer*), William Penn (*A Key, Opening the Way to every Capacity. . . .* [1692]) and, of course, Jeremy Taylor (*The Rule and Exercises of Holy Living and Holy Dying* [1650] and *The Golden Grove* [1655]).[164] These were

---

[164] For a survey of this literature during the Restoration refer to C. John Sommerville, *Popular Religion in Restoration England*, (Gainesville: University Presses of Florida, 1977), 33-59.

popular works that were optimistically directed toward the renewal of personal piety in a society many considered by many to be in moral decline.

On Clemens Alexandrinus' Description of a Perfect Christian, if nothing else, is evidence of a revived interest among a small group of young English clergy (Oxford Methodists) in the merits of personal transformation and holy living. More significantly, it is suggests that Wesley's thoughts on holiness in particular had early on been shaped by an acquaintance, whatever the circumstances surrounding it, with Clement's perfect Christian.

B. The Letter to Lloyd's Evening Post

In 1767 Wesley found himself in the midst of a serious and all-too-public controversy concerning the doctrine of Christian perfection. It seems as though William Dodd, editor of the provocative but short-lived *Christian Magazine* had accused Wesley and the Methodists of promoting 'sinless perfection', a condition of grace that theoretically makes sin improbable if not impossible, and extraordinary religious manifestations.[165] Dodd's accusations had their basis partially in the 'enthusiasm' issue that had dogged Methodism from its inception.

The Methodist Conferences between 1758 and 1763 had formally addressed the way Christian perfection was being taught. Wesley had attempted to correct those who misunderstood the doctrine in *Thoughts on Christian*

---

[165] Ward and Heitzenrater, eds., *Journal and Diaries V*, vol. 22 of *The Works of John Wesley* (Nashville: Abingdon, 1993), 71-73. See also Telford, *Letters of John Wesley*, 5: 42-44. Dodd's *Christian Magazine* had a relatively short life of seven years (1760-67). On his colorful and somewhat tragic life see Ward and Heitzenrater, *Journal and Diaries V*, 22: 71, n. 27. Although Dodd had been ordained by the Anglican Church and had served in several ministry settings, he had a penchant for living beyond his means. After being caught committing forgery, Dodd was tried, convicted, and imprisoned for a time, then executed in 1777. In spite of Dodd's accusations, Wesley obviously respected him, so much so that in 1783 he published "Some Account of the Late Dr. Dodd" (Jackson, *Works*, 11: 454-56) — a commendable effort that includes a brief but moving account of Wesley's pastoral visitation of Dodd prior to the latter's execution.

Perfection in 1759.[166] In 1767 Wesley incorporated that tract into his larger work *A Plain Account of Christian Perfection*, the design of which was to describe in concise and clear language what he had consistently taught from 1725.[167] Still, misunderstandings abounded.

Three issues attended the controversy. First, there was the question of whether sanctification (i.e., 'Christian perfection' or 'perfection', as Wesley preferred) may be achieved instantaneously or, as those in the Reformed tradition had long maintained, it is to be conceived as gradual and progressive over time. In *Plain Account* he writes:

> Q. When does inward sanctification begin? A. In the moment a man is justified (Yet sin remains in him, yea, the seed of all sin, till he is sanctified throughout.) From that time a believer gradually dies to sin, and grows in grace.[168]

Although there may be other differences on such issues as baptism, all Protestant churches agreed that following the evangelical conversion of the individual gradual moral improvement is expected. Wesley continues:

> Q. Is this [inward sanctification] ordinarily given till a little before death? A. It is not, to those who expect it no sooner. Q. But may we expect it sooner? A. Why not? For, although we grant, (1.) That the generality of believers, whom we have hitherto known, were not so sanctified till near death; (2.) That few of those to whom St. Paul wrote his former Epistles were so at that time; nor, (3.) He himself at the time of writing his former Epistles; *yet all this does not prove, that we may not be so to-day.* [169]

---

[166] Wesley refers to this pamphlet in "A Plain Account of Christian Perfection," Jackson, *Works*, 11: 394.

[167] See Rack, *Reasonable Enthusiast,* 333-42 for an assessment of this period and the issues at stake for the Methodist movement.

[168] "A Plain Account of Christian Perfection," Jackson, *Works*, 11: 387:

[169] Ibid. Italics mine.

The doctrine justification is not at issue. The controverted issue was whether entire inward sanctification is to be expected only at death, as all branches of the church generally agree, or may one obtain it sooner — perhaps many years before death. Wesley had always been cautious with regard to instantaneous perfection; yet he had also been open to the idea as well. Some claimed to have experienced an immediate cleansing of heart and motives from sin; and Wesley was not willing to rule it out. Though he maintained that sanctification is normally experienced as a lifelong process culminating at death, Wesley admitted that he could see no reason why one could not expect entire sanctification instantaneously well before death of the physical body.[170]

A second and related issue was the extent to which Christians may expect to be delivered from sin prior to death. The holiness theme, which had been so critical in the formation of Wesley's own religious consciousness, had grown in importance among Methodists. Though Wesley had never before defined sanctification as absolute sinlessness, now disagreements over the degree of holiness Christians may expect threatened to divide the movement. Does entire sanctification imply absolute holiness with no sin remaining, or does it refer to something else? Wesley did not agree with the absolutists, and he immediately set about to correct such notions.

A third and more complex issue was the role of subjective religious expressions in evangelical experience. The controversy over 'enthusiasm' not only attracted harsh criticism from outside the movement, but it also involved

---

[170] Wesley's acceptance of instantaneous perfection becomes much more apparent later when in a letter to his brother Charles (Telford, *Letters* 5: 39) he writes: "I believe this perfection is always wrought in the soul by a simple act of faith; consequently in an *instant*. But I believe a gradual work, both preceding and following that instant. . . . I believe this instant generally is the instant of death, the moment before the soul leaves the body. But I believe it may be ten, twenty, or forty years before. I believe it is usually many years after justification; but that it may be within five years or five months after it, I know no conclusive argument to the contrary." Italics mine.

disagreement within Methodist ranks over the role, if any, that visions and religious ecstasies should play in perfecting the believer's faith. Wesley had always believed and taught that those who receive salvation may reasonably expect an inward assurance of forgiven sins, but he had learned to be wary of outward displays of religious fervor.

His caution was justified in 1762 when the revival in London was enjoying great success with both sinners and backsliders finding deliverance. Wesley feared that in such an emotionally charged atmosphere aberrant religious behavior might arise that would destroy the good work that had been accomplished. He therefore cautioned that emotional displays spring most often not from true faith but rather from false spiritual pride. Sure enough, immediately upon his departure his fears came true. As he writes:

> "[A]s soon as I was gone enthusiasm broke in. Two or three began to take their own imaginations for impressions from God, and thence to suppose that they should never die; and these, labouring to bring others into the same opinion, occasioned much noise and confusion. Soon after, the same persons, with a few more, ran into other extravagances; fancying they could not be tempted; that they should feel no more pain; and that they had the gift of prophecy, and of discerning spirits"[171]

As we noted earlier, enthusiasm as a troubling issue had dwelt on the periphery of Methodism as far back as the movement's very beginning in 1739.[172] What seems to have heightened Wesley's concern by the late 1750s and into the 1760s was the increase in negative publicity from outside the Methodist camp. There was a growing perception on the part of outside observers that Methodism might be related to various enthusiastic religious movements of the past. Such groups had regularly appeared throughout history, usually in times of crisis and spiritual renewal.

---

[171] "A Plain Account of Christian Perfection," Jackson, *Works*, 11: 406.

[172] See remarks for January 17 and July 31, 1739 in Ward and Heitzenrater, *Journals and Diaries, II*, 19: 31-32; 82-87.

As a result of these rumblings, perfection was a topic of focused discussion at the Methodist Conferences of 1758 and 1759, then again in 1761. Finally, in 1762 two preachers, Thomas Maxfield and George Bell, publicly scandalized the Methodist movement. Rack observes that the actions of these two insurgents gave rise to the "suspicion that Methodism was simply a new version of the wild sects of the Interregnum or the more recent French Prophets."[173] Maxfield and Bell represented a tiny wing of perfectionist doctrine extremists. Before it was all over they and a handful of followers had seceded from the Methodists. The Maxfield and Bell affair, though relatively minor in terms of the actual number of individuals affected, kept the enthusiasm charge alive among critics of Methodism, making it a sensitive issue for Wesley in years yet to come.

It is with these events as background that Wesley responded to William Dodd's charge that Methodism represented an 'enthusiastic' sect. The vindication of his position that Wesley publishes in *Lloyd's Evening Post* are not only crucial in providing additional evidence of what he taught concerning Christian perfection, but they also provide the context in which, for the first time, Wesley refers directly to the influence that Clement of Alexandria had upon the formation of his doctrine of sanctification and Christian existence. He writes:

> The occasion of his [Dodd's] late attack is this: *Five or six and thirty years ago I much admired the character of a perfect Christian drawn by Clemens Alexandrinus. Five or six and twenty years ago, a thought came into my mind of drawing such a character myself, only in a more scriptural manner and mostly in the very words of Scripture. This I entitled the 'Character of a Methodist',* believing that curiosity would incite more persons to read it and also that some prejudice might be

---

[173] Rack, *Reasonable Enthusiast,* 337. The French Prophets had their origin in the unsuccessful Huguenot rebellion of the Camisards in France during the years 1702-05. A small number of the sect made their way to England ca. 1707. The French Prophets were charismatic enthusiasts who reveled in ecstatic devotion, visionary experiences and outrageous prophecies. Their movement was short lived, however, when in 1708 one of their deceased members failed to rise again from the dead as prophesied. See E. G. Rupp, *Religion in England 1699-1791,* 216-17.

> removed from candid men. But that none might imagine I intended
> a panegyric either on myself or my friends, I guarded against this in
> the very title-page, saying both in the name of myself and them, 'Not
> as though I had already attained, either were already perfect.' To the
> same effect I speak in the conclusion: 'These are the principles and
> practices of our sect; these are the marks of a true Methodist' (i.e., a
> true Christian, as I immediately after explain myself). 'By these
> alone do those who are in derision so called *desire* to be
> distinguished from other men' (p. 11). 'By these marks do we *labour*
> to distinguish ourselves from those whose minds or lives are not
> according to the gospel of Christ' (p. 12).[174]

Given the historical context in which Wesley published this response, his remarks concerning Clement of Alexandria and the writing of *Character of a Methodist* are all the more significant.

By appealing to a leading and prolific father of the ancient church as the inspiring source for one of his own early tracts, which by then had been reprinted many times, Wesley distanced Methodists from the fanatical 'enthusiasts' that had raised questions in the public mind. Wesley's comments are not merely a situational ploy, but they demonstrate that from the beginning Methodism had been established on the counsel of the church fathers. Even though as a religious society Methodism was barely two and one-half decades old, it had not been built upon the shifting ground of spurious or novel notions. This was a brilliant move really. The Anglican Divines once argued in full view of the Roman magisterium that England's church had been established on the bedrock of the fathers. Now Wesley stood in the public eye, arguing that sanctification, the heart of Methodist teaching and the real focus of Dodd's attack, had been established in complete accord with one of the best known church fathers. The analogy was not lost on those who understood the nature and implications of the debate; and it was those persons upon whom Wesley was counting.

---

[174] Ward and Heitzenrater, *Journals and Diaries, V*, 22: 72. Italics mine.

C. *"Character of a Methodist"*

1. Background

Character of a Methodist was first published in 1742. It was reprinted eighteen times during Wesley's lifetime and many more after his death. It was translated into French at Wesley's behest in 1743, and before he died in 1791 two German editions had been published. In the years following his death *Character* appeared in Polish, Swedish, and Dutch versions.[175] Rupert Davies comments that Wesley had three reasons for writing it:

> First, he wished to demonstrate that Methodism is just genuine Christianity, not some new-fangled theory. . . . Second, he wished to put into more scriptural terms the description of a perfect Christian he had found in the *Stromateis* (or Miscellanies) of Clement of Alexandria (150-215). . . . Third, he wishes [*sic*] to give the proper meaning to the term 'Methodist', which, he points out, was not one that Methodists had assumed, but one that had been thrust upon them in Oxford at the time of the Holy Club.[176]

Character of a Methodist is a crucial document, not only because it reflects the core beliefs and practices of Methodists during the earliest years of the revival, but also because it offers a rare glimpse of how John Wesley adapted theological sources to meet the needs of his audience. Of all the church fathers that Wesley mentions, the only one he specifically cites as inspiring something he wrote is Clement of Alexandria.

---

[175] Bibliographical information for "Character of a Methodist" is found in Frank Baker, *A Wesley Bibliography: An Introduction to the Publications of John and Charles Wesley,* 1981, TD [photocopy], pp. 393-405 which will eventually be published as part of *The Bicentennial Edition of the Works of John Wesley,* volumes 32 and 33. See also Frank Baker, comp., *A Union Catalogue of the Publications of John and Charles Wesley,* 2nd ed. (Stone Mountain, Georgia: George Zimmerman, 1991), 43-45.

[176] *"The Character of a Methodist" (1742),* An Introductory Comment," Rupert E. Davies, ed., *The Methodist Societies: History, Nature, and Design,* vol. 9 of *The Works of John Wesley,* (Nashville: Abingdon Press, 1989), 31.

In 1767, twenty-five years after the initial publication of *Character of a Methodist* and several years after the enthusiasm schisms of the early 1760's abated, Wesley published a defense of Christian perfection in two places — the letter to *Lloyd's,* which we have already examined, and the treatise *A Plain Account of Christian Perfection.* In *Plain Account* Wesley states that *Character of a Methodist* was the first treatise he had ever written on the subject of perfection, though he admits that he had avoided using the term 'perfection' in the title of the work, so that "none might be prejudiced before they read it."[177]

Written scarcely four years after Aldersgate, Wesley states that his overall objective in *Character of a Methodist* was to set forth in the clear language "the *principles* and the *practice* whereby those who are called 'Methodists' are distinguished from other men."[178]

2. Content

In attempting to understand why *Character of a Methodist* held such broad appeal, we shall examine some of its salient theological and structural features.

Methodism Defined in Context

First, Wesley intends to describe Methodism in terms of what it is an in relation to other movements within the larger church tradition. At the beginning and then again near the end, Wesley notes that this treatise concerns "the *distinguishing marks* . . . [and] the *principles* and *practices* of our 'SECT'.[179] According to Davies, Wesley capitalized 'sect' in order to emphasize the falsity of the innuendoes concerning the Methodist revival.[180] Wesley was especially

---

[177] "A Plain Account of Christian Perfection," Jackson, *Works,* 11: 370.

[178] "Character of a Methodist," Davies, *The Methodist Societies,* 9: 32.

[179] "Character of a Methodist," Davies, *The Methodist Societies,* 9: 33, 41.

[180] "Character of a Methodist," Davies, *The Methodist Societies,,* 9: 32. See n. 2.

sensitive to the charge that Methodists were sectarian and separatist. He takes
pains to clarify that Methodists are by no means heterodox in their beliefs and
practices. They are not in any way akin to ancient heretical sects such as the
Socinians and Arians.[181] Nor, he insists, is Methodism marked by "*words or
phrases. . . actions, customs*, or *usages* of an *indifferent* nature."[182] Methodists
cannot be accused of "laying the *whole stress* of religion on an *single part* of it."[183]

Of course, this does not mean that Methodists have no distinguishing
beliefs. Methodism is justifiably distinguished from other branches of
Christianity, especially the Roman Church, by the authority it accords the Bible.
Against the "Romish Church," Wesley asserts that Holy Scripture is "the only and
the sufficient rule both of Christian faith and practice."[184] The Fourth Session of
the Council of Trent (convened April 8, 1546) affirmed that Scripture and holy

---

[181] "Character of a Methodist," Davies, *The Methodist Societies*, 9:33. Socinianism denies the
Trinity and the distinguishability of the persons of the Godhead. As a sect, it took its name
from Lelio Sozini (1525-62) and his nephew Fausto Sozzini (1539-1604). Natives of Italy,
both were rationalists who were eventually exiled to Switzerland and then Poland for their
unorthodox views. Their denial of medieval scholasticism, coupled with an appeal to natural
reason and Scripture, won them a group of supporters, especially among certain aristocrats.
Socinianism entered English thought primarily through the efforts of John Biddle (1615-62) of
Gloucester. (See Rupp, *Religion in England*, 245). Arianism is much older, deriving from the
teachings of Arius (256-336), a priest of the church in Alexandria. Arius and his followers
taught that the Son holds a metaphysically subordinate position to the Father by virtue of his
begottenness. Christ, according to the Arians, was of a divine but lesser substance than the
Father, making him a creature of God somewhere between pure divinity and created humanity.
A complex theory with many far-reaching implications, Arianism, like Socinianism, is
essentially a speculative theology that attempts to explain the historical appearance of Jesus
Christ without resorting to supernatural categories and the concept of divine mystery. Its
greatest failing is that it does not do justice to the historical record (Scripture) containing what
the church has always held to be the self-revealing acts of God. In the case of Socinianism,
the result is a unitarian conception of God. In the case of Arianism, the result is two gods, one
greater than the other.

[182] "Character of a Methodist," Davies, *The Methodist Societies*, 9: 34.

[183] "Character of a Methodist," Davies, *The Methodist Societies*, 9: 35.

[184] "Character of a Methodist," Davies, *The Methodist Societies*, 9: 34.

tradition together form the single deposit of the apostolic faith.[185]   Although Wesley followed the well-worn path of Anglican reverence for church tradition, he nonetheless remained an evangelical Protestant in his view of Scripture.

As we noted, Wesley's emphasis on the term 'SECT' likely is employed as a denial that Methodism is sectarian. His emphasis on the term 'FAITH' serves the opposite purpose. There are two places where 'FAITH' is capitalized in the text. The first is set within a discussion of how the believer is justified and comes to know it:

> For 'he now that believeth hath the witness' of this 'in himself'; being now 'the son of God' by FAITH, 'because he is a son, God hath sent forth the Spirit of his Son into his heart, crying out, Abba, Father.' And 'the Spirit itself beareth witness with his spirit that he is a child of God.'[186]

The second occurrence falls within a discussion of evangelism:

> [A Methodist works] . . . to awaken those that sleep in death; to bring those who are awakened to the atoning blood, that 'being justified by 'FAITH' they may have peace with God; and to provide those who have peace with God to abound more in love and in good works.[187]

If, as Davies suggests, 'SECT' emphasizes the false nature of accusations being made concerning Methodism, 'FAITH' emphasizes the authority and orthodoxy of the movement.

Wesley hoped that individuals living in a religiously tepid culture would recognize in Methodism the spark of true Christianity. The juxtaposition of 'SECT' and 'FAITH' is a tacit denial that Methodism was just another misguided utopian experiment. On the contrary, the emphasis in *Character* upon a faithful,

---

[185]   H.G. Schroeder, trans., *The Canons and Decrees of The Council of Trent* (Rockford, IL: Tan Books; reprint, St. Louis: B. Herder, 1941), 18-19.

[186]   "Character of a Methodist," Davies, *The Methodist Societies,* 9: 36.

[187]   "Character of a Methodist," Davies, *The Methodist Societies,* 9: 41.

entirely practical life of holiness suggests a community not in isolation from the world, but rather one that embraces the world with realistic optimism. From the beginning, Methodism had a profound social conscience. *Character of a Methodist,* if nothing else, is a mandate to genuine Christian living for to those who found themselves engaging the world of ordinary living and commerce.

Holiness Based on Love

A second feature of this treatise is the exceptional moral standard it upholds, which is based upon the idea of Christian love. Wesley lists ten character traits that mark a Methodist. In summary fashion they are:

1. Full and complete love for God.
2. Happiness in God.
3. Gratitude to God that produces contentment in every life situation, whether good or ill.
4. Unceasing prayer — a particular quality of heart disposition toward God, the exercise of love for God
5. Love for fellow human beings.
6. Heart purity — a cleansing of disposition that purges ill passions and affections, that produces humility and an ethical quality of life.
7. Full desire for and complete obedience to the will of God.
8. Obedience to the moral commands that springs from love for God.
9. A desire to glorify God in everything, avoiding any practice (even some considered indifferent by society-at-large) that would hinder one from reaching this goal.
10. Practical love toward others expressed as clothing the poor, visiting the sick, evangelizing all who will listen.[188]

These ten 'marks' of a Methodist begin and end with love. The stress upon love, of course, is first full and unreserved love for God. Citing the Gospel

---

[188] "Character of a Methodist," Davies, *The Methodist Societies,* 9: 35-41.

reiteration of the Old Testament command to love the Lord God with all of the heart, soul, mind and strength, Wesley elaborates with further citations from Scripture on the profound and all-devouring love with which the Methodist Christian is to love God.[189] Twice more in the litany of virtues, at the middle and the end, love for 'neighbor' is enjoined.[190] The New Testament links love of one's fellow human being to self-love, though the latter certainly not in a narcissistic sense. The command to love neighbor as self is really a matter of according as much regard for the well being of others as one does for oneself. Wesley's interpretive point is that love for God motivates moral virtue. The vertical relationship based upon the believer's love for God is set on a horizontal plane as the foundation of moral behavior. Wesley was aware that such ideas could potentially produce significant transforming effects in the church and in society. He also recognized that Christian perfection, defined as purity of intention and love, had been revered by the early church fathers, and that this is the only true perfection attainable in this life.

Happiness as the Telos of Religion

A third important feature of *Character* is Wesley's discussion of happiness as the true end of religion. Wesley writes:

> [The Methodist] . . . is therefore happy in God, yea, always happy, as having in him "a well of water springing up into everlasting life", and "overflowing his soul with peace and joy".[191]

While the 'blessed' or happy person has always formed the Judeo-Christian notion of the redeemed, happiness as the *telos* of human existence is also found in

---

[189] Ibid. See Mark 12:30; Matthew 22:37; and Deuteronomy 6:5: "You shall love the Lord your God with all your heart, and with all your soul, and with all your might." Known by tradition as the *Shema* (Hebrew imperative, "Hear!"), next to, "The Lord our God, the Lord is one," there is no greater statement in the Old Testament of the essence of Israel's faith.

[190] See Mark 12:31; Matthew 22:39.

[191] "Character of a Methodist," Davies, *The Methodist Societies,* 9: 35.

the writings of the ancient Greek philosophers. Plato and Aristotle both describe the final end of human existence as happiness. Both teach that happiness is ultimately related to the good or virtue. For Plato, happiness is achieved through contemplation of eternal forms such as justice and beauty. While Platonic thought contributed a great deal to Christian apologetics in the church's early centuries, Plato's idealism makes reality an abstraction and necessarily reduces human experience to something less than the happiness of the redeemed individual depicted in the Jewish and Christian Scriptures.

Aristotle, on the other hand, conceived of the good as grounded in the real, concrete world. Happiness is not a state of being; for Aristotle, it is a goal toward which the individual is directed. Getting there is a process that involves human beings fulfilling their role or function. Noted interpreter of Aristotle Sarah Broadie writes:

> Aristotle connects the function of a thing with the good at which it characteristically aims . . . . Human beings have an ultimate end or good — this (it is assumed) we already know; they are capable of excellence or of being good in themselves; and they reach their good, in the sense of human *perfection*, through attaining their end.[192]

Aristotle regards human happiness as "'that for the sake of which we do everything else', or 'that which renders life complete and lacking in nothing.'"[193]

For Aristotle, proper functioning is what brings about the desired end. Aristotle proposes that human beings, who are directed toward a *telos* consisting of happiness, will achieve this end only through the practice of the good, which in the real world exists as moral virtue. We will have much more to say about this in our discussion of Clement of Alexandria in Chapter 4. It is sufficient now simply

---

[192] Sarah Broadie, *Ethics with Aristotle* (New York: Oxford University Press, 1991), 34-35. Italics added.

[193] Ibid., 37.

to note that herein we discover the fundamental distinction between Platonic and Aristotelian ethics. Is human happiness a *state of being* as Plato argued, or should it be conceived as a *telos* achieved by means of *virtuous actions* as Aristotle contends?

In Scripture describes both a virtuous ideal and a practical end. The *Sermon on the Mount* discourse in Matthew's Gospel Jesus speaks of a piety grounded in the passive virtues of humility and meekness. But he also ascribes 'beatitude' or blessing to those who worship God, an activity that has its roots in the Hebrew notion of sacrifice, and actions such as peacemaking.[194]. Two characteristics of blessedness stand out however, which relate directly to the Christian's happiness. They are righteousness and purity of heart (Mt. 5:6,8). The fact that these characteristics are arguably synonymous demonstrates that they are to be regarded as conjoined in the experience of kingdom happiness.

Righteousness is the essential metaphor for salvation in the New Testament.[195] The linking of righteousness, purity of heart, and happiness strongly suggests that the idea of Christian salvation necessarily includes the believer's being made actually righteous. Wesley wove happiness as a thread throughout *Character of a Methodist* because he knew that it stands as the heart of the gospel, but also because he understood that the primitive fathers, unlike the Protestant Reformers over a millennium later saw little difference between justification and sanctification. They could not have anticipated the developments that led to the Reformation and the ideas that guided Luther, Calvin, Zwingli, and the Radical Reformers. Because they lived at a time that was historically much closer to the apostles and their successors — the sources and interpreters of tradition — they naturally viewed Christianity through a different lens. Specifically, salvation was

---

[194] Matthew 5:1-12. The term *makarios* is commonly translated "happy" or "blessed." See Liddell & Scott, *Lexicon*, s.v. μακαρία, μακαρίος.

[195] Gr. δικαιοσύνη. See Rudolph Bultmann, *Theology of the New Testament,* trans. K. Grobel (New York: Scribner's Sons, 1951), 1: 270-71.

not patently a justification/sanctification issue; it was an initial sanctification/sanctification issue. Initiation sanctification, of course, was the core of the baptismal rite, which corresponded to the actual grace received by the baptized for the washing by water from sin and a light for the illumination of the soul.[196] The Western Latin church began to move away from these ideas as early as Tertullian and definitely by the time of Augustine. The Eastern church however did not; and to this day the Orthodox tradition remains largely unchanged.

Synthesis of Catholic and Protestant Concepts of Justification

This conveniently brings us to a fourth notable feature of *Character of a Methodist*, which is that Wesley carefully follows a line between the holy living catholicism of the fathers and the *sola fide* doctrine of Protestantism. On the Protestant side, as we have seen, he affirms canonical Scripture as "the *only and the sufficient* rule of Christian faith and practice."[197] He argues that the Methodist "thinks *we are saved by faith alone*" minus any prior, meritorious works.[198] Wesley embraces the Reformers' standard that salvation is received solely by faith, that in a moment of time an otherwise sinful individual is justified. An infinitely merciful God legally declares the one who believes righteous, which is nothing other than salvation.

On the catholic side, however, Wesley moves well beyond the limits of forensic justification and asserts that salvation cannot consist simply of positional righteousness; it must and does in fact include grace that makes the believer

---

[196] On how light comes to be associated with the baptismal rite in the early church and particularly in Clement of Alexandria see Arkadi Choufrine, *Gnosis, Theophany, Theosis: studies in Clement of Alexandria's Appropriation of His Background,* Patristic Studies (New York: Peter Lang Publishing, 2002).

[197] "Character of a Methodist," Davies, *The Methodist Societies,* 9: 34.

[198] "Character of a Methodist," Davies, *The Methodist Societies,* 9:35.

actually righteousness. He writes: "By *salvation* he [the Methodist] means holiness of heart and life. And this he affirms to spring from true *faith alone*."[199] Whereas Luther and the Reformers were wary of connecting unmerited justification to good works, Wesley refuses to sever justifying faith from actual holiness. His mentors in the Anglican tradition taught him that faith and holy living are coordinate aspects of a unified doctrine of salvation. Wesley found that the primitive ante-Nicene fathers held similar views. As noted earlier, prior to the sixteenth century the line between saving faith (justification) and moral virtue (sanctification) had never been as sharply fixed as it came to be with Luther, Calvin and their followers.

By defining salvation as holiness of heart and life, Wesley distinguishes Methodism from Reformed and Lutheran thought. He insists that any doctrine of salvation that disconnects personal faith from personal holiness is inadequate. Though he always encouraged sincere seekers after God, he denies that anyone can be reasonably certain of salvation if their faith does not manifest itself outwardly in love.[200] Mere sincerity is not enough.[201] Thus, in *Character of a Methodist* we observe that the overall distinguishing trait of a Methodist is that he strives for and achieves loving obedience to God.

In addition to some of the striking features we have noted, there is a less obvious one that is necessary to include here. We refer to the 'theological virtues' — faith, hope and love — which form a subtle secondary structural feature of the treatise. The Methodist is a "Son of God by *FAITH*."[202] The Holy Spirit has

---

[199] Ibid.

[200] Gal. 5:6 was one of Wesley's favorite Scripture verses which we shall discuss below. References to it appear twenty-seven times in the sermons alone.

[201] "Character of a Methodist," Davies, *The Methodist Societies,* 9: 35. Note the illustration of the woman who thinks she is virtuous because she is not engaged in prostitution, or the man who believes himself to be honest because he does not commit theft.

[202] "Character of a Methodist," Davies, *The Methodist Societies,* 9: 36. Italics mine.

produced in him a "living *hope* . . . full of immortality."[203] The Methodist "exercises his love to God;" thus, "he who *loveth* God, *loves* his brother also."[204]

Faith, hope, and love, — the theological virtues — are distinguished from the intellectual and moral virtues in that they specifically have God as their object and are known to humankind only through the self-revelation of God.[205] Found prominently in 1 Corinthians 13, esp. v. 13, the theological virtues were said to govern every other aspect of the believer's character.[206] The classical theologians had taught that the theological virtues foster perfection of moral character that in turn leads to the eternal happiness of the individual. In the thirteenth century Thomas Aquinas expanded greatly the discussion of the virtues in what would be recognized as the epitome of their consideration. Thomas began with St. Augustine who had defined faith as an intellectual assent to revealed truth. He added to Augustine's definition an analysis grounded in Aristotelian ethics, arguing that assent involves the will, and that unaided faith is incapable of presenting to the will the necessary good that moves it to assent. Therefore, God 'infuses' a disposition to believe *(fides infusa)* that presents to the will the eternal reward of salvation. The will in turn actualizes faith, enabling it to give assent, thus bringing about justification of the believer.[207]

There were two aspects of the doctrine of *fides infusa* that troubled the Protestant Reformers. First, they argued that movement of the will to act is by

---

[203] Ibid. Italics mine.

[204] "Character of a Methodist," Davies, *The Methodist Societies,* 9:37. Italics mine.

[205] See C. G. Herbermann *et al.,* eds., *The Catholic Encyclopedia,* 15 vols. (New York: Robert Appleton Co., 1912), s.v. "Virtue," by Augustine Waldron. High medieval Catholicism held that the theological virtues are infused into the human soul.

[206] See also Col. 1:4-5

[207] See summary discussion by Reinhold Seeberg, *Textbook of the History of Doctrines,* 2 vols., (Grand Rapids: Baker Book House, 1958), 2: 103, 195.

definition a work. Therefore, faith might be construed as a work whereby the individual obtains merit toward salvation. For example, the Church had taught from apostolic times that baptism is the outward sign of faith. The baptismal act might not be regarded simply as an outward evidence of what had already taken place inwardly, but it could be viewed as a meritorious work prior to justification. Luther and Calvin, of course, rejected any the notion that justification can be secured by any prerequisite works of merit. The concept of infused faith, they believed, would endanger the notion that salvation is received from God solely on the basis of unmerited favor.

Secondly, the Reformers believed that *fides infusa* conflates the forensic notion of justification (being counted righteous even though one is not) with sanctification (being made actually righteous). Indeed, the outcome of the Sixth Session of Trent was unambiguous on this matter: faith alone is insufficient to save. Hope and love added to faith together are essential to justification.[208] In formal theological language, the debate had taken place on the difference between *imputed* and *imparted* righteousness, that is, between justification defined in the Lutheran and Calvinian sense as a legal declaration of righteousness, and justification defined in an older catholic sense as actual righteousness. In *Character of a Methodist* Wesley avoided the problems that taking sides would involve.

First, he departs from the Continental Reformers when he declares that salvation cannot be defined in any other way than "holiness of heart and life."[209] Herein, he is in agreement with Trent. Wesley believes that salvation's *formal* cause — the purpose for which a Holy God justifies — is to make holy those

---

[208] *Canons and Decrees of The Council of Trent,* 34: "For faith, unless hope and charity be added to it, neither unites man perfectly with Christ nor makes him a living member of His body." For a glimpse at how Lutherans responded to Trent on this issue, see Martin Chemnitz, *Examination of the Council of Trent,* trans., Fred Kramer, 2 vols. (Springfield, IL: Concordia Seminary, 1964; reprint, St. Louis: Concordia Publishing House, 1971), 1: 517-19.

[209] Ibid.

whom He saves.[210] Although upheld by Trent, the idea is actually much older. Lutheran defender Martin Chemnitz (1522-86) observed that the church fathers had early on defined the word *justify* as 'making just or righteous.'[211] Chemnitz in effect admitted that Luther's idea of justification as merely a forensic or positional change in relationship with God was too narrow and that it cannot be substantiated by appealing to the church fathers. Wesley, on the other hand, agrees with the fathers' notion that justification involves more than just a positional change with God; it also marks the beginning of personal moral renewal.

Secondly, Wesley agrees with the Reformers' teaching that works done prior to justification have no merit. In other words, Wesley does not agree with the Roman Catholic doctrine of infused faith. Faith alone is the condition of justification. Good works prior to justification are still good in themselves, but they accrue no merit on behalf of the individual performing them toward salvation.

It is this synthesis of theological traditions — justification as the beginning of sanctification achieved through faith alone — that underlies Wesley's argument in *Character of a Methodist*. The same combination is also found in the Wesleyan hymnody. In the first three editions of *Character* published at Bristol, Charles' hymn *The Whole Armour of God* was appended at the end of

---

[210] *Canons and Decrees of The Council of Trent,* 33: "[T]he single formal cause [of justification] is the justice of God, not that by which He Himself is just, but that by which He makes us just, that, namely, with which we being endowed by Him, are *renewed in the spirit of our mind,* and not only are we reputed but ware truly called and are just, receiving justice within us, each one according to his own measure, which the Holy Ghost distributes to everyone as He wills, and according to each one's disposition and cooperation."

[211] Chemnitz, *Examination of the Council of Trent,* 1: "But the papalists simply argue that the word justify properly signifies a movement, or change, from unrighteousness to righteousness, as when in natural movements one quality is driven out and another is brought in. . . *I am not ignorant of the fact that the fathers often employ the word 'justify' in this sense,* . . . ." Italics mine.

the treatise.[212] Inspired by Ephesians 6, the poem creates an image of a soldier preparing for battle as it describes the victory a faithful believer wins over the bondage of sin and moral incapacity. The fifth strophe is of particular interest:

> Let faith and love combine
> To guard your valiant breast;
> The plate be righteousness divine
> *Imputed* and *impressed.*[213]

The combination of faith and love undoubtedly points to Galatians 5:6.[214] More significantly, however, one notes the reference to divine righteousness "imputed and impressed" upon the believer. In other words, righteousness is both "imputed" or reckoned to the believer (its condition being faith) and "impressed" or imparted as a moral grace.

Perfection as a Realizable Goal

A fifth interesting feature of *Character* is Wesley's assertion that perfection is achievable in this life. We already noted that perfection is always to be understood as maturity of intention and love. Wesley follows the use of the New Testament writers when they employ words such as τελείοω, τελέωσις, τελειότης. These terms connote completion, maturity, and fulfillment. They are appropriately translated in English as 'to make perfect' and 'perfect.'[215] Though he would speak with greater clarity in later treatises concerning Christian perfection, Wesley's usage of the term 'perfect' in *Character* demonstrates that he always regarded it something attainable by all believers, not just a few.

---

[212] In contemporary hymnals, the title *Soldiers of Christ, Arise* often appears. For the complete text see "Character of a Methodist**Error! Bookmark not defined.**," Davies, *The Methodist Societies,* 9: 43-46. See esp. n. 30. Farley published at Bristol the original edition in 1742 and then republished it two more times in 1743.

[213] "Character of a Methodist," Davies, *The Methodist Societies,* 9: 44, stanza 5. Italics mine.

[214] References to Gal. 5:6 appear twenty-seven times in Wesley's sermons alone.

[215] Liddell & Scott, *Lexicon,* s.v.

It should be noted that perfect love for Wesley is never a static state of being; rather, it is love grown and nurtured through practice. In fact, Wesley believed that faith itself is formed and validated when it is filled with active love.[216] Perfection is loving God with all one's being and loving neighbor as self. Because it depends solely upon the gratuitous working of God, perfection, like justification, has as its instrumental cause faith. Thus, Wesley unhesitatingly declares that "holiness of heart and life. . .spring[s] from true *faith alone.*"[217]

Love is the perfection of human character and existence; it is the motivation for all other religious and moral actions. As he proceeds in *Character* to discuss prayer, purity of heart, obedience to the commands, conformity to God's will, relationship to others — we see that all are motivated by and directly linked to love for God. The reader comes away with a strong sense of the dynamic, supernatural work of God that brings about the perfection of character.

3. Conclusions

One thing that can be concluded from a careful reading of *Character of a Methodist* is that Wesley, as he stated in the *Letter to Lloyd's,* indeed created a portrait "of the character of a perfect Christian . . . in the very words of Scripture."[218] *Character of a Methodist* is peppered with quotations and allusions to the biblical text — all very deliberate on Wesley's part. He was a man dedicated to the interpretation and application of Scripture in everyday life.

---

[216] See "Catholic Spirit," Outler, *Sermons, II,* 2: 88: "Is thy faith ἐνεργουμένη δἱ ἀγάπης — filled with the energy of love?" See esp. ibid., n. 32. Wesley's reversal of the Greek syntax of Galatians 5:6, πίστις δἱ ἀγαπης ἐνεργουμένη, indicates acceptance of the Catholic doctrine of *fides caritatem formata,* faith formed by love. See also "The Almost Christian," Outler, *Sermons, I,* 1: 139, n. 58.

[217] "Character of a Methodist," Davies, *The Methodist Societies,* 9: 35.

[218] Ward and Heitzenrater, *Journals and Diaries, V,* 22: 72.

Second, Wesley obviously viewed scriptural righteousness as *actual* righteousness. We see in *Character of a Methodist* numerous allusions to biblical pericopae that refer to righteousness, renewal, and heart and life purity. These were his favorite themes. Wesley believes that scriptural perfection is achievable. He does not allow this ancient doctrine to be forced into the category of a utopian, unreachable ideal. As he writes: "[The Methodist Christian's] . . . soul is 'renewed after the image of God', 'in righteousness and in all true holiness'. And 'having the mind that was in Christ' he 'so walks as' Christ 'also walked'."[219] Wesley is careful not to be too rigid in his discussion of perfection, for he never here or elsewhere will argue that it not properly to be viewed as a process and therefore progressive over time. This is the meaning of the parenthetical note he adds to the treatise's title, a quotation lifted from St. Paul's Epistle to the Philippians: "Not as tho' I had already attained."[220]

Finally, if Wesley wrote *Character of a Methodist* based upon his reading of Clemens Alexandrinus' portrait of Christian perfection, then by mirror-reading Wesley's thoughts we may conclude that he found Clement's concept of real moral transformation very appealing. The holy living theme that permeated Wesley's thinking should not be simply regarded as originating with his Puritan family roots, 18th century German pietism, or even 17th century Anglican thought. As important as these sources were in Wesley's theological formation, we must not overlook his indebtedness to Clement of Alexandria. Is it conceivable that Wesley found in Clement's portrait of Christian character a description of perfection that predated and substantiated all that he later encountered in his

---

[219] "Character of a Methodist, Davies," *The Methodist Societies,* 9:41.

[220] The title page of the original 1742 edition of the tract is reproduced in Davies, *The Methodist Societies,* 9: 30. See also p. 32 and n. 1. In the context of a discussion in which he states his aspiration to know Christ Jesus, the power of his resurrection and the fellowship of his sufferings, the Apostle writes: "Not that I have already obtained this or have already reached the goal; but I press on to make it my own, because Christ Jesus has made me his own" (Philippians 3:12).

investigation of other branches of Christianity? Though at this point one may only speculate, we will attempt to point out as our investigation progresses that such a notion is plausible.

D. Correspondence with Miss March

1. Background

There is a fourth reference to Clement of Alexandria that appears in the context of an extensive written correspondence Wesley carried out with Miss J. C. March.   The citation itself and those leading up to and following it chronologically would seem to suggest that Wesley not only had read Clement's works, but that he had critically reflected on them.   The history of this correspondence provides a window into the development of Wesley's theology from the days of primitive church idealism at Oxford to well into his career and the end of the period described by Rack as "the consolidation of Methodism."[221]

Beginning in 1760, Wesley wrote at least forty letters to Miss March over a seventeen-year period, which he published. The last letter was dated December 10, 1777. This correspondence is important if, for no other reason than it provides some insight into the kind of pastoral care Wesley gave to persons. The letters to Miss March reveal one Methodist's struggle with the doctrine of perfection. The literary exchange culminates with a reference to Clement of Alexandria.

Very few details of Miss March's biographical background exist. Curnock notes that she was "a lady of fortune and piety in London," but he does not indicate where he obtained this information.[222] Telford, citing Jackson, writes:

---

[221] Rack, *Reasonable Enthusiast,* 331 s.v.

[222] Nehemiah Curnock, ed., *The Journal of the Rev. John Wesley, A.M.,* 8 vols., (London: Epworth, 1938), 6: 427, n. 2.

> Miss March was a lady of good education; and, having a small independent fortune, devoted her life and all she had in doing good. She sometimes made excursions to Bristol and other parts of the country, where she met classes, & c.[223]

Tyerman includes a portion of an unpublished letter attributed to Miss March that includes discussion of the 1774 Methodist Conference.[224] Also present is evidence suggesting that she had been a Methodist lay worker in London.

2. Content

As one of Wesley's many correspondents, more than just news passed between the two. On numerous occasions Wesley wrote Miss March on theological topics. The tone of the letters is quite pastoral. If we reconstruct Miss March's concerns based upon Wesley's responses, her struggle seems to have centered on the issue of personal piety and her own apparent inability to achieve a level of passivity with respect to her emotions. It is fairly obvious that she held the notion that absence of all spontaneous or undesirable emotions (i.e., *apatheia*) is the moral equivalent of Christian perfection.

As early as his second letter, dated March 29, 1760, the issue of perfect love appears in the trail of correspondence. The occasion is an apparent dispute Miss March had been involved in with another individual.[225] Several months later Wesley states that a believer may be "sanctified in an instant, yet undoubtedly

[223] Cited in Telford, *Letters,* 4: 85.

[224] Luke Tyerman, *The Life and Times of the Rev. John Wesley, M.A., Founder of the Methodists,* 3 vols. (New York: Harper and Brothers, Publishers, 1872), 3: 177.

[225] "To Miss March, March 29, 1760," Telford, *Letters of John Wesley,* 4: 90: "You may undoubtedly remain in peace and joy until you are perfected in love. You need neither enter into a dispute, when persons speak wrong, nor yet betray the truth; there is a middle way. You may simply say, 'I believe otherwise; but I think, and let think; I am not fond of contending on this or any other head, lest I receive more hurt than I can do good.'"

grows by slow degrees."[226] Nine months later Wesley alludes to holiness conceived as increasing love. He cites St. Paul's discussion of love in 1 Corinthians 13 as the source of this notion.[227] Wesley mentions the same passage again in 1771. This time his meaning is unambiguous: "In the 13th of [First] Corinthians you have the height and depth of genuine perfection; and it is observable St. Paul speaks all along of the love of our neighbour, flowing indeed from the love of God."[228]

By June 1761, evidence appears for the first time that Miss March had communicated to Wesley her concern that she had not yet received the grace of holiness. Wesley responds:

> I apprehend your great danger now is this — to think you never shall receive that blessing because you have not received it yet; nay, perhaps you may be tempted to believe that there is no such thing, and that those who thought they had received it were mistaken as well as you. . . . As yet you are but a babe. Oh, what heights of holiness are to come![229]

The same issue carries over into April 1763, when Wesley writes: "Thus is certain: they that love God with all their heart and all men as themselves are scripturally perfect."[230]

The discussion takes a new turn a little over a year later when Wesley suggests that Miss March has been so concerned with achieving a state of perfection, she risks negating it altogether. He writes:

---

[226] Ibid., 4: 100. The theme degrees of salvation recurs about eight years later in another letter. Cf. "To Miss March, March 14, 1768," ibid., 5:81: "There are innumerable degrees, both in a justified and a sanctified state, more than it is possible for us exactly to define."

[227] Ibid., 4: 124.

[228] "To Miss March, July 13, 1771," Telford, *Letters*, 5: 268.

[229] "To Miss March, June 17, 1761," Telford, *Letters*, 4: 157.

[230] "To Miss March, April 7, 1763," Telford, *Letters*, 4: 208.

94

> You was [*sic*] in a measure a living witness of the perfection I
> believe and preach — the only perfection of which we are capable
> while we remain in the body. To carry perfection higher is to sap
> the foundation of it and destroy it from the face of the earth."[231]

The issue is sharpened when Wesley finds it necessary to address the distinction between outward and inward piety. Apparently, Miss March had begun to lean toward outward *perfectionism* rather than inward, biblical perfection expressed outwardly in love. He writes: "To your outward walking I have no objection. But I want you to walk inwardly in the fullness of love, and in the broad light of God's countenance."[232]

Six years later, Wesley again writes to Miss March concerning holiness, sanctification, purity of heart, and perfect love. He advises her to "remember [that] the essence of Christian holiness is simplicity and purity; one design, one desire — entire devotion. But this admits a thousand degrees and variations, and certainly will be proved by a thousand temptations."[233] Four months later he encourages her, when he writes:

> To devote all our thoughts and actions to God, this is our highest
> wisdom; and so far as we inwardly or outwardly swerve from this,
> we walk as fools, not as wise. . . . Take more of His fullness, that
> you may love Him more, praise Him more, and serve Him better.[234]

In spite of Wesley's counsel, Miss March's inner turmoil continues. Somehow, she is unable to discriminate between biblical perfection and emotional perfectionism. Things begin to come to a head by early summer 1774, when Wesley writes:

---

[231] "To Miss March, June 24, 1764," Telford, *Letters,* 4: 251.

[232] "To Miss March, August 31, 1765," Telford, *Letters,* 4: 310.

[233] "To Miss March, April 14, 1771," Telford, *Letters,* 5: 238.

[234] "To Miss March, August 3, 1771," Telford, *Letters,* 5: 270.

You are a living witness of two great truths: the one, that there cannot be a lasting, steady enjoyment of pure love without the direct testimony of the Spirit concerning it, without God's Spirit shining on His own work; the other, that setting perfection too high is the ready way to drive it out of the world."[235]

Two weeks later, he once again cites 1 Corinthians 13 on the subject of Christian love.[236]

Wesley's remarks reveal that Miss March apparently had been judging her piety by the outward appearances of devotion manifested by two contemporaries, Elizabeth Johnson (1721-1798) and Penelope Newman.[237] A letter posted by Wesley in mid-September of 1774 admonishes Miss March to seek inward and outward holiness motivated by faith and love.[238]

After many years of correspondence, Wesley's counsel to Miss March arrives at the question of whether perfect Christian character is better defined as a stoic lack of passion or an energetic outworking of love. The crucial letter comes on November 30, 1774; the occasion is the ongoing conflict between Miss March and Elizabeth Johnson. Apparently, Miss March had begun to doubt whether she could continue as Mrs. Johnson's friend. Wesley responds to her feelings of self-abnegation and regret with insight, as he relates her perceptions to the larger themes of Christian experience, friendship, increasing love, and holiness. He writes:

---

[235] "To Miss March, June 3, 1774," Telford, *Letters,* 6: 88.

[236] "To Miss March, June 17, 1774," Telford, *Letters,* 6: 92.

[237] Elizabeth Johnson was renowned for her fervent piety. See *An account of Mrs. Elizabeth Johnson* (London: W. Pine and Son, [1799]). Mrs. Johnson's piety is mentioned by Alexander Knox in his "Letter to Joseph Butterworth, Esq.," *The Remains of Alexander Knox,* 3rd ed., 4 vols. (London: Duncan and Malcolm, 1844), 1: 76.

[238] "To Miss March, September 16, 1774," Telford, *Letters,* 6: 113.

> I 'sum up the experience' of persons, . . . in order to form their
> general character. But in so doing this we take a different way of
> making our estimate. It may be [that] you chiefly regard (as my
> brother does) the length of their experience. Now, this I make little
> account of; I measure the depth and breadth of it. Does it sink deep
> in humble, gentle love? Does it extend wide in all inward and
> outward holiness? If so, I do not care whether they are [Christians]
> of five or five-and-thirty years' standing.[239]

Apparently, Miss March had not had as long an 'experience' of evangelical faith
as her friend Miss Johnson. Elizabeth Johnson, whom everyone agreed possessed
an admirable character, nonetheless possessed certain characteristics that Wesley
regarded as flaws, the most prominent of which was a stoic and austere
disposition. In a moment of surprising candor, Wesley utilizes these peculiarities
to illustrate *via negativa* an important theological insight:

> Yet some things in [Elizabeth Johnson's] . . . character I do not
> admire; I impute them to human frailty. Many years ago I might
> have said, but I do not now,
>
> > Give me a woman made of stone,
> > A widow of Pygmalion.
>
> And just such a Christian one of the Fathers, *Clemens Alexandrinus*,
> describes; but I do not admire that description now as I did formerly.
> *I now see a Stoic and a Christian are different characters;* and at some
> times I have been a good deal disgusted at Miss Johnson's *apathy*.[240]

By late 1774, Miss March had begun to construe Christian perfection as
analogous to stoic apathy or passionlessness. In a follow up letter on December
27, 1774 Wesley again holds up Mrs. Johnson as a somewhat skewed example of
Christian perfection:

---

[239] "To Miss March, November 30, 1774," Telford, *Letters*, 6: 129.

[240] Ibid. Italics mine. Butler's *Hudibras*, 1.iii.28 is the source of the citation.

> There is a great calmness in Betty Johnson; but I want more softness
> and tenderness; I want more of human mingled with the divine. . . . I
> desire no apathy in religion; a Christian is very far from a Stoic.[241]

The implication is clear. Wesley rejects passionlessness as a suitable analogy of Christian perfection. He advises Miss March to do the same.

One wonders how Miss March had come to associate passionlessness with Christian perfection. Had it come from her reading? Or, had she heard such issues discussed among the Methodist bands? The historical context that gave rise to these letters will probably never be known, but one additional communication between Wesley and Miss March may help shed light on the question. In a letter dated June 9, 1775 Wesley discusses the distinction between cognitive knowledge and heartfelt love in relation to Christian perfection. In a candid and pastoral tone he writes:

> I am less careful about your increase in knowledge any farther than
> it tends to love. There is a danger of your laying more stress on this
> than sound reason requires. . . . I feel that [you are] more [in] want
> of heat than light. I value light; but it is nothing compared to love.
> Aim at this [i.e., love], my dear friend, in all public exercises, and
> then you will seldom be disappointed. Then you will not stop on the
> threshold of *perfection* (I trust that you do not now), but will press on
> to the mark, to the prize of the high calling of God in Christ Jesus,
> till you *experimentally* know all that love of God which passeth all
> (*speculative*) knowledge.[242]

Finally, he exhorts: "Take up your cross, woman! Remember the faith! Jesus went before you, and will go with you. Put off the gentlewoman; you bear an higher character."[243] There are six letters that follow after this one, the last dated December 1777. A few touch upon theological issues, but none address the

---

[241] "To Miss March, December 27, 1774," Telford, *Letters,* 6: 133.

[242] "To Miss March, June 9, 1775," Telford, *Letters,* 6: 153. Italics mine.

[243] Ibid.

doctrine or experience of perfection. So far as we know, this matter had settled for Miss March.

3. Conclusions

What conclusions can be drawn from Wesley's correspondence with Miss March? First, the November 30, 1774 letter proves decisively that Wesley had read Clement of Alexandria and that his reading had been thorough. The reference to *apatheia* as a defining mark of Christian character shows that he had more than a cursory acquaintance with Alexandrian theology. Clement's *Stromateis* in its historical context had been an important defense of orthodox Christian faith against second century Hellenistic Gnosticism; but more than that, it was known for its description of Christian perfection by means of the philosophical virtue of *apatheia*. Having read Clement's works while at Oxford, Wesley was undoubtedly familiar with this feature of the Alexandrian's soteriology. That Wesley sought to discourage Miss March from holding philosophical, idealistic *apatheia* as a goal for her own spiritual development demonstrates that he was familiar with the finer nuances of Clement's thought.

Second, the letters demonstrate that the doctrine of Christian perfection continued for many years as a real pastoral issue among Methodists. Moreover, there appears to have been a tendency on the part of some within the movement — Miss March and Elizabeth Johnson serving as good examples — to conceive of perfection in philosophical rather than biblical terms. This is not to suggest that these women had read Clement of Alexandria, although they may have.[244] Rather, it may point to the existence of a philosophical trend in Methodism whose roots in the apologetics of the ancient church may or may not have been understood among Methodist lay persons. What is certain, however, is that

---

[244] Up to and including Wesley's lifetime, only one of Clement's treatises, *Quis Dives*, had been translated into English and published. See J. Jones, trans., *A Discourse Concerning The Salvation of Rich Men* (London: Phillip Guillim, 1711).

Wesley himself grasped the doctrinal analogy; for he obviously had sought to derail Miss March's intentions to become a stoic 'woman of stone' before she fell into even greater despair over her spiritual condition. Indeed, Wesley's admission to having once admired the ideal of 'passionless' Christianity based upon a philosophical ideal may very well indicate that he felt some personal responsibility for the promulgation of such notions among Methodists.

Finally, the letters to Miss March do not contradict the relevance of Alexandrian Christianity for *Character of a Methodist.* What they do is sharpen our insight into the larger questions of development and transition in Wesley's thought. Wesley may have "much admired" Clement's portrait of Christian character, but he does not specify the *loci* within the Clemens Alexandrinus corpus which had captured his imagination. We know that Wesley at one time was attracted to ancient Eastern Christianity. By the 1760s his views had been changing. We cannot ignore this transition. The fact that it occurred with reference to Clement of Alexandria, makes the need for a careful examination of Wesley's reading of Clement all the more essential.

E. Other References

In addition to the substantial references to Clement we have examined, Wesley made several of lesser importance. Two times he cites Clement in his 1749 *Letter to Dr. Conyers Middleton.* The first is to respond to Middleton's charge that Clement was as obligated to the Greek mystery religions as he had the Hebrew and Christian Scriptures. Wesley's reply, as expected, is that citing an extra-biblical source does not prove that one reveres that source in its entirety.[245]

---

[245] "Letter to Conyers Middleton," Jackson, *Works*, 10: 31-32. Middleton had charged that Justin Martyr (2nd c.) "'with treating the spurious books, published under the names of the *Sibyl* and *Hystaspes*, with the same reverence as the prophetic Scriptures' and that Clement of Alexandria had later added support. Wesley responds: "That 'these books were held in the highest veneration by the Fathers and Rulers through all succeeding ages,' is in nowise proved by that single quotation from Clemens Alexandrinus, wherein he urges the Heathens with the

The second reference is typical of the way Wesley tended to cite all the church fathers; that is, he includes Clement in a list. His purpose of listing authorities is obviously an attempt to add the weight of the patristic tradition as a whole to his argument.[246]

There is also a reference to Clement in the short treatise *A Roman Catechism*. Published originally in 1756 at Bristol, it appears to be a revision of a work by an earlier author. Though carrying less evidential weight, the fact that Wesley kept the treatise intact suggests approval. The citation itself is taken from *Stromateis* 7 and is concerned with establishing a sound hermeneutical method. Clement writes: "The way for understanding the Scriptures, is to demonstrate out of themselves, concerning themselves."[247]

In 1756, Wesley published *An Address to the Clergy* in which he assumes the role of pastor to pastors. In Wesley's day many pastors were ill equipped educationally for the task of parish ministry. Wesley addresses this matter by identifying the skills that every capable pastor ought to possess. Knowledge of Scripture is mandatory; but one cannot have a sound grasp of the Word without training in "the original tongues."[248] Acquaintance with the history of ideas and culture, geography, science, logic, metaphysics, mathematics, psychology (which Wesley describes as "a knowledge of men, of their maxims, tempers, and manners such as they occur in real life."), and the ability to reason correctly — all are fitting components of a pastor's educational background.[249] In addition to the minister's learning, Wesley considers the gifts of divine grace in effecting the

---

testimonies of their own authors, of the Sibyl and Hystaspes. . . . We cannot infer from hence that he himself held them 'in the highest veneration;' much less that all the Fathers did."

[246] Ibid., 10: 79.

[247] Cit. "Roman Catechism," Jackson, *Works*, 10: 94.

[248] "An Address to The Clergy," Jackson, *Works*, 10: 482-83.

[249] Ibid., 10: 483-85 *passim*.

minister's work, writing: "For what are all other gifts, whether natural or acquired, when compared to the grace of God?"[250]

Singled out for special consideration in Wesley's ideal curriculum are the earliest interpreters of Scripture, the church fathers. Wesley felt that an acquaintance with the controversies and settlements that occurred in the early centuries of church history was essential for anyone who is to preach and comment on the Scriptures.[251] He exhorts his readers to self-examination, as he writes:

> Am I acquainted with the Fathers; at least with those venerable men who lived in the earliest ages of the Church? Have I read over and over the golden remains of Clemens Romanus, of Ignatius and Polycarp; and have I given one reading, at least, to the works of Justin Martyr, Tertullian, Origen, *Clemens Alexandrinus*, and Cyprian?[252]

The implication, of course, is that Wesley himself had read these fathers and that he had employed them as sources for interpreting Scripture and modeling the Christian faith. Wesley's familiarity with the writings of the church fathers cannot reasonably be doubted.

Two additional references to Clement occur in Wesley's published writings. Both are found in sermons. The first, *Hypocrisy in Oxford*, was originally prepared for delivery at St. Mary's Chapel in 1741. Outler includes the necessary background in his introduction and gives plausible reasons why the

---

[250] Ibid., 10: 486.

[251] Ibid., 10: 484: "Can any who spend several years in those seats of learning, be excused, if they do not add to that of the languages and sciences, the knowledge of the Fathers? the most authentic commentators on Scripture, as being both nearest the fountain, and eminently endued with that Spirit by whom all Scripture was given. It will be easily perceived, I speak chiefly of those who wrote before the Council of Nice."

[252] Ibid., 10: 492. Italics mine.

102

sermon was never preached as planned.[253] As the title suggests, *Hypocrisy in Oxford* is a diatribe against the university, specifically, the lapse of moral and intellectual excellence among Oxford's faculty and students. In one section Wesley laments the general intellectual malaise of Oxford's scholars, observing that they have made themselves willfully ignorant. It is in this context that the following lines are found:

> How many whose ignorance is not owing to incapacity, but to mere laziness! How few . . . of the vast number who have it in their power are truly learned men! Not to speak of the other eastern tongues, who (almost) is there that can be said to understand Hebrew? Might I not say, or even Greek? A little of Homer or Xenophon we may still remember; but how few can readily read and understand so much as a page of *Clemens Alexandrinus*, St. Chrysostom, or Ephraem Syrus?[254]

The implication is that Wesley himself had not let down the high standards he commended to others. The fact that he authored his own concise Latin, Greek and Hebrew grammars suggests that there was no demonstrable hypocrisy in the charges he was bringing against his colleagues.[255] Since he mentions Clement, it is logical to conclude that Wesley had read him; otherwise, he would not have had the moral ground upon which to level such charges.

Another reference to Clement occurs in a 1777 sermon on the occasion of the laying of the cornerstone for New Chapel. Reviewing the history of the Methodist movement, Wesley states: "Methodism, so called, is the old religion, the religion of the Bible, the religion of the primitive church, the religion of the

---

[253] "Hypocrisy in Oxford, An Introductory Comment," Outler, *Sermons, IV,* 4: 389-92. As part of the requirements for his B.D. degree, Wesley transcribed this sermon in Latin. The entire Latin text appears in Outler, *Sermons, IV,* 4: 408-19.

[254] "Hypocrisy in Oxford," Outler, *Sermons, IV,* 4: 402. Italics mine.

[255] See Wesley's short grammars in Jackson, *Works,* 14: 1-160.

Church of England."[256] The name Clement of Alexandria appears in a list of church fathers. As he writes:

> This [Methodism] is the *religion of the primitive church*, of the whole church in the purest ages. It is clearly expressed even in the small remains of Clemens Romanus, Ignatius, and Polycarp. It is seen more at large in the writings of Tertullian, Origen, *Clemens Alexandrinus*, and Cyprian. And even in the fourth century it was found in the works of Chrysostom, Basil, Ephrem Syrus, and Macarius. It would be easy to produce a cloud of witness testifying the same thing, were not this a point which no one will contest who has the least acquaintance with Christian antiquity.[257]

These are the same fathers that the Wesley read with the Oxford Methodists during the 1725-35 period. Forty and fifty years later he still regarded these writers as bedrock sources for the theological formation of the Methodist movement.

F. Critical Assessments

Recent scholarship has gradually come to recognize that the question of how Wesley employed the fathers is now more important than whether he read them, since the latter question is hardly in doubt. Two attempts, in particular, have shed some light on matters we have already discussed.

In *John Wesley and Christian Antiquity*, Ted Campbell offers a broad analysis of Wesley and the fathers; and in the process he notes the affinity that Wesley had for Clemens Alexandrinus. Campbell bases his analysis on an examination of the poem *On Clemens Alexandrinus' Description of a Perfect Christian* and on Wesley's testimony concerning the composition of *The*

---

[256] "On Laying the Foundation of the New Chapel," Outler, *Sermons, III*, 3: 585.

[257] Ibid., 3: 586. Italics mine.

104

Character of a Methodist.[258] Campbell follows the assumption that Wesley borrowed something from Clement's discussion of character in Book 7 of *Stromateis.* Because of the broad scope of his research, Campbell does not treat Clement's theology in depth. While affirming that the references to Clement "represent a case in which Wesley's religious vision was consciously inspired by that of an ancient Christian work," Campbell states that "Clementine emphases such as the Christian's passionlessness and contemplation of the divine find no place in Wesley's work."[259] Despite leaving open many questions, Campbell demonstrates that Wesley consistently affirmed Clement's theology throughout his career, beginning with the period of 1738-48, through the middle years 1749-70, and into the latter stage following 1770.[260]

David Bundy has written more specifically concerning the influence of Alexandrian theology upon John Wesley.[261] He too turns up key textual evidence with respect to the poem *On Clemens Alexandrinus' Description of a Perfect Christian* and the treatise *The Character of a Methodist.* On the former text, Bundy concludes "there is . . . a reasonable likeness to the portrayal of the quest of perfection described in *Stromata* 4 and *Stromata* 7, albeit without any indication of the larger context of Clement's work."[262] Bundy observes with respect to

---

[258] Campbell, *John Wesley and Christian Antiquity,* 42.

[259] Ibid.

[260] Ibid., 40-52 *passim.* I am indebted to Prof. Campbell for his work in appraising Wesley's overall patristic vision. Since his task was of a survey nature, Campbell was not able to spend a great amount of capital on any individual writer. The abundance of allusions to Clement of Alexandria he turned up, however, is certainly some indication of the Alexandrian's impression upon Wesley's theological vision. It is even more significant, as Campbell's work shows, that this impression was made near the beginning of Wesley's career and that it seems to have endured in some form throughout.

[261] David Bundy, "Christian Virtue: John Wesley and The Alexandrian Tradition," *Wesleyan Theological Journal* 26, no. 1 (Spring 1991): 139-63. Bundy examines the relationship between Wesley and the Alexandrian tradition as a whole in this article.

[262] Ibid., 144.

Character of a Methodist that "that had Wesley not noted that Clement was his source, we might not have guessed it to be the case."[263]

Nonetheless, Bundy finds interesting similarities between Wesley's doctrine of perfection the portrait of Christian character drawn by Clement in *Stromateis.* Yet he is curiously skeptical that Wesley had actually read Clemens. Instead, he proposes that Alexandrian ideas were mediated to Wesley through later writers such as the Anglican divines, mystics such as John Cassian and Thomas à Kempis, and the seventeenth century Cambridge Platonists.[264] Bundy does not believe that Wesley had ever seriously undertaken a reading of the primary text.

We would agree that Alexandrian thought has been employed in the formulation of doctrine as an analogue to Christian faith, but it is doubtful that Clement's theology was principally mediated to Wesley through the sources that Prof. Bundy suggests. [265] One criticism of such a position that the road from late second century Alexandria to eighteenth century England would have passed through so many hands that is doubtful it could have come to Wesley in a form that could be clearly identified with Clement. Perhaps more significantly, we know that Wesley had access to some of the best the primary source patristic texts of his day during the Oxford years, including the works of Clemens Alexandrinus. Furthermore, we believe it can be shown that he had a special interest in the works of Clement.

The main problems that exacerbate discovering a simple solution to Wesley's appropriation of Clement's portrait of Christian character are as follows. First, there is Wesley's penchant for dropping the names of his sources while

---

[263] Ibid.

[264] Ibid., 141-42.

[265] Ibid., 142.

giving only scant or no indication of the textual loci involved. This is a major obstacle that some of Wesley's interpreters have mistaken as a sign of careless eclecticism. Those who have followed this line of reasoning have been forced to argue that Wesley simply was not a very sophisticated theologian.

A second problem is the apparent inconsistency between Wesley's views of holiness and the views held by Clement. Wesley argued that Christian perfection consists primarily in an attitude of perfect love for God and for neighbor. Clement, on the other hand, most often described perfection in philosophical terms, employing such abstract concepts as *apatheia* among others. As we already have seen, *apatheia* may have played some role in shaping Wesley's thought during the Oxford Holy Club days, but does not characterize his later views. If Wesley rejected philosophical *apatheia* as an apt analogy of biblical perfection, then it necessarily falls upon anyone who intends to maintain Wesley's reliance upon Clement to show that Wesley continued to hold Clement in high regard, while at the same time dealing honesty with his reservations. One could scarcely argue that *Character of a Methodist* depicts an 'apathetic' view of Christianity. And there is no evidence that Wesley ever retracted any part of the treatise or his *Letter to Lloyd's*. So any suggestion that Wesley may have experienced a significant change of opinion concerning the truly essential worth of Clemens' work between the year 1742, when *Character* was published, and 1774, when he disparaged *apatheia* in two letters to Miss March, is not plausible.

Finally, there is the problem of mediation. Is it plausible that Wesley could have imbibed so much Alexandrian theology second or third hand that he would boldly state in an open letter that a church father whose writings he had never read had inspired him?

G. Summary

In summarizing the findings of this chapter, we must admit that the amount of direct textual evidence for Wesley's use of Clement is relatively small.

There are a total of eight significant references appearing in seven loci. This scarcity, however, does not mean that proof is wanting for drawing decisive conclusions. On the basis of the textual references alone the case can be made that Wesley had read Clement. There is among this material clear evidence that Wesley held Clement's portrait of Christian character in such high regard that it inspired his 1742 apologia *Character of a Methodist.* Additional evidence accrues from the *Miss March* correspondence, indicating that Wesley's concept of Christian perfection had been conditioned in part by Clement's doctrine of *apatheia.* Admittedly, Wesley rejects the concept of passionless perfection.

The suppositions of such capable scholars as Ted Campbell and David Bundy cannot be overlooked. In fact, our views may prove to be in the minority of scholarly opinion when all has been said. Entering the mind of a past figure and trying to grasp how that individual may have actually read and synthesized the thought of an even older figure is impossible. Examining the available textual evidence, however, and drawing reasonable conclusions is something that can be accomplished. It is therefore on these objective grounds that we shall proceed.

Chapter 4
Clement Of Alexandria

There are many reasons why Clemens Alexandrinus has remained one of the more important fathers of the church. He is certainly one of the most prolific of the early Christian apologists. Clement lived and wrote theology barely one century after the he apostolic age had ended. He reflects the thinking of the church prior to the rise of formal ecumenism symbolized by the Council of Nicaea a century and a quarter later and the beginning of Christendom via the rule of Emperor Constantine. Clement was intimately acquainted with Christianity's struggle to survive with and evangelize the ancient pagan world. He employed his skills as a classically trained philosopher to translate Christianity into terms that were familiar to his age. More importantly, his mission was to convince a Hellenistic audience that the quest for wisdom, which the Greeks had given to the world, had indeed been fulfilled in the coming of Jesus of Nazareth, a crucified yet risen Palestinian Jew, who is the Anointed One (maschiach, christos) and the world's only Savior. Clement reflects the environment of ancient Alexandria, whose cosmopolitan and academic reputation among the leading cities of the Near East afforded an excellent venue for Christianity's ascent among intellectuals. His work was a model for his pupil Origen and for others in the Eastern tradition who would follow.

Clement is important for this present study because John Wesley apparently found in his thought a portrait of Christian character that was adaptable to the needs of the Methodist revival. The exact nature of Wesley's appropriation will be proposed in the concluding chapter. It is important to investigate first something of Clement's background in order to draw the parallels.

A. Biography and Historical Setting

There is an unfortunate lack of biographical information concerning Clemens Alexandrinus. What there is comes primarily from his own writings. Later sources such as Eusebius of Caesarea (ca. 260-340) give a more complete picture of Clement's overall work. Titus Flavius Clemens was born around 150 A.D. in either Athens or Alexandria.[266] His parents were not Christians, which probably means that he entered the church as an adult through conversion and baptism. Whatever has been suggested about his conversion to Christianity is speculation, since there is no written evidence concerning the date or circumstances surrounding it.[267] Clement's writing, however, suggests that his conversion was weighted toward the intellectual side of his personality. As a student of philosophy and religion, Clement had gained familiarity with the various religions of the ancient Near East by the time he had come to embrace

---

[266] See Everett Procter, *Christian Controversy in Alexandria: Clement's Polemic Against the Basilideans and Valentinians,* American University Studies. Series VII, *Theology and Religion,* vol. 172 (New York: Peter Lang Publishing, Inc., 1995), 3 and esp. n. 10. The fourth century writer Epiphanius of Salamis (Isle of Cyprus) suggested that Clement was born either in Athens or Alexandria. The proposed date of 150 A.D. for Clement's birth, as Procter notes, is largely an educated guess based upon the more dependable knowledge of the time of his residence and ministry in Alexandria.

[267] Such speculation is a weakness of R. B. Tollington's approach in *Clement of Alexandria: A Study in Christian Liberalism,* 2 vols. (London: Williams and Norgate, 1914) 1: 13: "Conversion was perhaps as natural and untroubled to Clement as to any of the educated heathen who found their way within the Church's doors. He does not seem to have had gross sins to surrender. Great renunciations were not apparently involved." I can find no historical evidence leading to such conclusions.

Christianity. Though his writing often shows a pastor's concern, his major works are dedicated to defending the Christian faith in a diverse religious climate.

Following his conversion, Clement traveled throughout Greece, southern Italy, Syria, and Palestine seeking Christian teachers who might satisfy his quest for knowledge. At Alexandria he found a Christian philosopher by the name of Pantaenus (d. 200 A.D.), whose lectures in theology captured his interest and imagination.[268] Clement writes of his mentor:

> I fell in with a final one [teacher] — supreme in mastery. I tracked him down to his hiding-place in Egypt and stayed with him. He was the true Sicilian bee, culling out of the flowers from the meadow of prophets and apostles a pure substance of true knowledge in the souls of his hearers.[269]

Around 200 A.D. Clement succeeded his master as head of the catechetical school at Alexandria, but his tenure was short lived. A general persecution of the church in Egypt under Septimus Severus ca. 202-203 AD forced Clement to flee the city; he never returned. Taking refuge in Cappadocia for the remainder of his life, he probably died just before 215 A.D.

Alexandria, though smaller than Rome in total population, was a large city by ancient standards in the late second century.[270] It had been founded by

---

[268] On the catechetical school at Alexandria and Pantaenus see Quasten, *Patrology*, 2: 2-5. The standard ancient source on Clement is Eusebius of Caesarea's *Ecclesiastical History*. In English translation see *Eusebius: The History of the Church from Christ to Constantine*, trans. G.A. Williamson (Baltimore: Penguin Books Inc., 1965; reprint, Minneapolis: Augsburg Publishing House, 1975), 213-14.

[269] *Strom.* 1.1:11.2; *FC*, 85: 30. Citations of Clement's works will include both the standard Migne references and, when employed, the published English translations. Clement's works will be abbreviated in this fashion: *Strom.* = *Stromateis*, in Engl. trans. often *Misellanies* or *Carpets*; *Paed.* = *Paedagogus* or in translation *Christ the Education/Instructor*; *Prot.* = *Protrepticus*, in translation *Exhortation to the Greeks*. The loci of English translations will be abbreviated in this fashion: *ANF* = *Ante-Nicene Fathers* series; *FC* = *Fathers of the Church* series; *LCL* = *Loeb Classical Library* series.

[270] The slave population alone may have numbered more than three quarters of a million persons, according to Tollington, *Clement of Alexandria*, 1: 36.

112

Alexander the Great in 331 B.C. for two mundane yet equally powerful motives — the empire's economic prosperity and the emperor's self-aggrandizement.[271] Ancient Alexandria was located on the Mediterranean coast of northern Egypt just west of the Nile delta. Protected by the island of Pharos from the silt that disgorged from the mouth of the Nile, the city had two fine harbors. Convenient access to both land and sea trade routes made it a center for commerce. Alexandria's excellent location, coupled with the fact it was the capital from which the Ptolemies ruled the eastern Mediterranean, caused it to grow and prosper.

Sociologically, Alexandria bore many of the same traits common to modern cities, including a large population, thriving economy, and a libertarian bent that manifested itself in a variety of available entertainments and vice.[272] As its name and founding suggest, Alexandria was a Greek city culturally, though several distinctly non-Greek ethnic populations lived within its environs. The diversity of the populace is partially reflected in the various religions known to have thrived there.

P. M. Fraser identifies five categories of religions active during the reign of the Ptolemies: (1) the cults of the traditional Olympian and Greek deities; (2) the royal family cults which worshipped Alexander and the Ptolemies; (3) the Egyptian cult deities of Serapis, Isis, Harpocrates; (4) the non-Egyptian oriental mysteries; and (5) Judaism.[273] Although the cults had their individual characteristics, none remained untouched or unchanged by this religious environment. Syncretism had characterized Alexandria's religions from the earliest days of the Ptolemies. There was one sect, however, which avoided the

---

[271] P. M. Fraser, *Ptolemaic Alexandria,* 2 vols. (London: Oxford University Press, 1972), 1: 3

[272] Tollington, *Clement of Alexandria,* 1: 39 politely refers to Alexandria's reputation for immoral amusements. The historical context has a significant impact upon some of the topics Clement addresses.

[273] Fraser, Ptolemaic Alexandria, 1: 192.

many, but not all of the tendency toward syncretism — the Jews. As one of the more prominent religions in Alexandria, Judaism had consistently played an important role in the city's intellectual life. Having adopted much that Greek philosophy and thought had to offer, Hellenistic Judaism created a superior culture in comparison to the city's other ethnic populations, while retaining its identity as a community formed by the Torah.[274]

The quality of Alexandria's intellectual life was second to none in the ancient world. Such would not have been possible had it not been for the patronage of the Ptolemaic kings. The reigns of Philadelphus (285-246 BC) and Euergetes I (246-221 BC) were crucial in fostering a sophisticated environment. Philadelphus is credited with founding the celebrated Royal Library at Alexandria. Under the patronage of successive Ptolemaic rulers, an incredible 490,000 plus papyrus rolls were cataloged.[275] A fire in 48 B.C. destroyed as many as 400,000 rolls, an unfortunate consequence of Julius Caesar's conflict with the local opponents of Cleopatra. Mark Antony, however, apparently donated as many as two hundred thousand books as a gift to the alluring queen. In any case, scholarship at Alexandria seems to have been mostly unaffected by the loss. Erudition continued in the various branches of science, which included medicine, mathematics and astronomy.

The early history of Christianity in Alexandria is ambiguous from lack of documentation. Tradition holds that St. Mark the Evangelist founded the first Christian community in the city. If true, this would date the church's establishment to the middle of the first century A.D. What is quite certain, however, is that catechesis and the role of the teacher were valued from the

---

[274] Ibid., 1: 54-58. The rise of anti-Semitism during the Roman period lends credibility to the notion that Alexandrian Jews remained a prominent yet unassimilated ethnic group after the demise of the Ptolemaic kingdom in 31 B.C.

[275] Ibid., 1: 328-35.

beginning in the Alexandrian church. The famous catechetical school at Alexandria probably began shortly after the establishment of Christianity there as a means of satisfying the critical need for doctrinal instruction and the training of pastors. The school came under the direction of Pantaenus ca. 180 A.D., resulting in its influence spreading outward to the larger church. Pantaenus had been educated in Stoic philosophy, which he combined with a zeal for Christian doctrine.

Though a discussion of early Christian catechesis lies beyond the scope of the present study, it serves our purpose to make two general observations. First, catechesis and the catechetical school were important during the pre-Constantinian period because of intermittent periods of persecution Christians were forced to endure. Whether widespread or more localized, persecution not only resulted in the loss of church leaders, but it tended to scatter the faithful, demoralize the newly converted, and drive the visible local church underground. Catechesis kept the church alive so long as there were still believers who could faithfully pass on to the next generation the doctrines of the Christian faith.[276]

Second, catechetical instruction insured the accuracy of faith's content as it was handed down. This was especially important at Alexandria. The newly converted more often than not came from polytheistic backgrounds; many had drunk deeply from the wells of trendy philosophical religions. These individuals The ancient model of the *paedagogus* or 'instructor' provided a convenient, culturally understood and accepted backdrop for Christian instruction.

Catechesis remained an important feature of Alexandrian Christianity for the next two hundred years. The fourth century under Constantine the Great saw Christianity become the official religion of the Roman Empire, and with this development the day-to-day life of the church became considerably more stable. Increasing numbers of persons were born into the church and lived their entire

---

[276] *tradere* — 'to hand over, pass on'; *traditio* — 'tradition.'

lives as Christians. The urgency for rigorous catechetical training diminished. As the need for formal catechesis waned, so did the need for the catechetical school. By the end of the fourth century the school at Alexandria ceased to exist.

In the late second century, however, the need for instruction was great. A natural teacher like Clement was welcome. His dedication to the Scriptures made him an important leader and thus insured for him a place in the succession of apostolic teaching. Eusebius writes: "In his time Clement was noted at Alexandria for his patient study of Scripture. He bore the same name as the former head of the Roman church [Clement of Rome], the pupil of the apostles."[277] This association of names would not have been lost on a second century catechumen. The importance of the succession of apostolic teaching and the handing down of an accurate interpretation of the Scriptures had been deemed crucial from the beginning of Christianity's spread. Eusebius' remarks are an echo of the reverence that had been accorded Clemens Alexandrinus already for over two hundred years.

B. Clement's Sources

Clement's approach to theology is embedded in both his training as an eclectic philosopher and his cultural climate.[278] He had a broad acquaintance with an array of classical Greek and Hellenistic sources ranging from Plato and Aristotle to Philo. In many ways, Clement's role as a Christian theologian is analogous to the role played in Hellenistic Judaism by Philo Judaeus (20 B.C. – 50 A.D.). As Philo had attempted to reconcile Judaism and Greek thought, so

---

[277] Williamson, *Eusebius: History of the Church,* 214.

[278] Henry Chadwick (*Early Christian Thought and The Classical Tradition* (Oxford: Oxford University, 1966), 36) notes that "Clement belongs to the world he is addressing."

Clement tries to do for Christianity.[279] Clement believed that Holy Scripture is generally compatible with Greek categories of thought, though he recognized that there were some irreconcilable differences.[280] When faced with such differences, Clement comes out on the side of biblical Christianity.

However, as an apologist living in a time when the church's faith demanded competent defenders, Clement often finds himself walking a fine line between philosophical and biblical categories of truth, yet not as though the two are mutually exclusive. Clement believed that natural revelation and special revelation are reconcilable. Philosophy, which is based on experience of the natural world, is the highest achievement of human thought. Clement's argument is that philosophy is compatible with the highest achievement of religion, the Judeo-Christian revelation. Clement viewed his task as defending the faith not as a philosopher who happened to be a believer in Christ, but as a believer in Christ whose formal education had been in philosophy. The subtlety of this fact makes all the difference when attempting to understand Clement's theology. His particular task, as he sees it, is to defend Christianity using the tools and language of philosophy.

As already noted, Clement of Alexandria was an eclectic philosopher; that is, he borrowed freely from various philosophical schools. Henry Chadwick notes that Clement took his metaphysics from Plato, his ethics from the Stoics, and his descriptive logic and terminology from Aristotle.[281] It is this eclecticism that often makes Clement's thought so difficult to engage for modern readers.[282] Yet if we

---

[279] See Tollington, *Clement of Alexandria,* 1: 166 where it is suggested that "Clement could [not] have been a Christian Platonist unless Philo had been a Jewish Platonist before him."

[280] For a helpful though brief analysis of Clement's biblical hermeneutic see Manlio Simonetti, *Biblical Interpretation in the Early Church,* trans., J. A. Hughes; eds., A Berquist and M. Bockmuehl (Edinburgh: T&T Clark, 1994), 35-39.

[281] Chadwick, *Early Christian Thought,* 41.

remember that Clement's primary theological source is Holy Scripture, his arguments begin to make sense.

Using St. Paul's encounter with the philosophers at the Areopagus (Acts 17:22-28), Clement illustrates the relationship between faith and philosophy. Like Paul, Clement accepts the premise that philosophy enabled the Greeks to deduce in part, the truth about God.[283] On the other hand, also like Paul, he does "not regard philosophy as a *sine qua non*."[284] Both philosophy and Christianity are engaged in the search for true knowledge, but the knowledge of God gleaned by the Greeks through investigation of the natural world could not approach the revelation of God mediated through his incarnate Son. Although philosophy helped humankind to achieve a measure of righteousness, it could not perfect righteousness, since it is only an ancillary source of ethical reasoning. According to Clement, philosophy neither enhances nor detracts from the truth revealed in Christ; its purpose rather is to serve revealed truth by "reduc[ing] . . . the power of the sophistic attack on it."[285] Clement is not blind to the glaring deficiencies of philosophy. Rather, he argues that Christianity must appropriate the best of philosophy in defending the Christian faith; as he puts it: "Take the best of the philosophers.[286]

---

[282] Scholars are generally agreed that Clement cited from anthologies of philosophical sources. See Tollington, *Clement of Alexandria*, 1: 155 f.; also, Salvatore R. C. Lilla, *Clement of Alexandria: A Study in Christian Platonism and Gnosticism*, Oxford Theological Monographs (London: Oxford University Press, 1971), 123.

[283] *Strom.* 1.19:91.1-5; *FC*, 85: 92. Clement illustrates from St. Paul's encounter with the philosophers at the Aeropagus (Acts 17:22-28) the relationship of philosophy and Scripture.

[284] *Strom.* 1.20:99.1; *FC*, 85: 98.

[285] *Strom.* 1.20:100.1; *FC*, 85: 98.

[286] *Strom.* 2.1:1.2; *FC*, 85: 157.

Clement is indebted to some philosophical schools more than others. He especially admires Plato, whom he regards as a "fellow-worker in the search [for God]."[287] At the same time he recognizes Plato's limited perspective. Citing a line from the *Timaeus*, Clement writes: "It is a hard task to find the Father and Maker of this universe, and when you have found Him, it is impossible to declare Him to all."[288] In other words, Clement believes that Plato came close to true knowledge of God, but not close enough to proclaim his insights as gospel or revelation.

Clement is less indebted to Aristotle and the Peripatetic School's concept of the divine. He criticizes Aristotle for having described God as "the soul of the universe."[289] Positively, however, Clement finds that Aristotle's precision regarding ethical conduct is analogous to the moral qualities of the redeemed depicted in Scripture.[290] Since the focus of Clement's soteriological thought is the moral transformation of believers in Christ, it is to be expected that he would find analogies to Christian perfection in the Stoic virtues.[291]

Like Justin Martyr (d. 165) a half century earlier, Clement believed that the Greeks received their ideas about God — imperfect though the reception may have been — from the Old Testament.[292] Philo had argued similarly much earlier. But Clement's contribution extends well beyond Philo's. Clement established

---

[287] *Protr.* 6:67.2; *LCL,*92: 153.

[288] *Protr.* 6:68.1; *LCL,* 92: 153,55.

[289] *Protr.* 5:66.4; *LCL,* 92: 151.

[290] See for example *Strom.* 5.13:86.1-3; *ANF,* 2: 464-65 and how Clement weaves Aristotle's distinction between doing (ποιεῖν) and practicing (πράττειν) into a definition of faith.

[291] See *Strom.* 5.14:110.2; *ANF,* 2: 470 where Clement cites the early Stoic philosopher Cleanthes (ca. 331-233 B.C.) on the nature of the good.

[292] Clement alludes to this in many places, e.g., *Strom.* 1.17:81.1-5; *FC,* 85: 85. See *Strom.* 1.1:1.1; *FC,* 85: 157: "We shall . . . prove that they plagiarized our most important doctrines and debased them . . . in matters concerning faith, wisdom, revealed knowledge, and scientific knowledge, hope and love, and concerning repentance, self-control, and above all fear of God (really a swarm of the virtues of the truth)."

philosophically the compatibility of Hebrew, Greek, and Christian thought. Divine providence, Clement argues, prepared both Jews and Greeks for the ultimate revelation of God in Jesus Christ. He writes:

> So, before the Lord's coming, philosophy was an essential guide to righteousness for the Greeks. At the present time, it is a useful guide towards reverence for God. It is a kind of preliminary education for those who are trying to gather faith through demonstration. 'Your foot will not stumble,' says Scripture, if you attribute good things, whether Greek or Christian, to Providence. God is responsible for all good things: of some, like the blessings of the Old and New Covenants, directly; of others, like the riches of philosophy indirectly. *Perhaps philosophy too was a direct gift of God to the Greeks before the Lord extended his appeal to the Greeks. For philosophy was to the Greek world what the Law was to the Hebrews, a tutor escorting them to Christ.* So philosophy is a preparatory process; it opens the road for the person whom Christ brings to his final goal.[293]

The coming of humankind to the true knowledge of God is an educational process that began with the self-revelation of God to Israel. Subsequently and indirectly, God revealed himself to the Greeks by providentially guiding them in the philosophical search for truth. The divine purpose overall was to include the entire human race in salvation, not just the Jews.

For Clement, the convergence of the Old Testament revelation and Greek philosophy was achieved in the revelation of Jesus Christ. Philo could have had no stake in this achievement. Christ is the culmination of humankind's quest for truth. In a remarkable passage, Clement writes:

> Wherefore it seems to me, that since the Word Himself came to us from heaven, we ought no longer to go to human teaching, to Athens and the rest of Greece, or to Ionia, in our curiosity. If our teacher is He who has filled the universe with holy powers, creation, salvation, beneficence, lawgiving, prophecy, teaching, this teacher now

---

[293] *Strom.* 1.5:28.1-3; *FC,* 85: 41-42. Italics mine.

instructs us in all things, and *the whole world has by this time become an Athens and a Greece through the Word.*[294]

Clement unequivocally affirms the superiority of the Christian revelation to Greek philosophy, yet he will not discard Greek thought. He continues:

[P]hilosophy, as the elders say, is a lengthy deliberation, that pursues wisdom with a never-ending love. But 'the commandment of the Lord shines afar, giving light to the eyes.' Receive the Christ; receive power to see; receive thy light; . . . .[295]

Clement's task is to clarify and universalize the biblical revelation by reconciling the philosophical search for truth with the self-revelation of God in Jesus Christ.

C. Works

The most reliable edition of the works of Clemens Alexandrinus was published by Otto Stählin over the years 1905-09.[296] Prior to this Clement's works were collected in Migne's *Patrologia Graeca.*[297] R. B. Tollington's classification of Clement's extant and lost works is still helpful and shows something of the breadth of the Alexandrian's interests.[298] Three of Clement's treatises traditionally have been grouped as a trilogy. They are *Protrepticos, Paedagogos* and *Stromateis.* These writings serve as the focus of this study.

---

[294] *Protr.* 11:112.1-2; *LCL,* 92: 239. Italics mine.

[295] *Protr.* 11:113.1,2; *LCL,* 92: 241.

[296] Otto Stählin, ed., *Clemens Alexandrinus,* 4th ed., 4 vols., *Die Griechischen Christlichen Schriftsteller der Ersten Drei Jahrhunderte* (Berlin: Akademie-Verlag, 1960-80). Hereafter, this series will be abbreviated *GCS.*

[297] J. P. Migne, *Patrologiae cursus completus. . . Series Graeca,* vols. 8, 9 (Paris: Migne, 1857-66).

[298] Tollington, *Clement of Alexandria,* 1: 195-202. Tollington divides the collection into four categories: (1) commentaries on Scripture; (2) controversial writings; (3) philosophy of doctrine; (4) pastoral writings. By "philosophy of doctrine" one should understand systematic theology. Tollington also lists lost treatises whose titles only are known.

1. Protrepticos

Protrepticos, is the abbreviated title for Προτρεπτικός πρός Ἕλληνας, *An Exhortation to the Greeks*. *Protrepticos* is an evangelistic treatise directed toward Greek-speaking polytheists. Its thesis is that the Christian revelation is the ultimate revelation of God in human history. The author exhorts his readers to cease searching for wisdom in philosophy and striving for salvation the gods. Christ is the true wisdom and only salvation of God. The one who turns *from* worldly wisdom and false worship *to* faith in Christ and obedience to God will emerge from hopeless darkness. He will become a "disciple of the Light, the friend of Christ and joint-heir with Him."[299] Clement's purpose is to exhort his Hellenistic audience to receive "the greatest of good things — salvation."[300]

2. Paedagogos

The three books of *Paedagogos* or *The Instructor* form the second work in the trilogy. Whereas the purpose of *Protrepticos* had been to evangelize, *Paedagogos* was written to instruct those who had already embraced faith in Christ, but as yet had not achieved spiritual maturity. Thus, the author addresses his readers as children who need guidance and instruction toward living as followers of Christ.[301]

The image of a teacher of children is found historically in Hellenistic culture. The roleof the παιδαγωγός (*paedagogos* — 'teacher, instructor') had originally been defined as that of a servant dwelling in an affluent household, whose task was to shepherd the master's children to and from school. Later, the

---

[299] *Protr.* 11:115.4; *LCL*, 92: 247.

[300] *Protr.* 12:123.2; *LCL*, 92: 263.

[301] Tollington (*Clement of Alexandria*, 1: 195) classifies *Paedagogus* among Clement's writings of a pastoral nature.

role of *paedagogos* took on greater responsibility. The *paedagogos* was an educated servant who actually taught or at least supervised the learning of the master's children. But the *paedagogos'* primary task was to oversee the formation of the children's moral character, to make sure that they progressed in the development of virtue. Clement employs the image of the *paedagogos* and his charges as an analogy of the relationship between Christ and the newly converted.

Apparently, this approach was not perceived as condescension. We must remember that Clement's audience was made up of affluent persons who had been immersed in the culture and moral environment of Alexandria.[302] These individuals, having come to faith in Christ, were drawn to Clement's catechetical school. Though acquainted with the Greek classics and knowledgeable about pagan religions, they were uninstructed in the newfound Christian faith.[303] True, they needed to learn the essential doctrines of the faith, but their greater need was to learn how to practice Christianity. In addition to a cognitive grasp of the faith, they needed to embrace its ethical demands if they were to experience the fullness of salvation and live as true Christians in the world.

The writer calls his readers 'children' (reminiscent of 1 John), though they are not children in terms of their knowledge of God.[304] In fact, they already 'know' God because they have been reborn, regenerated (*anagennao*), enlightened (*sotizo*), and made perfect (*teleios*).[305] To knowledge however they must acquire virtue. *Paedagogos* is therefore a moral treatise. Drawing upon the

---

[302] See esp. *Paed.* 3.1-6; *FC*, 23: 199-229. Clement's discussion here and there affords an interesting glimpse into the kind of city late second century Alexandria was.

[303] For the sake of greater clarity, we shall distinguish the speculative philosophical religion historically known as Gnosticism from Clement's paradigm of the sanctified Christian believer whom he terms a 'Gnostic'. The former will be referred to as Hellenistic Gnosticism, the latter 'Christian Gnostic'.

[304] See *Paed.* 1.6:25.1-52.3; *FC*, 23: 24-49.

[305] *Paed.* 1.6:25.1-3; *FC*, 23: 24-25. This countered the teaching of the Hellenistic Gnostic sects, which claimed that Christians were children in terms of personally apprehending God.

ancient idea of *paideia* (instruction), Clement argues that the Son of God, the *Logos*, is the divine educator (*paedagogus*). The role of Christ as educator is distinguished from that of Christ as teacher (*didaskalos*):

> Let us call Him, then, by the one title: Educator of little ones, an Educator who does not simply follow behind, but who leads the way, for His aim is to improve the soul, not just to instruct it; to guide to a life of virtue, not merely to one of knowledge. Yet, that same Word does teach. It is simply that in this work we are not considering Him in that light. *As Teacher* [didaskalos], *He explains and reveals through instruction, but as Educator* [paedagogos] *he is practical.* First He persuades men to form habits of life, then He encourages them to fulfill their duties by laying down clear-cut counsels and by holding up, for us who follow, examples of those who have erred in the past. Both are most useful: the advice, that it may be obeyed; the other, given in the form of example, has a twofold object — either that we may choose the good and imitate it or condemn and avoid the bad.[306]

Without denying the need for instruction in doctrine (Christ the *didaskalos*) in this treatise Christ is the educator of character.[307] It is striking in the above citation that, while Clement affirms that both intellectual and moral instruction are essential, only moral education is salvific. Reminiscent of the Epistle of St. James, Clement argues that faith alone will not save. True faith produces moral transformation, which in turn results in the practice of good.

---

[306] *Paed.* 1.1:1.4-2.2; *FC*, 23:4. Italics mine.

[307] Quasten (*Patrology*, 2: 12) regards the move to attribute to the Word the tasks of exhorting (*protrepto*), educating (*paidagogeo*) and teaching (*didasko*) as evidence that Clement intended volume three of the trilogy to consist of a work by the title of *Didaskalos*; but this is speculation only. Clement's emphasis was on the development of moral virtue, not systematic doctrine. *Stromateis* is more likely the third volume, if indeed there was supposed to be one. But see also citation for n. 755, which would seem to validate Quasten's argument.

124

3. Stromateis

Principal among Clement's extant writings is *Stromateis*. The full title in translation is *Miscellanies of Notes of Knowledge According to the True Philosophy*, which aptly reflects not only the treatise's philosophical character, but also its sometime disorganized structure and approach. The term στρωματεῖς (*Stromateis* — 'carpets, miscellanies') in ancient times originally described a patchwork bedspread. At some point, it was appropriated by the literati of Greece as a descriptive title for a genre of popular literature. Structurally, 'miscellanies' as a genre treated ideas in no particular order with no attempt to systematize. It was favored as a form for the writing of philosophy.[308]

There are several reasons why *Stromateis* might easily be written off as an eccentric piece not worth the effort. First, Clement's logic is often difficult to follow. The Western mind is by nature ill-disposed toward prose that contains non-sequiturs. Until one is willing to live with a more cyclical Eastern style of argumentation, frustration with *Stromateis* is inevitable. Second, acquaintance with Hellenistic philosophy is a prerequisite in order to understand the subtleties of *Stromateis*. Clement's method is twofold: (1) to employ the classical philosophers and poets to support theological points whenever it is useful; and (2) as an apologetic tactical move to empty philosophical terminology of its meaning and fill it with Christian content. This methodology affords him the tools to counter the claims of polytheism and overcome challenges orthodoxy. A final reason that makes for difficulty in reading *Stromateis* is owing to the fact that a new critical English translation is sorely needed. Such a project would make the treatise much more accessible to scholars and would serve to help those who work with the Greek text to do so more efficiently.

---

[308] See Quasten, *Patrology*, 2: 12; Ferguson's introduction to *Stromateis, FC*, 85: 10; and, Tollington, Clement of Alexandria, 1: 186-87.

At first glance, *Stromateis* appears to be what the title implies, a pastiche of topics that meander across the author's idiosyncratic interests. Upon closer examination, however, we find that Clement's purpose is to produce a philosophy of the Christian faith. *Stromateis* is intended to serve as a collection of notes on topics that Clement himself had valued as part of his own education. On this issue, he winsomely writes:

> This work is not a writing rhetorically shaped for exhibition. It is a collection of memoranda, a treasure for my old age, a remedy against forgetfulness, a mere reflection, a sketch of vividly alive originals, words I was thought worthy to hear, and blessed and genuinely memorable men from whom I heard them.[309]

The notion of 'instruction' governs *Stromateis* in a way reminiscent of *Paedagogos*, only more expansively. In *Stromateis* Clement strives to preserve and make known "the tradition of revealed knowledge" which opposes the "thorns and . . . weeds" of the false knowledge of God promoted by the Hellenistic Gnostic sects.[310] All true learning comes from God by "the grace of the Spirit."[311] *Stromateis* is an attempt to show the ultimate dependence of all the branches of human knowledge upon the self-revelation of God that can only be received by faith. In many ways, *Stromateis* is a prototype of the Christian faith and learning motif that will subvert and assimilate the classical world, eventually leading to the rise of the European university.

A mirror reading of *Stromateis* reflects an educated audience that was familiar with the nuances of philosophical discourse. These were persons who had embraced Christ and were now moving on toward maturity in the faith. In making the connection between philosophy and faith, Clement compares classical

---

[309] *Strom.* 1.1:11.1; *FC*, 85: 30.

[310] *Strom.* 1.1:15.2; *FC*, 85: 33.

[311] *Strom.* 1.1:14.1; *FC*, 85: 32.

126

philosophy to water that prepares the hard earth for seed: "[W]e use the pure water of Greek philosophy to water in advance the earthly part of our readers, to make them fit to receive the sowing of the spiritual seed and enable it to grow without difficulty."[312] He rejects the opinion of those well intentioned but misinformed believers "who think that philosophy comes from an evil source"; instead, he affirms that philosophy was given to humankind by divine providence.[313] *Stromateis* is designed to "embrace the truth which is mixed in with the dogmas of philosophy . . . [and] which is covered in and hidden within them."[314] Philosophy does not harm faith; it is instead "a clear likeness of truth, a gift granted to the Greeks by God."[315]

However, Clement also recognizes philosophy's limitations. Following an extensive review of the history of classical thought, Clement summarizes its strengths and weaknesses:

> Greek philosophy in the view of some teaches truth in one way or another by accident, but obscurely and without the whole truth. Others would have it as set in motion by the devil. Some have supposed that all philosophy is inspired by inferior powers. But even if Greek philosophy does not grasp the magnitude of the truth, and further, is too weak to fulfill the Lord's commandments, still it prepares the way for the supremely royal teaching; in one way or another it produces a sense of discipline, foreshadows right character, and prepares the person who has an inkling of Providence to receive the truth.[316]

Clement's confidence in philosophy's ability to assist, not harm the Christian faith is grounded in his conviction that the ultimate sources for Greek philosophy were

---

[312] *Strom.* 1.1:18.4; *FC*, 85: 35.

[313] *Strom.* 1.1:18.3; *FC*, 85: 35.

[314] *Strom.* 1.1:18.1; *FC*, 85: 35.

[315] *Strom.* 1.2:20.1; *FC*, 85: 36.

[316] *Strom.* 1.15:80.5,6; *FC*, 85: 84-85.

the prophets of ancient Israel. Using the myth of Prometheus' theft of the divine spark as an analogy, he describes the supposed relationship between the beginning of philosophy and Hebrew prophecy:

> So there is in philosophy, stolen as it were by Prometheus, a little fire which blazes up helpfully into a useful light; a trace of wisdom, an impulse about God. In this way only could the Greek philosophers be called "robbers and bandits," *taking from the Hebrew prophets fragments of the truth before the Lord's coming,* but without full knowledge, rather appropriating them as personal doctrine, defacing some, twisting others in an ignorant excess of enthusiasm while actually discovering some fully.[317]

One would have to say that overall Clement sees more value in philosophy than danger. By later standards, some might say (and have said) that he has accorded it too much worth. Nonetheless, Clement remains one of the best of the early Christian apologists, if for no other reason than he took seriously the challenge of reconciling Greek and Christian thought and wrote extensively on the subject.

As we noted, the logical flow of *Stromateis* may at times appear convoluted to Western logic; but there is one theme that draws together all its extraneous ends. It is Clement's description of the true Gnostic or 'perfect' Christian. The theme of perfection is its underlying ground. One of Clement's nineteenth century interpreters, Anglican Bishop John Kaye, observes:

> The object of Clement in composing the Stromata [*sic*], was to describe the Gnostic and perfect Christian, in order at once to furnish the believer with a model for his imitation, and to prevent him from being led astray by the representations of the Valentinians, and other Gnostic sects.[318]

---

[317] *Strom.* 1:17:87.1,2; *FC*, 85: 88-89. As we saw earlier, Justin Martyr and Philo both believed that Greek philosophy owed its existence to Hebrew thought. Italics mine.

[318] John Kaye, *Some Account of the Writings and Opinions of Clement of Alexandria* (London: Rivington, 1835), 229.

Hellenistic Gnostic sects such as those founded by Valentinus and Basilides flourished in Alexandria during the late second century. These movements were highly syncretistic, attempting to combine speculative philosophical mysticism with catholic Christianity. Apparently, the chief arguing point of Valentinus and the others was the claim to superior spiritual knowledge. *Gnosis*, the ordinary word for 'knowledge', was the term these sects employed in referring to their gospel of 'secret' salvific knowledge. The chief social feature of the Gnostic sects was an elitist attitude toward the rest of humanity grounded in a highly deterministic worldview. Gnostics tended to think of themselves as spiritually privileged and more sophisticated than catholics.

Clement opposed Gnosticism's elitist claims on the basis of its sheer hubris, and because Gnostic teachers failed to deal responsibly with the Christian doctrine of salvation. Gnostics denigrated the catholic faith as an inferior knowledge of God. In attempting to meet the challenge, Clement posed a detailed argument for the perfect *gnosis* of God that comes only by faith in Christ. He not only rejects his Gnostic opponents' arrogant claims, but he subverts the ground of their arguments by taking over their favorite term, *gnosis*, and filling it with Christian meaning. This was a brilliant move. In effect, Clement declares a rhetorical war. He writes: "It is . . . our purpose to prove that the [Christian] Gnostic alone is holy and pious, and worships the true God in a manner worthy of Him; and that worship meet for God is followed by loving and being loved by God."[319] There is a "perfection in faith," he insists, which stands in contrast to "ordinary faith."[320]

Although the tone of the discussion is consistently philosophical, his approach to theological discourse is invariably grounded in Scripture, and his

---

[319] *Strom.* 7.1:2.1,2; *ANF*, 2: 523.

[320] *Strom.* 4.16:100.6; *ANF*, 2: 427.

purpose and worldview are distinctly biblical. Such distinctives are evident to the careful reader of *Stromateis*.

4. Miscellaneous Works

Next in the manuscript tradition are two smaller works, *Excerpta ex Theodoto* and *Eclogae propheticae*. Both appear in Stählin's edition, but only *Excerpta* has been translated into English.[321] These works consist primarily of extracts Clement took from Gnostic texts, possibly for illustrative purposes or as preliminary studies. They are not significant.

A more important work is the sermon *Quis Dives Salvetur?* or *Who is the Rich Man that is Saved?* based upon Mark 10:17-31.[322] Not only does it provide insight into Clement's pastoral ministry, but *Quis Dives* also provides further confirmation that Clement's readers were drawn from the wealthier classes of Alexandria.

Finally, a number of fragments of writings that are now lost have been attributed to Clement. Quasten lists these works, noting that most are of doubtful origin.[323]

D. Soteriology

Clement addresses a variety of theological issues, some of which have had scholarly treatment over the years, many have not.[324] For the purposes of this

---

[321] R. P. Casey, trans., *The Excerpta Ex Theodoto of Clement of Alexandria* (London: Christophers, 1934).

[322] Stählin, *GCS*, 17: 157-91. English translations include W. Wilson, *ANF*, 2: 589-604 and Butterworth, *LCL*, 92: 270-367.

[323] Quasten, *Patrology*, 2: 16-19. For a complete listing of the fragments see Stählin, GCS, 17: XI-XXXVIII.

[324] Among the various attempts at scholarly interpretation, older surveys by R.B. Tollington and John Kaye (*op. cit.*) are recommended. Among recent writers, John Ferguson's efforts stand

130

study, however, we will limit our investigation to soteriology. As we might expect, Clement's discussion of salvation is clothed in the philosophical language of his historical location.

1. Faith

Clement teaches that faith is the foundation of salvation and the beginning of the believer's being made righteous. He writes:

> [F]aith appears to us as the *first leaning* towards salvation; fear, hope, and penitence develop in the wake of faith, in association with self-control and patience, and lead us to love and knowledge.[325]

Faith is essential to knowing God; for Clement, faith in the incarnate Word of God is a decisive act:

> For the gates of the Word being intellectual [*logikai*], are opened by the key of faith. No one knows God but the Son, and he to whom the Son shall reveal Him. And I know well that He who has opened the door hitherto shut, will afterwards reveal what is within; and will show what we could not have known before, had we not entered in by Christ, through whom alone God is beheld.[326]

As we already noted, Clement was by nurture and training drawn to classical Greek philosophy and the search for wisdom. As a Christian however, he recognized that the ultimate source of knowledge and wisdom is the one God who

---

out in *Clement of Alexandria* (New York: Twayne, 1974) and in "The Achievements of Clement of Alexandria," *Religious Studies* 12 (1976): 59-80. Also recommended is Walter H. Wagner, *After the Apostles: Christianity in the Second Century* (Minneapolis, MN: Fortress Press, 1994), 171-86.

[325] *Strom.* 2.6:31.1; *FC*, 85: 179. Italics mine.

[326] *Protr.* 1:10.3; *ANF*, 2: 174. See also *LCL*, 92: 27: "For the gates of the Word are gates of reason [*logikai*], opened by the key of faith." The use of the term *logikai* here does not mean that Clement views faith as speculative. Rather, its use suggests the inherent relationship between faith and reason. Faith is an act of reason empowered by grace. Clement is saying that God chooses to reveal himself only to those who believe in his Son, which is a reasonable action to take.

has revealed himself as Father, Son, and Holy Spirit.[327] Clement's task is to prove that the salvation offered in Christ was the goal for which the philosophers so arduously had strived. Faith in the Incarnate Son, he asserts, is the sole condition to achieving this end.

Clement's doctrine of faith is built upon a philosophical epistemology, which he then attempts to reconcile with biblical concepts and terminology. H. A. Wolfson observed that Clement's concept of faith is a synthesis of ideas held by Aristotle and the Stoics, what he termed a theory of "double faith."[328] First, there is faith as an *a priori* consciousness, that is, an immediate kind of knowledge grounded either in perceptions or first principles. This faith is incapable of being demonstrated or proven.[329] It exists as an innate awareness and conviction prior to experience. When directed toward God, the object of religion, it exists as a simple, initial kind of faith in the Christian revelation.[330] A second kind of faith is that which is possessed entirely on an *a posteriori* or derived basis. This is faith

---

[327] Clement's prayer to the Paedagogos is a tribute to the early Trinitarian concept of God. *Paed.* 3.12:101.1,2; *FC*, 23: 275.

[328] See H.A. Wolfson, *Faith, Trinity, Incarnation*, vol. 1 of *The Philosophy of the Church Fathers* (Cambridge, MA: Harvard University Press, 1970), 112-19. On the influence of Aristotle's thought upon Clement's theology in general see Elizabeth A. Clark, *Clement's Use of Aristotle: The Aristotelian Contribution to Clement of Alexandria's Refutation of Gnosticism* (New York and Toronto: Edwin Mellen Press, 1977).

[329] Aristotle first spoke of this type of faith as a *strong assumption* (ὑπόληψις ἰσχυρά). The Stoics used the same definition for a different term, *assent* (συγκατάθεσις). Wolfson believes that the Stoic writers borrowed and extended Aristotle's idea of faith to include *assentError! Bookmark not defined.*.

[330] Lilla maintains that Clement used the term faith in three major ways, not two. In Lilla's view, Clement differentiates faith in undemonstrated first principles from simple religious faith. See *Clement of Alexandria: A Study in Christian Platonism and Gnosticism,* 120 f., 136 f. In my opinion, Lilla has created an artificial distinction that Clement did not intend. Clement's purpose is not to develop new insights into the philosophical doctrine of faith. Rather, he is simply trying to show that the philosophical concept of undemonstrated faith in first principles is analogous to the believer's undemonstrated faith in the Gospel. In my view, undemonstrated faith and simple religious faith are equivalent for Clement.

demonstrated either through scientific confirmation, syllogism, or opinion.[331]   In theological terms, it is faith grounded in the subjective experience of one who has become conscious of having been acted upon by the divine.   Though it is arguable whether properly speaking any synthesis can be considered a duality, Wolfson's observations do have merit in that they perhaps are the first real attempt to deal logically with Clement's epistemology.

Though a full treatment of Greek epistemology lies beyond our concerns, the following observations are pertinent. First, the philosophical concept of faith is based upon an epistemological realism, which postulates that all truth claims must conform to the real, external world.[332] To put it conversely, no faith claim is valid whose object does not exist.   Second, faith conjoins the action of the speculative intellect with the practical intellect.[333]   To believe is to render a judgment concerning the truth and moral goodness of a thing. Faith accounts for the rational capacity to recognize these qualities and act upon them. Third, the exercise of faith is a free and uncoerced choice.   It is an entirely free and voluntary movement of the will. Because faith involves choosing to believe, the exercise of faith is a moral act.[334]

---

[331] Science (*scientia*) here refers to knowledge derived from experience, not science in the modern sense derived through hypothesis and experimentation.

[332] On Aristotle's realism see Frederick Coppleston, *A History of Philosophy*, vols. 1-3 (Westminster, MD: The Newman Press, 1962, 1963; reprint, New York: Image Books, 1985), 1: 278. See also primary source discussions in Aristotle *Met.* 13.10.1087a; *De An.* 2.5.417a. All citations of Aristotle are from Jonathan Barnes, ed., *The Complete Works of Aristotle,* 2 vols. (Princeton, NJ: Princeton University Press, 1984).

[333] This was the main modification of Aristotle's theory of knowledge made by the Stoics. See Wolfson, *Faith, Trinity, Incarnation,* 117. Whereas Aristotle held that philosophy is the *intellectual* search for truth, Stoic writers argued that the primary purpose of philosophy was *practical,* that is, having to do with ethical conduct, virtue, and happiness. On Stoic ethics in general see Coppleston, *A History of Philosophy,* 1: 394-400.

[334] This is made possible by Clement's description of faith (πίστις) as *assent* (συγκατάθεσις), which is discussed below.

Two Levels of Faith

As he explored the relationship between Christianity and philosophy, Clement found partial agreement on the notion that, properly understood, there are degrees or levels of faith. Citing Romans 1:17, he writes: "The apostle [Paul]. . . manifestly announces a *twofold faith,* or rather *one which admits of growth and perfection*; for the *common faith* lies beneath as a foundation."[335] He describes these as *simple* and *scientific* faith.

Simple Faith

The first level, simple faith, is *a priori* in nature. Clement views *simple* faith as fundamentally an epistemological category, but a very important one, for simple faith is the sole prerequisite of Christian salvation. Two Greek concepts combine to form Clement's definition of *simple* faith.

Prolepsis

Prolepsis or 'preconception' is a philosophical term, but Clement uses it with a biblical analogy in mind.[336] He writes:

> Faith, which the Greeks think alien and useless and which they consequently malign, is in fact *preconception* [*prolepsis*] by the will, an act of *consenting* [*sungkatathesis*] to religion and, as the divine Apostle puts it, 'the assurance of things hoped for, the conviction of things not seen.'[337]

---

[335] *Strom.* 5.1:2.4-6; *ANF,* 2: 444. Italics mine.

[336] Liddell & Scott, *Lexicon,* s.v. "προλημψις."

[337] *Strom.* 2.2:8.4; *FC,* 85: 162. Italics mine. Probably the "Greeks" he has in mind here are the Hellenistic Gnostic sects, but he also may be thinking of the philosophical schools that placed little value on *a priori* ways of knowing. The biblical text cited is Hebrews 11:1-2. Characteristic of the Alexandrian church, Clement assumes that the Apostle Paul authored the Epistle to the Hebrews. See *Strom.* 6.8:62.2; *ANF,* 2: 494.

Simple proleptic faith involves a movement of the will toward its object. The object of Christian faith is God. Therefore, proleptic faith is, according to Clement (quoting Hebrews 11:1), a sure evidence of the object to which it points.

The long history of development behind the concept of *prolepsis* is of no real concern to us here, but a brief overview may be helpful. The way Clement uses *prolepsis* is the result of a synthesis of ancient philosophical thinking. Properly understood, *prolepsis* is an *a priori* concept or mental image that is held in memory and into which subsequent experiences are placed.[338] This is significant, for it opens the door for faith to be defined as a substantive kind of knowing. Such is reflected in Clement's identification of *prolepsis* with the definition of faith found in Hebrews 11.

Clement agreed with the Greek apologists who had made the case for interpreting the God of the Bible in the idiom of Greek philosophy. It is reasonable to believe in a God who has revealed himself in history, though absolute knowledge of that God is necessarily incomplete. Creatures cannot know fully the infinite uncreated Creator who in his essence stands in relation to the world as utterly transcendent.[339] Yet the Creator, because he has chosen to reveal himself, can be known; and since Scripture mandates that faith alone is the means by which human beings may know God, there must be a way of reconciling the transcendent God of philosophy with the self-revealing God of Scripture.

---

[338] See Coppleston, *History of Philosophy,* 1: 403. The Epicureans viewed *prolepsis* somewhat like Aristotle's *first principles.* However unlike Aristotle, they did not treat it as *a priori* in nature. Rather, they held that *prolepsis* is *a posteriori* in nature, specifically, something conceived in sensory experience and held in memory as an image to be called up later. The synthesis of the later Greek schools saw *prolepsis* revert to its original *a priori* usage.

[339] See *Strom.* 2.2:5.1-6.4; *FC,* 85: 160-61 where Clement argues that God cannot be known because: 1) The "unborn and uncreated" cannot be known by "a creature subject to birth"; and, 2) "[h]e is beyond space and time and anything belonging to created beings."

Clement's solution is simple proleptic faith, which does not depend upon the human ability to know, but rather upon God's disclosure of himself.[340] Clement argues that the idea of God is present in an *a priori* fashion to the human mind. He writes:

> For there was always a *natural manifestation* of the one Almighty God among all right-thinking men; and the most, who had not quite divested themselves of shame with respect to the truth, apprehended the eternal beneficence in divine providence. . . . Far from destitute of a divine idea is man[kind], who, it is written in Genesis, partook of inspiration being endowed with a purer essence than the other animate creatures.[341]

Proleptic faith is incapable of being proven, according to Clement; it needs no proof other than its own immediate existence.[342]

Clement stresses the importance of proleptic faith in relation to eschatology and the final destination of all believers. *Prolepsis* is an anticipation of the fulfillment of salvation's goal. In Clement's day, the Gnostic sects had claimed that the faith of catholics was imperfect and inferior. Clement responds by showing that the very premise of their argument is flawed. He writes:

> [T]hey [the Gnostic sects] object . . . [that the Christian] man has not yet received *the gift of perfection* [τὴν τελείαν δωρεάν – 'the perfect gift']. I agree with them, except that I insist *he is already in the light* and that darkness does not overtake him. There is nothing at all in

---

[340] This is in part why hope and faith are so similar for Clement. *Strom.* 5.3:16.1; *ANF*, 2: 448: "For he who hopes [*elpizo*], he who believes [*pisteuo*], sees intellectual objects and future things with the mind."

[341] *Strom.* 5.13:87.2, 4; *ANF*, 2: 465. Italics mine.

[342] Clement used *prolepsis* both epistemologically and theologically. He argues that from an epistemological perspective *prolepsis* is essential to know anything at all. The individual who exercises *prolepsis* demonstrates a willingness to be taught and an openness to learning the truth. The exercise of proleptic faith is the equivalent of "attention or comprehension or teachability"; he adds, "then clearly no one will learn without faith, since no one will learn without a preconception [*prolepsis*]. (*Strom.* 2.4:17.3; *FC* 85: 168)

between light and darkness. Perfection lies ahead, in the resurrection of the faithful, but it consists in obtaining [now] the promise which has already been given to us.[343]

Clement agrees that the believer's faith at a proleptic stage has not yet reached perfection. He insists, however, that even proleptic faith is salvific because it secures the promised perfection in advance, which by definition is eternal life. Faith," he

explains, "is begotten in time . . . while the completion is the possession of the promise, made enduring for all eternity."[344] Faith is a *prolepsis*, a willing anticipation, of the arrival of faith's object. "In believing," he writes, "we already anticipate in advance what we will receive as an actuality after the resurrection, ..."[345]

To grasp the import of Clement's argument here, we must recall that it occurs within an apologetic context. The Gnostic sects held a hierarchical view of humankind, teaching that the soul of every individual falls into one of three categories. The souls of *hylikoi* ('material ones'; *hylikos* — 'material, belonging to matter';) are persons whose fate is the fallen material world. The souls of the *hylikoi* are utterly incapable of salvation; they are condemned to imprisonment in the evil substance of the material universe. The *psychikoi* ('soulish'; *psuche* — 'soul') are individuals whose souls are partly spiritual and partly material. The *psychikoi* may or may not be saved according to their ability to receive saving *gnosis*. Finally, there are the *pneumatikoi* ('spirituals'; *pneuma* — 'spirit') who belong to the highest order. The *pneumatikoi* are irreducible spirits, pure souls trapped in material bodies, which once released through physical death, are irrevocably destined to a salvation instrumentally brought about by their

---

[343] *Paed.* 1.6:28.3; *FC*, 23: 28. Italics mine.

[344] *Paed.* 1.6:28.5; *FC*, 23: 28.

[345] *Paed.* 1.6:29.2,3; *FC*, 23: 39.

possession of inborn secret *gnosis* — something that the *hylikoi* can never own and that the *psychikoi* may only receive through missionary efforts. Saving *gnosis* enables the soul of the *pneumatikos'* self, which is nothing other than a divine spark, to negotiate passage through concentric spheres of the spiritual realm lying just beyond the material world. Each sphere ruled by a daemon or archon represents a challenge to the soul, threatening it with a return and imprisonment once again in the material world. Only by employing the secret *gnosis* may the soul negotiate its way through each of these spiritual authorities on its way to perfection, blessedness in the divine *pleroma*(lit. 'fullness') and unity with the world-soul.

Hellenistic Gnosticism was a highly speculative, mystical, and elitist system. Catholics quickly realized that Gnostic teachers were charlatans who regarded themselves as the true *pneumatikoi*. They regarded Christian catholics as *psychikoi* who might be converted to a syncretistic amalgam of Christianity and Gnostic myth. Practitioners of all other religions and cults they categorized among the *hylikoi* souls who were irretrievably condemned to the material world. As we have seen, the Gnostic sects believed that they alone possessed the saving *gnosis*, and while they may have theoretically at least allowed for the salvation of Christians, in practice most Gnostic teachers taught that salvation for catholics was at best doubtful.[346]

Clement responds to their assault upon catholic Christianity with a finely nuanced theological argument. Faith, he says, is inherently proleptic in nature; it contains within itself the assurance of perfection, which is synonymous with personal eternal salvation. Faith is not the end; rather it is the certainty of a good and perfect end. Clement writes:

---

[346] For a comprehensive introduction to Gnosticism see Kurt Rudolph, *Gnosis: The Nature and History of Gnosticism,* trans. P. W. Coxon and K. H. Kuhn, ed. R. M. Wilson (San Francisco: Harper Collins, 1983, 1987), esp. 91-92.

138

> We say emphatically that both of these things cannot co-exist at the
> same time: [namely, the] *arrival* at the goal and the *anticipation*
> [*prolepsis*] of that arrival in the mind. Eternity and time are not the
> same thing, nor are the beginning and the completion. But both are
> concerned about the same thing, and there is only one person
> involved in both. *Faith, . . . begotten in time, is the starting point, . . .
> while the completion is the possession of the promise, made enduring for
> all eternity.*[347]

Faith anticipates the promise of salvation that shall appear at the bodily
resurrection of the dead, which is tantamount to the perfection of the saved.
Clement writes:

> Nothing is lacking to faith, for of its nature it is *perfect* [*teleia*] and
> complete. If there is anything lacking to it, it is not wholly *perfect*,
> nor is it truly faith, if defective in any way. . . . In believing, *we
> already anticipate in advance what we will receive as an actuality after
> the resurrection*, that the words may be accomplished: 'Be it done
> unto thee according to thy faith.' In this world, we have the promise
> of what we believe; the enjoyment of that promise will be
> *perfection.*[348]

The proleptic nature of simple faith is an important concept for Clement. Faith is
its own perfection; it constitutes in and of itself evidence of the eschatological
fulfillment of the promise secured by believing. The perfection of faith achieved
on earth is a proleptic anticipation of a blessed future.

Assent

Clement also defines simple faith as 'assent' (Gr. *sungkatathesis*), a move
which marks a decisive departure from Aristotle's epistemology. In the
Aristotelian system assent only had relevance with regard to the practical intellect,
which imparted to it a task that was entirely ethical in nature – judging matters of
right and wrong, good and evil, justice and injustice. Aristotle held faith separate

---

[347] *Paed.* 1.6:28.4,5; *FC*, 23: 28. Italics mine.

[348] *Paed.* 1.6:29.2,3; *FC*, 23: 29. Italics mine. Cit. Matthew 9:29.

from assent, limiting its task to judging only what is true and false, not what is good. So long as knowledge of what is true is held in sharp distinction from knowledge of what is good, faith and assent also must be kept apart, according to Aristotle.

Change in Aristotle's formulation was on the horizon when the Stoic school combined assent and faith in an epistemological synthesis that gave faith the added connotation of judging goodness as well as truth. Since as we observed earlier, to choose is in fact decisively moral act, it is possible for one to believe with less than comprehensive knowledge of faith's object, but this does not in any way lessen the ethical implications of the faith-assenting act. When the object of faith is the self-revealing God of human history, less than perfect knowledge is to be expected; but faith is nonetheless a supreme moral action taken on the part of the one who believes.

The role of assent in Clement's soteriology cannot be underestimated, for it is very much analogous to the biblical term *pistis* or trust. We hear echoes of Hebrews 11:1 as Clement declares:

> The *assent* given willingly . . . is not a hypothetical conjecture; it is an act of *assent* to someone reliable.[349]

The God to whom Christians assent, in whom they trust, is not based on conjecture. Clement explains:

> [W]e have *faith* [*pistis*] in the one in whom we have trusted, for the glory of God and his saving power. We have *believed* [*pepoithotes*] in the one and only God. We know that he will not fail to fulfill his high promises to us, and all that he has created because of those promises, and all that he has given us in his benevolence.[350]

---

[349] *Strom.* 2.6:27.4; *FC*, 85: 176. Italics mine.

[350] *Strom.* 2.6:28.2; *FC*, 85: 177. Italics mine.

140

The power to save and the reliability of the One to whom assent is directed, Clement argues, is the essence of saving faith.

Summary of Simple Faith

By joining *prolepsis* and assent within a conceptual framework of simple faith, Clement creates a profound, theologically accurate analogue to the biblical idea of faith. Consider the following. First, simple faith in the gospel is salvific. It is not necessary to have grasped the full breadth and meaning of Christian teaching in order to be saved. Faith alone is the foundation of salvation and the beginning of the Christian life. Clement writes:

> [T]he Apostle [Paul] exhorts, 'that your faith may not be in the wisdom of human beings' who promise to persuade, 'but in the power of God' which alone and without *demonstration* is able to save.[351]

In one place Clement excoriates those who demand empirical proof before they will believe: "For many demand the demonstration as a pledge of the truth, not satisfied with the simple salvation by faith."[352] In another he writes: "Faith is an internal good, and without searching for God, confesses his existence, and glorifies Him as existent."[353] This is not to suggest that simple faith is based upon a vague concept of God. Rather, "believing [in Christ] . . . is the foundation and the superstructure, by whom are both the beginning and the ends."[354]

Second, Clement believes that it is not sufficient for the believer to remain perpetually in a state of simple faith. "Faith, . . ." he writes, "must not be inert and alone, but accompanied with investigation."[355] What lies beyond simple faith in

---

[351] See *Strom.* 5.1:9.2. Translation mine.

[352] *Strom.* 5.3:18.3. Translation mine. See also *ANF*, 2: 448.

[353] *Strom.* 7.10:55.2; *ANF*, 2: 538.

[354] *Strom.* 7.10:55.5,6; *ANF*, 2: 538.

[355] *Strom.* 5.2:11.1; *ANF*, 2: 446-47.

God and the gospel of Christ? In the vernacular of the evangelical church it is called 'growth in grace.' The Bible uses the term 'perfection'. Because Hellenistic Gnostic teachers were attempting to draw away from Christ and the church the philosophically sophisticated yet theologically naïve catholics in northern Egypt by proclaiming salvation through *gnosis*, we contend here that Clement pilfered their favorite term, emptied it of its superstitious and obscure implications, and filled it with a very apt description of the biblical conception of perfection. Did he do this well? Yes. Was he able to find accurate biblical analogues for every facet of hellenistic *gnosis*? If we are to give an honest appraisal, we would have to answer 'No'. Nevertheless, Clement was able to show the important parallels between philosophy and Scripture as he discusses faith and its relation to Christian gnostic perfection.

Scientific Faith

Simple faith is to *scientific* faith in Clement's system as 'choice' is to 'conviction'. Simple faith produces scientific faith, but it does so indirectly. As we have seen, Clement defines simple faith as *proleptic assent* — a choice, an act of the will. The decision to exercise simple faith sets in motion a series of causes and effects that produce scientific faith. The idea of scientific faith or scientific knowledge derives from the Greek term *episteme,* which Aristotle had defined as experiential knowledge.[356] Scientific faith is faith that has been proven true in the real world. It is therefore *a posteriori* (post-experiential) in nature.

There are two issues that need to be addressed with regard to the nature of scientific faith. The first is what Clement calls *scientific demonstration* or sometimes simply *demonstration.* Scientific demonstration is the ground of

---

[356] *Met.* 1.981a.1. See also Liddell & Scott, *Lexicon,* s.v. ἐπιστήμη. In classical Greek thought, επιστήμη opposes δόξα, 'opinion.'

scientific faith. The second issue is the meaning he ascribes to the important term *gnosis*.

Demonstration

Demonstration (Gr. *apodeixis*) is the bridge from simple faith to scientific faith. Simple faith, as we saw above, is indemonstrable because it is entirely *a priori* in nature. Once simple faith has become an act of the will however, it immediately becomes scientific and therefore *a posteriori* in nature. The experience that follows the act of believing is a demonstration of the efficacy of the very act, which includes inward regeneration and the beginning of true moral transformation. The demonstration, i.e., the experience of the believer, is now itself the basis for continued faith.

Before examining further how Clement relates these ideas to Scripture and the Christian life, we must examine the philosophical foundations of demonstration (*apodeixis*). We find that Clement again has turned to Aristotle, who said that all truth is limited to demonstrability through experience in the real world. Nothing is true that cannot be related to the material realm. Every effect has its cause, every movement its source of motion, every being its source of being. Aristotle recognized of course the danger in such an approach that lay in the logical fallacy of infinite regression. In order to avoid this problem he was forced to admit that there are some causes, sources of motion and origins of being that are grounded in realities that cannot be demonstrated. In fact, all knowledge that can be proven through experience must derive ultimately from realities that are indemonstrable.[357] These indemonstrable realities Aristotle called 'primary' or

---

[357] Aristotle, *An. Post.* 1.2.71b20-24: "If, then, understanding [ἐπιστήμη] is as we posited, it is necessary for *demonstrative* understanding in particular to depend on things which are true and primitive and immediate and more familiar than and prior to and explanatory of the conclusion (for in this way the principles will also be appropriate to what is being proved). For there will be deduction even without these conditions, but there will not be *demonstration*; for it will not produce understanding." Italics mine. See also *An. Pr.* 2.16.64b30f.

'first principles'.[358]   The doctrine of first principles was designed chiefly to address epistemological issues in logic; but Aristotle extended it to include theological inquiry, arguing in his *Metaphysics* that there exists a First Principle of the universe which moves all things but which itself is not moved. This Unmoved Mover, he concluded, must be named God.[359]

It is at this point in Aristotle's thought that Clement points out a nexus between Christianity and philosophy.[360] Clement argues that the God who initially revealed himself to Israel, and then later to the world through the coming of his Son, is the same God who was understood from afar by the philosophers. It follows then that simple faith is a proleptic assent to the content of revelation, which in philosophical language constitutes knowledge of the divine. This same knowledge in biblical language, according to Clement, is knowledge of God.[361]

Now it is possible to return to our discussion of demonstration. When simple faith has been exercised, there is produced a *demonstration* or *experience* of salvation that is the basis of scientific faith.. Of what does this experience consist? It is important to note that Clement always describes salvation in ethical terms — i.e., transformation, moral improvement, regeneration, and holiness. Scientific faith/knowledge is produced when the believer who has exercised simple faith experiences the presence of God and a decisive change and

---

[358] ἀρχή, ἀρχαί. Cf. Aristotle *Top.* 1.1.100a30f.: "Things are true and primitive which are convincing on the strength not of anything else but of themselves; for in regard to the first principles of science it is improper to ask any further for the why and wherefore of them; each of the first principles should command belief in and by itself."

[359] Aristotle *Met.* 1.1.983a6-11; 12.1072a19-1072b13. See also Clark, *Clement's Use of Aristotle*, 18. Unless I am missing something in her analysis, Prof. Clark is mistaken when she asserts that Aristotle had not identified the one *first principle* of the universe as God.

[360] See discussion in *Strom.* 5.12:78.1-82.4; *ANF*, 2: 462-64.

[361] *Strom.* 2.4:14.1; *FC*, 85: 166: "By faith alone is it possible to arrive at the first principle of the universe."

144

improvement in moral character. The *demonstration*, which is the experience of having been saved and morally renewed, produces scientific faith. This faith in turn manifests itself as continuing moral transformation and spiritual growth.

Clement describes the relationship between demonstration and scientific faith as follows: "In the most proper sense . . . *demonstration* is said to be that which inspires *scientific faith* in the souls of learners."[362] Scientific faith can only be produced by demonstration. He writes:

> There is a trustworthy form of knowledge; one might call it a *scientific demonstration* of the *traditions of true philosophy*. . . . [which is] a rational approach to providing, on the basis of *accepted truths*, an account in which we can put our faith in relation to matters in dispute.[363]

The above excerpt is the opening salvo of a focused argument on the saving efficacy of Christian faith. The phrases "traditions of true philosophy" and "accepted truths" are euphemisms for Holy Scripture.

Demonstration vis-à-vis Scripture

For Clement, simple faith is directed toward the self-revealing God, but since the record of divine revelation is contained only in canonical Scripture, faith cannot be separated from Scripture's content and meaning. Clement's view of Scripture in this regard is interesting in that he places it nearly on a par with revelation. It not only records revelation, it somehow becomes the mystery of revelation re-enacted to the one who approaches it in faith. Scripture for Clement is more sacramental than the Western mind conceives it.

It is with this understanding that he says one must exercise simple faith (both proleptic and assenting) in Scripture in order to be saved. Out of that initial

---

[362] *Strom.* 8.3:5.3. Translation mine. Clement admits that there are two kinds of demonstration: one results in *episteme*, the other results in *doxa*. The former is certain because it relies upon things as they really are. The latter is conjectural since it is applies to rhetoric and is therefore subject to errors in judgment. See *Strom.* 2.11:48.1-49.4; *FC*, 85: 191-92.

[363] *Strom.* 2.11:48.1; *FC*, 85: 191. Italics mine.

act of faith will come a demonstration, viz., salvation experienced as moral transformation, which serves to verify the authenticity and efficacy of the act itself. Clement writes:

> Is there any doubt that the *demonstration* we provide alone leads to truth, when it is provided out of divine Scripture, sacred writings, and the wisdom the Apostle describes as 'God-taught'?[364]

Scripture is the voice of the living God to the one who believes. Clement writes: "If a person has faith in the divine Scriptures and a firm judgment, then he receives as an irrefutable demonstration the *voice of God* who has granted him those Scriptures."[365] Canonical Scripture is the sole means by which the believer hears God. It is nothing less than God speaking.[366]

Although at first glance this argument appears fatally convoluted, its internal logic holds up, provided one accepts faith as a valid means of knowing.[367] Scripture is the indemonstrable first principle of faith that communicates God's will to humankind. Its reliability is impossible to demonstrate *a priori* the initial exercise of faith, but in exercising faith the believer experiences salvation, which consists of inward transformation and moral improvement. The experience of salvation is nothing other than proof that the content of what one has believed is

---

[364] *Strom.* 2.11.48.3; *FC*, 85: 191. Italics mine.

[365] *Strom.* 2.2.9.6; *FC*, 85: 163. Italics mine. The phrase "voice of God" here ("voice of the Lord" in other places) is undoubtedly a metaphor describing the authoritative teaching of God communicated either through Jesus Christ or the apostles (*Strom.* 6.6:47.3; *ANF*, 2: 491), or the Holy Spirit through an apostle (*Paed.* 1.6:49.2; *FC*, 23: 46), or in the Old Testament as a direct impression given to the prophet who speaks on God's behalf (*Strom.* 6.3:34.3; *ANF*, 2: 488).

[366] Simonetti concurs: "Clement . . . regards Scripture as the actual voice of the divine Logos . . . ." (*Biblical Interpretation in the Early Church*, 35)

[367] In the late second century, given Clement's audience and its sophistication concerning Aristotelian and Stoic metaphysics and epistemology, faith was a valid epistemological premise, as we have shown. The modern severing of faith and reason was still sixteen centuries away.

the voice of the living God. All subsequent faith the believer exercises is by definition scientific because it occurs *a posteriori* the *a priori* act of faith and the confirming experience of salvation.

Clement's discussion of Christian faith in philosophical language aligns conceptually fairly well with a New Testament understanding of saving faith, the new birth, and regeneration. The emphasis in the New Testament is upon initial faith as the instrumental means to the reception of saving grace, which brings about inward transformation and the beginning of moral improvement. Clement agrees of course, but what is especially interesting is that he defines transformation not primarily as performance, but rather as love. He writes:

> I assert that faith, whether it is founded on *love* or, . . . on fear, comes from God, and is not torn apart by any other worldly affection or dissolved by any present fear. For *love* creates *faithfulness* [i.e., obedience] by its attraction to faith, while *faith by the benefits it introduces is the foundation of love.*[368]

The practice of faith is the only real demonstration of salvation's efficacy, and for Clement there is no more concrete evidence of having believed than to practice what Scripture teaches. Practice is not an issue however, so long as faith produces love. Here, it is clear that he is specifically of love for God. Although the above excerpt almost sounds proverbial, it is nonetheless a truism that love which has God as its object generally results in faithfulness.

So far in our discussion of scientific faith, we have defined and established the role of demonstration in Clement's system, and we have examined the role he assigns to it in relationship to Scripture and salvation. To briefly summarize: the fact that the believer experiences moral regeneration marked by increasing obedience to God is the demonstration that his initial act of simple faith is both true and good; and this demonstration transmutes the believer's simple faith into scientific faith, for the latter will always be confirmed by the ongoing experience

---

[368] *Strom.* 2.6:30.2-3; *FC*, 85: 178-79. Italics mine.

of the one who believes. Now, we are ready to examine how scientific faith, which consists of *a posteriori* knowledge of God in the form salvation and regeneration, forms the bridge to higher level of Christian existence.

Gnosis

The second issue we must examine with regard to scientific faith is *gnosis*(Gr. 'knowledge'), a term laden with superstition and speculative mystery for Clement's gnostic opponents; but for Clement who emptied it of these connotations and filled it with new meaning, *gnosis* became a powerful metaphor for Christian perfection and the biblical concept of sanctification . Stated in the barest terms, this portion of Clement's *ordo salutis* can be outlined in this fashion: simple faith produces scientific faith through demonstration; and scientific faith produces *gnosis*. Of course, we have left out many details, but since it is perfection, the doctrine of holiness and sanctification, that concern us most here, we may be allowed to move forward.

As we have seen, Clement describes the experience or demonstration of salvation in practical moral terms.[369] Clement's Christian Gnostic is the epitome of the ethically and spiritually mature believer. The progression from faith (simple and scientific) to *gnosis* is seen in the following excerpt from *Stromateis* 7:

> Therefore, since we reasonably have embraced by *faith* the indemonstrable first principle and have received out of an abundance the *demonstration* by the first principle itself concerning the first principle, we are being instructed in the *knowledge* [*epignosis*] of the truth.[370]

---

[369] For example, see *Strom.* 2.11:48.4; *FC,* 85: 191: "The process of learning consists in obedience to the commandments, or in other words, faith in God. And faith is a power of God, having the strength of truth."

[370] *Strom.* 7.16:95.6. Translation and italics mine. In this citation 'knowledge' translates a cognate of *gnosis* — *epignosis,* which in this context carries essentially the same meaning.

Having believed in the gospel, Clement argues, the believer must assume the role of learner, being instructed in "the knowledge of the truth."[371] The *gnosis* that proceeds from scientific faith serves as the foundation upon which Clement builds his portrait of Christian character. We will investigate this issue further after saying a few more things about his views on faith.

The Dynamics of Faith

Clement views faith as always active, never static. linking the term *pistis* (Gr. 'faith, trust') with such words as (*dunamis*) ('power') and *ergon* ('work'). Through faith the believer receives the power to do God's will and to live a holy life. For example, in *Protrepticus* 11 Clement recalls St. Paul's exhortation in Ephesians 6:14-17 to put on the "armour of peace" which consists of "the breastplate of righteousness, . . . the shield of faith, . . . [and] the helmet of salvation."[372] He then exclaims:

> O this holy and blessed *power,* by which God has fellowship with men! Better far, then, is it to become at once the imitator and the servant of the best of all beings; for only by *holy service* will any one be able to *imitate* God, and to serve and worship Him only by *imitating* him.[373]

The power to which Clement refers is the presence of God, which accompanies the one who has put on the armor that repels the attack of the Evil One.

Dynamic living faith enables the believer to be righteous; it confers the ability to judge things accurately, "to receive the words of God," to be free of sin and to do good.[374] Clement explicitly states that faith necessarily precedes and

---

[371] Ibid.

[372] *Protr.* 11:116.3; *ANF,* 2: 204.

[373] *Protr.* 11:117,1,2; *ANF,* 2: 204. Italics mine.

[374] *Strom.* 1.1:8.2-4; *FC,* 85: 28.

empowers good works. He cites the Apostle Paul who wrote in the Epistle to the Romans that Abraham, the archetype of the faithful man, was justified not by works but by faith.[375] The difference between faith and good works is akin to the difference between:

> [s]omeone talking about the truth and truth giving an account of herself. . . . The first is a likeness, the second the actuality. The first survives by learning and discipline, the second by power and faith. Instruction in religion is a gift [*dorean*], faith is a *grace* [*charis*].[376]

In describing the stages of Christian living leading from initial salvation to gnostic holiness, Clement argues that by its very nature faith advances a process of growth. "Faith," he writes, "is a force leading to salvation, a power [*dunamis*] leading to eternal life."[377]

As a careful exegete of St. Paul's thought, Clement discusses the Apostle's classic statement on the relationship between faith and moral character: "For in Christ Jesus neither circumcision nor uncircumcision counts for anything; the only thing that counts is *faith working through love*."[378] Clement is sensitive to the issue of individual responsibility within the larger community of faith. As head of a catechetical school, he writes of the importance of handing down to succeeding generations the teaching tradition of the church: "If two people preach the word, one in writing, one orally, receive them both: *they have made the faith operative* [*energon*] *by their love.*[379] The term *energos* may be taken in several ways including

---

[375] *Strom.* 1.7:38.1-5; *FC*, 85: 49, 50.

[376] *Strom.* 1.7:38.4-5; *FC*, 85: 50. Italics mine.

[377] *Strom.* 2.12:53.5; *FC*, 85: 195.

[378] Gal. 5:6. Italics mine.

[379] *Strom.* 1.1:4.1; *FC*, 85: 25.

"active, effective, actual (as opposed to potential)."[380] The point is that faith is put into action by love.

Clement is fond of the concept of 'faith working through love.' In *Protrepticos*, his evangelistic appeal to the Greeks, Clement enumerates the benefits of faith, which include deliverance from sin, enlightenment, and the ability to live virtuously. He writes:

> He who obeys Him has the advantage in all things, follows God, obeys the Father, knows Him through wandering, loves God, loves his neighbour, fulfills the commandment, seeks the prize, claims the promise.[381]

The one whose faith is followed by loving obedience is the one who fulfills the command to be perfect as the Father is perfect (Matthew 5:48). In *Paedagogus* Clement defines faith in terms of love, writing:

> Faith is not the possession of the wise according to the world, but of the wise according to God; it is taught without written letters; its book, which is both commonplace and divine, has been called *love*, which is a spiritual treatise.[382]

Love is faith's true expression. The origin of all love is God. Love's act is a "spiritual treatise" for Clement.[383]

In numerous other places Clement refers to the relationship between faith and love. He believes that faith expressed through loving acts is the essence of the Christian life.

---

[380] Liddell & Scott, *Lexicon*, s.v. ἐνεργός.

[381] *Protr.* 11:115.5; *ANF*, 2: 204.

[382] *Paed.* 3.11:78.2,3. Translation and italics mine. Cf. *ANF*, 2: 290.

[383] Ibid. The term σύνταγμα ('treatise') connotes 'work, book, body of doctrine' as in a collection of works. Clement's point is that that love sums up the collected works of faith.

Summary

Clement's doctrine of dynamic, twofold faith suggests that salvation, properly conceived, is progressive. Simple faith, a proleptic assent to the content of revelation, is the entranceway to redemption. Lacking such faith, Clement would argue, salvation is impossible. The initial *a priori* act of believing produces the clearest evidence of salvation — inward transformation and moral improvement. It is at this point in Clement's *ordo* that simple faith becomes scientific; all further acts of believing are based upon the fact that a real change in character has already begun as a result of having exercised simple faith. Scientific faith, which proceeds from the initial act, becomes the bridge to an ever-increasing *gnosis* or knowledge of God. Having discussed Clement's twofold notion of faith and its finer distinctions, we now are at liberty to examine the second clear movement in Clement's soteriology.

2. Gnosis

Because Clement's definition of salvation falls on the side of process and transformation rather than a forensic or mere positional change in relationship with God, it is especially important for him to articulate carefully the ongoing nature and growth Christians normally experience as they walk in faith. Protestantism, in its attempt to throw off late medieval scholastic doctrines of infused faith and prerequisite human merit unto salvation, found it expedient to differentiate between the biblical doctrines of justification and sanctification, even though both ideas arguably refer to being made actually righteous or holy.[384] As the Reformers saw it, justification consists primarily of the legal reconciliation of the believer to God, sanctification the believer's actual moral improvement and

---

[384] δικαιόω — "to justify; to set right; pronounce or treat as righteous'; δικαιοσύνη — 'justification, righteousness.' ἁγιάζω — 'to make holy, sacred'; ἅγιος — 'sacred, holy, pure.' See Liddell & Scott, s.v.

increase in personal righteousness. Many centuries earlier long before the rise of medieval theology, writers in the Christian East, especially, did not make such a sharp distinction. For Clement and the fathers who followed, salvation is a fabric in which the mainly identifiable pieces consist of initiating faith symbolized by baptism, and progressive sanctification symbolized by faithful reception of the Eucharist.

The care that Clement takes in developing the philosophical analogies necessary to express the biblical concept of faith is also employed in his treatment of the biblical doctrine of Christian maturity and holiness. Given the polemical context in which he lived and the concerns of the faith community, *gnosis* was the philosophical metaphor Clement employed; and it is no surprise that, like his doctrine of faith, he treats imparts to *gnosis* several different shades of meaning..[385]

From a broader perspective though, faith and *gnosis* function as complementary ideas. As we have already seen, simple faith is an *a priori* volitional response to the content of revelation and the sole entrance into salvation. Simple faith does not stand alone; it also produces an demonstration of inward transformation and gradual moral improvement. The content of salvation's experience produces the scientific faith that accompanies the gradual maturation of character and increase in righteousness that Clement calls *gnosis*. He writes:

> [The] [c]hoice [to believe], if it is inexorable, offers a strong impulse in the direction of *knowledge* [*gnosis*]. The practice of faith immediately becomes *knowledge* [*episteme*] based on strong foundations."[386]

The choice accompanying simple faith is a decisive advance toward *gnosis*.

---

[385] Among contemporary scholars none has handled this better than S. Lilla in *Clement of Alexandria*, 142-89.

[386] *Strom.* 2.2:9.3; *FC*, 85: 163. Italics mine. For all practical purposes, scientific knowledge [ἐπιστήμη] is not really all that different from *gnosis*, which is the mark of the perfect Christian. The demonstration of faith that results from the former also produces the latter.

Like salvation itself, faith is the sole condition of Christian *gnosis*; there can be no maturing of one's character without it. In *Stromateis* 7 Clement illustrates the relationship between the two:

> *Faith* therefore is an interior good; and, without undertaking a philosophical search for God, *faith* confesses that he exists and it magnifies him as existing. Beginning from this *faith* and having been strengthened by the grace of God itself, it is possible to receive the *knowledge* [*gnosis*] of him [within the limits of our ability].[387]

A couple of lines later he continues: "[B]elieving is the foundation stone of knowledge [*gnosis*]."[388] Such excerpts typify Clement's view of Christian spirituality. The believer begins with simple faith, the initial stage of salvation, then advances via grace and experience toward Christian *gnosis*, which is maturity of character and personal virtue. The process of gnostic ascent results in the believer becoming like God both inwardly and outwardly.

Gnosis is the leading metaphor for sanctification (itself a metaphor for a divinely formed reality) in Clement's theological system. His Christian Gnostic is not a follower of one of the speculative Gnostic sects led by Valentinus, Basilides, or Isidore. Rather, he is a Christian actively pursuing an intimacy with God that results in increasing personal righteousness. The inward effects of Christian *gnosis* remain mysterious and sublime, since they can be known only as personal and subjective experience. The outward effects however are measurable, as they consist of an increasing excellence in moral character.

With these introductory thoughts in mind, we can now examine more closely Clement's views on Christian *gnosis* and the ideas he brings into association with it.

---

[387] *Strom.* 7.10:55.2-4. Translation mine.

[388] *Strom.* 7.10:55.5. Translation mine.

Associated Metaphors

Perfection

In *Stromateis*, Clement speaks to believers who aspire to full *gnosis* and a godly life. Though he maintains the relationship between gnostic perfection and moral behavior, Clement does not view perfection as a state of being, but instead he sees it more in biblical and dynamic terms. Absolute perfection was a reality only for Christ Jesus. Clement declares: "I do not know of anyone from among humankind perfect in all things, who is still a human being, except the one who clothed himself with humanity for our sake."[389]

Nonetheless, Clement does not gloss over the connection between obedience to the divine commands and the gospel of Christ, a relationship that he correctly calls 'perfection.' He writes:

> And yet according to the law alone, anyone may be perfect who professes abstinence from evil; and, this is both the way to the gospel and to doing good. But *gnostic perfection* resting on law is an acquisition of the gospel in order that one may become *perfect* according to the law.[390]

While biblical perfection is not perfect performance, at the same time Clement recognizes that the trajectory of the gospel is faithfulness and obedience to the moral demands of the law. These two, obedience and biblical perfection, can only be reconciled when the issue of heart motivation is considered, which we shall soon see.

In the meantime, let us observe that for Clement and other writers in the Christian East, it is possible for the believer to keep the commandments. Moral purity is the mark of one who knows Christ and is worthy of the kingdom of God. For example, in *Protrepticos* Clement writes:

---

[389] *Strom.* 4.21:180.2. Translation mine. Cf. also *ANF*, 2: 433.

[390] *Strom.* 4.21:180.2 f. Translation mine.

> Cleanse the temple, and abandon pleasures and amusements like a
> passing flower to the wind and fire; but sensibly cultivate the fruit of
> self-control and present yourself as first fruits to God in order that
> you may be not only the work but also the grace of God. Both are
> fitting for the one who is acquainted with Christ, even to have
> shown oneself worthy of the kingdom and to be counted worthy of
> the kingdom.[391]

Clement's argument is that there exists a certain synergism between the individual
and God. Salvation is a cooperative endeavor that involves an impartation of
grace on God's part, and on the believer's part responsive obedience. The
believer is saved *sola gratia per fidem*, solely by grace through faith. In the same
fashion grace and faith bring about the believer's perfection.

At this juncture, we should speak more specifically concerning Clement's
use of perfection language. The English word 'perfection' normally translates the
Greek term *teleios*.[392] *Teleios* and its cognates convey notions of maturity,
fulfillment, and completion.[393] When used in the New Testament in association
with the life of a believer, *teleios* describes maturity of a believer in Christ, not
flawlessness or sinlessness. A good example is found is found in the synoptic
account of Jesus' encounter with the young scribe.

> [A]nd one of them, a lawyer, asked him a question to test him.
> "Teacher, which commandment in the law is the greatest?" He said
> to him, "'You shall *love* the Lord your God with all your heart, and
> with all your soul, and with all your mind.' This is the greatest and
> first commandment. And a second is like it: 'You shall *love* your
> neighbor as yourself.' On these two commandments hang all the
> law and the prophets."[394]

---

[391] *Protr.* 11:117. 5. Translation mine. Cf. Butterworth, *LCL,* 92: 251.

[392] τέλειος

[393] See such New Testament loci as Mt. 5:48; 19:21; Phil. 3:15; Col. 4:12; Heb. 5:9.

[394] Mt. 22:35-40. Emphasis added. Cf. Mk. 28-34; Lk. 10:2-28

156

Arguably, every soteriological use of the term *teleios* or one of its cognates in the New Testament can be referred to one, the other, or both aspects of Jesus' response to the scribe — love for God, love for neighbor, or love for both God and neighbor.

The clearest illustration of the relationship between perfection and love is found in the Epistle of 1 John.

> Whoever says, "I have come to know him," but does not obey his commandments, is a liar, and in such a person the truth does not exist; but whoever obeys his word, truly in this person the love of God has reached *perfection*.[395]

John highlights the connection between obedience to the commands and love. Obedience is offered as evidence that the believer's love has been perfected. That love is central to the biblical idea of perfection is also seen in the way the apostle contrasts love with fear. He writes:

> Love has been *perfected* among us in this: that we may have boldness on the day of judgment, because as he is, so are we in this world. There is no fear in love, but *perfect love* casts out fear; for fear has to do with punishment, and whoever fears has not reached *perfection in love*.[396]

The believer's love for God stands in stark contrast to fear of judgment. Fear has to do with unrequited sinful deeds, but obedience that emerges out of heartfelt, uncoerced love for God displaces fear. Those who fear do so because their love is either misdirected or weak.

Clement's concept of perfection is decisvely shaped by the New Testament. Perfection is demonstrated by the object and quality of the believer's love. Assuming that the objects of love are God and the things of God, how completely or perfectly the believer loves forms the ground and content of *gnosis*.

---

[395] 1 John 2:4-5. Italics mine.

[396] 1 John 4:17-18. Italics mine.

Similarly, perfection is never considered apart from ethic. "The perfect man," he writes, "ought therefore to *practice* love, and thence to haste to the divine *friendship,* fulfilling the commandments from love."[397] The one who is "perfect" [*teleiosis*], he says elsewhere, is the one who "fulfills the command: 'Thou shalt love thy neighbor as thyself'."[398]

Though perfection is defined by the propr objects of a believer's love, viz., God and neighbor, as a theological construct Christian *gnosis* is not restricted to cognitive reasoning and discourse. It is a metaphor for a supernatural reality that encounters the soul with teaching that "goes beyond catechetical instruction."[399] Christian *gnosis* involves a maturing of faith through perspective and practice. He writes:

> For *knowledge* [*gnosis*], to speak generally, a *perfection* [*teleiosis*] of man as man, is consummated by acquaintance with divine things, in character, life and word, accordant and conformable to itself and to the divine Word. For by it faith is *perfected* [*teleioo*], inasmuch as it is solely by it that the believer becomes perfect [*teleios*].[400]

Simple faith of the believer, even though demonstrated through moral improvement, is at the same time immature. Perfection is the *telos* of salvation attained through faith.[401]

---

[397] *Strom.* 4.13.98.2 f.; *ANF,* 2: 426. Italics mine.

[398] *Paed.* 2.12.120.4,5; *FC,* 23: 192.

[399] *Strom.* 6.18:165.1; *ANF,* 2: 519.

[400] *Strom.* 7.10:55.1; *ANF,* 2: 538. Italics mine.

[401] *Strom.* 7. 2:11.2,3. See version by F.J.A. Hort and Joseph B. Mayor, *Clement of Alexandria: Miscellanies Book VII, The Greek Text with Introduction, Translation, Notes, Dissertations and Indices* (London: Macmillan, 1902), 19: "For he [Christ] leads different men by a different *progress,* whether Greek or barbarian [Jew], to the *perfection which is through faith.* But if any of the Greeks dispenses with the preliminary guidance of the Greek philosophy and hastens straight to the true teaching, he, even though he be unlearned, at once distances all competition, having chosen the short-cut, viz. that of *salvation through faith.*" See also *ANF,* 2: 526: "For by a different *process* of advancement, both Greek and Barbarian [i.e., Jew}, He

Habit

Another term that Clement employs in relation to Christian *gnosis* is 'habit'. Among the classical philosophers, 'habit' (Gr. *hexis*) connoted a state or condition achieved through repetition and practice.[402] For Clement, habit is vital to the believer's progress from simple faith to higher *gnosis*. Recalling an earlier citation:

> The practice of faith immediately becomes knowledge [*episteme*] based on strong foundations. The disciples of the philosophers define knowledge [*episteme*] as a state [*hexis*] which reason cannot shake.[403]

According to Clement, scientific knowledge (*episteme* — again, nearly synonymous with Christian gnostic holiness) is a 'habit' achieved through practice. However, the question must be asked, "The practice of what?"

Clement believes that holiness is achieved through the habituation of loving acts. As we noted in our discussion of scientific faith, he follows carefully St. Paul's argument that faith must be made active through love. He writes:

> If, for example, anyone should propose to the [Christian] Gnostic by way of supposition whether he should wish to choose the knowledge [*gnosis*] of God or eternal salvation, and if it should be possible to separate these things (which are ultimately identical), he would choose without any doubt whatsoever the knowledge [*gnosis*] of God, for he would have determined on account of the very same choice that the character of *faith through love leading to knowledge* [*gnosis*] is the higher principle.[404]

[Christ] leads to the *perfection which is by faith.* And if any one of the Greeks, passing over the preliminary training of the Hellenic philosophy, proceeds directly to the true teaching, he distances others, though an unlettered man, by choosing the compendious *process of salvation by faith to perfection.*" Italics mine throughout.

[402] Liddell & Scott, *Lexicon*, s.v. ἕξις.

[403] *Strom.* 2.2:9.3-4; *FC*, 85: 163.

[404] *Strom.* 4.22:136.5-137.1. Translation mine. Cf. *ANF*, 2: 434.

Clement declares that by comparison Christian *gnosis* (*gnosis*), which is achieved by faith made active through, is greater than eternal salvation – if it were possible to divide the two, which it is not. In biblical language, this is to say that holiness of heart and life on earth is of more value than certainty of heaven and eternal life. The logic of this assertion follows as he writes:

> This therefore is the first act of well doing by the perfect one [Christian Gnostic]. Whenever it [i.e., the performance of a morally good action] is done not on account of any benefits which might accrue to him, but because he has determined that it is honorable to do the good, the *energy* borne by each act freely produces good, not just in some things nor in others; but it is established in the *habit* [*hexis*] of doing good . . . in order that he should achieve a manner of living according to the image and likeness of the Lord.[405]

As with later writers of the Christian East, Clement places greater stress upon the restorative and regenerative effects of salvation than the legal or positional reconciliation of the believer with God. Whenever the Christian Gnostic does the good for the sake of the good and not for personal gain, the energy of the good act produces good and forms the basis of a habit. It is by the habituation of virtuous actions grounded in loving faith that the believer gradually achieves likeness to God, which is the essence of Christian holiness.

Much of the above excerpt, though controlled by biblical content, has its linguistic and conceptual origins in classical philosophy. We want to note especially the following terms:

1. *arete* — moral excellence, virtue
2. *ergon* — work, action
3. *hexis* — habit, state.[406]

---

[405] *Strom.* 4.22:137.1-2.

[406] Liddell & Scott, *Lexicon*, s.v. ἀρετή, ἕξις, ἐργόν.

Plato had described *hexis* as a state of being. Aristotle agreed, but departed from Plato on one essential point. Whereas Plato viewed *hexis* as a state of stasis and inactivity, Aristotle viewed it as a state of movement and action. Thus, when it came to discussion of the virtues, for Plato, *arete* is a static ideal to be pursued through contemplation. For Aristotle, on the other hand, *arete* is achieved through a habit (*hexis*) of good actions. S. Broadie compares and contrasts the two philosophers with regard to happiness. She observes that both Plato and Aristotle define *arete* as a "state [*hexis*] of the soul." Broadie adds, however, that "Aristotle constantly reminds his readers that happiness is activity: it is virtue in action, not virtue unused."[407] For Aristotle, the *arete* of the individual is determined not by whether he has achieved virtue as a state of being, but rather whether his life is characterized by the habit (*hexis*) of doing pure and virtuous works (*erga*).

Broadie's observations are supported by selections from the *Nicomachean Ethics*. In this foundational treatise Aristotle argues that the good produced by human beings is an activity of the soul that conforms to the *arete* of a perfect (*teleiosis*) life.[408] "Moral excellence," he writes, "comes about as a result of habit."[409] In other words, virtue is achieved through virtuous actions. Aristotle, in contrast with Plato, emphasizes that actions are the sole means of achieving as well as maintaining virtue. Conversely, the absence of virtuous activity contradicts the notion that one is virtuous. Aristotle observes:

> For the state [*hexis*] may exist without producing any good result, as in a man who is asleep or in some other way quite inactive, but the activity cannot; for one who has the activity will of necessity be acting, and acting well.[410]

---

[407] Sarah Broadie, *Ethics with Aristotle*, 57. Portions of this discussion are indebted to Broadie's analysis.

[408] Aristotle, *Nicomachean Ethics*, 1098a.16-18. Abbreviated *EN.* from now on.

[409] Aristotle, *EN.* 1103a.14-19.

[410] Aristotle, *EN.* 1098b.31-1099a.3.

There is no virtuous state for which virtuous activity is not essential. He concludes: "[T]he excellence (*arete*) of a man also will be the state [*hexis*] which makes a man good and which makes him do his own work [*ergon*] well."[411]

Clement finds that Aristotle's definition of *arete* as a *hexis* of virtuous action is an apt description of the Christian's practice of faith. This is seen in *Stromateis* 6.12 where he involves himself in a broad discussion of the perfectibility of human nature. Key to his argument is the doctrine of Adam's original righteousness and the logical problem presented by the fall. If Adam was created an imperfect creature, then the perfection of God who created him is harmed. On the other hand if Adam was created perfect, then it remains an impenetrable mystery why he disobeyed the divine command. Clement concludes that God did not fashion Adam to be a virtuous to a fault, but rather created him with the capability of receiving virtue.[412] The ability to become virtuous is crucial, because it places real value on human actions. The crux of Clement's ethical theory is existence determines essence; what an individual does determines what he is or will become. Clement is convinced that the habituation of virtue ought to characterize the believer's life because salvation depends upon it.[413]

Gnosis, the preeminent goal of the believer's faith, is unattainable without good works. "The works which share in knowledge [*gnosis*]," he writes, "are good and honorable acts."[414] Yet Clement's Christian Gnostic is not a boring moralist. The habit of gnostic holiness creates a quality of life that is marked by

---

[411] Aristotle, *EN*. 1106a.21-23.

[412] *Strom.* 6.12:96.2; *ANF*, 2: 502.

[413] *Quis Dives* 18.1; *LCL*, 92: 307: "Salvation does not depend upon outward things, whether they are many or few, small or great, splendid or lowly, glorious or mean, but upon the soul's virtue, upon faith, hope, love, brotherliness, knowledge, gentleness, humility and truth, of which salvation is the prize."

[414] *Strom.* 6.12:99.5. Translation mine.

162

joy now, and promises greater joy in the eschatological future. One does not live merely in order to become righteous; rather, one lives righteously in order to truly live.[415] The habituation of virtue through good works is the practical substance of Christian Gnosticism.

No habit is more important to develop than that of loving God. The believer who loves God initiates the process of becoming like God.

> If the divine majesty [i.e., godliness] is the habit [*hexis*] which preserves that which is appropriate to God, then *loving God* is the *habit* [*hexis*] which preserves that which is fitting for the godly person alone. This person is the one who knows what is fitting both according to knowledge [*episteme*] and life. It is necessary to live in this manner [i.e., *loving God*] for the one who will be and already is being made like God.[416]

Clement argues that there is symmetry between loving God and becoming like God. The believer becomes like God by forming the habit of loving God. He assumes in kind, not degree the moral qualities of God.

The validity of *hexis* as a metaphor for sanctification and Clement's model Christian Gnostic depends upon a true synergism between the working of God in the human soul and the believer's response. The believer must cooperate with God through loving obedience to God. As to specific means, Clement identifies prayer as one way in which the Christian Gnostic concurs with God in becoming good. He writes:

> Therefore, the Gnostic makes his prayer and request for the things that are truly good, the things concerning the soul; and, he prays while at the same time cooperating [*sunergeo*] to arrive at the *habit*

---

[415] See *Strom.* 6.12:100.2; *ANF,* 2:503: "Therefore, regarding life in this world as necessary for the increase of science [*episteme*] and the acquisition of knowledge [*gnosis*], he [the Christian Gnostic] will value highest, not living, but living well."

[416] *Strom.* 7.1:3.6. Translation mine.

[*hexis*] of goodness, that he may no longer have the good things
appended to certain lessons, but that he may *be* good.[417]

More than just private expressions of faith are required however; public
demonstrations in the form of loving one's neighbor are habits the Christian
Gnostic develops. Clement cites as one such habit almsgiving, which is a good
that even society at large associates with righteousness.[418] The Christian Gnostic
does such things not for promise of reward nor from fear of punishment, but
because he loves and desires to please God.[419] God and the believer work together
to bring about, maintain, and increase the believer's holiness. The concept of
hexis is critical to this relationship.

Likeness

Clement uses the term *exhomoiosis* ('assimilation, likeness') and certain
cognates to describe the goal of the Christian life — the *imitatio Christi.*[420] He
cites or alludes to Genesis 1:26 ("Let us make humankind in our *image*, according
to our *likeness* . . . .") no less than sixteen times, establishing the ideal toward
which believers are to aspire and the ethical standard by which they will be
judged. Clement was not the first to employ 'image' and 'likeness' in elaborating
Christian salvation. These terms were used earlier by Clement of Rome, Justin
Martyr, and in the Epistle of Barnabas. Each employed 'image' and 'likeness' as
near synonyms referring to the regenerative effects of salvation.

---

[417] *Strom.* 7.7:38.4. Translation mine. See also *Strom.* 7.7:43.1; *ANF,* 2: 535: "When, then, the man who chooses what is right, and is at the same time of thankful heart, makes his request in prayer, he contributes [*sunergeo*] to the obtaining of it, gladly taking hold in prayer of the thing desired."

[418] See *Strom.* 7.12:69.7; *ANF,* 2: 543.

[419] *Strom.* 7.12:70.2, 3; *ANF,* 2: 543.

[420] Liddell& Scott, s.v. ἐξομοιωσις Cognates include ὁμοιωσις and ὁμοιωτής.

164

Clement of Alexandria, however, was one of the earliest theologians to articulate a theological distinction between 'image' and 'likeness'. He suggests that the terms distinguish between humanity's intellectual and moral capacities respectively. An inkling of this usage appears in *Protrepticos,* where in defending the Christian doctrine of God against worship of the Pantheon, he writes:

> For "the *image* of God" is His Word (and the divine Word, the light who is the archetype of light, is a genuine son of Mind [i.e., the Father]; and an *image* of the Word is the true man, that is, the mind in man, who on this account is said to have been created "in the *image*" of God and "in His *likeness*," because through his understanding heart he is made like the divine Word or Reason, and so is reasonable.[421]

The perfect 'image' is Christ the Son, who is the Logos of the Father. Alluding to Genesis 1:26, he points out how Adam was created in the image of Christ. Here, 'image' refers to intellectual cognition. The hint that 'likeness' is to be distinguished from 'image' arises in the assertion that "through his understanding heart" the individual is made like Christ.[422] Clement is not merely repeating what he has already stated — i.e., that human beings bear the intellectual 'image' of Christ. Rather, he speaking of the moral likeness of Christ with which Adam was created.

In *Stromateis* Clement makes the distinction between 'image' and 'likeness' much clearer, when he writes:

> Wherefore also man is said "to have been made in [God's] *image* and *likeness.*" For the *image* of God is the divine and royal Word, the impassible man; and the *image* of the *image* is the human mind [*nous*]. And if you wish to apprehend the *likeness* by another name, you will find it named in Moses, a *divine correspondence.* For he

---

[421] *Protr.* 10:98.4; *LCL,* 92: 215. Italics mine.

[422] Ibid. The phrase τῇ κατὰ καρδίαν φρονήσει is better translated "through practical wisdom grounded in heartfelt desire."

says, "Walk after the Lord your God, and keep His commandments."[423]

The 'image' of God in which human beings have been created refers to the intellectual aspect of the soul. The human ability to know both the world and its Creator is borne by the 'image' of God. The 'likeness', however, has to do with the moral capacity of the soul to receive proportionately the moral character of God. Likeness to God is practically expressed in moral character and behavior. Clement writes:

> It is the Christian Gnostic who is "in the *image* and *likeness*," who imitates God so far as possible, leaving out none of the things which lead to the possible *likeness*, displaying continence, patience, righteous living, sovereignty over the passions, sharing his possessions so far as he can, doing good in word and deed.[424]

Human beings possess the 'image' of God by nature, but they attain 'likeness' only by actively cooperating with God in the sanctifying process. In biblical terms, cooperation necessarily entails obedience to the divine commands.

The theological distinction between 'image' and 'likeness' has some important advantages. First, it provides a framework for explaining how human nature can be morally transformed by grace, taking on the moral qualities of God, while in no way allowing that human beings can become substantially divine. Today, Old Testament scholarship largely regards the terms 'image' and 'likeness' as synonymous, a simple example of Hebrew parallelism. Though Clement was with doubt unaware of this issue, he was convinced that the

---

[423] *Strom.* 5.14:94.4-6; *ANF*, 2: 466. Italics mine. The reference is Deut. 13:4 (acc. to Stählin), but it is not a direct quote. Note that Clement says "likeness" is synonymous with a "divine correspondence." The *ANF* translation "divine correspondence" of the Greek idiom ἀκολουθιαν θείαν is too arcane. A better rendering of ἀκολουθιαν θείαν is "conformity to the divine", which better reflects Clement's view (and the Eastern view in general) of sanctification.

[424] *Strom.* 2.19:97.1; *FC*, 85: 221-22. Italics mine.

distinction was theologically amenable to the teaching of Scripture as well as true to Christian experience. By referring 'image' to the intellect and 'likeness' to moral virtue, salvation is depicted in therapeutic and progressive terms. Clement writes:

> Our nature is subject to passion, and needs continence, and uses it to practice reducing to needs in the effort to acquire a disposition not far from the nature of the divine. The good man . . . is on the border between a mortal and immortal nature.[425]

The goal of salvation is never in question: human beings are to put off sin and take on the moral character of God. Clement believes that through Christ humankind inherits the ability to become actually righteous. He declares as much when he states that the Christian Gnostic is "divine and already holy, God-bearing and God-borne."[426]

A second advantage of this distinction is that it assists Clement in combating Hellenistic Gnostic falsehoods. Some of the Gnostic sects had misapplied Scripture in order to support of their claim to possess an elite *gnosis*. Valentinus and Basilides taught that the bulk of humanity was formed by an inferior creator according to an inferior image, while they, having been created by an invisible Aeon, possessed an immortal likeness.[427] Clement ridicules such far-fetched ideas, arguing that true likeness to God "[is found] . . . in the habit of doing good, neither for glory, nor, . . . for reputation, nor from reward either from men or God."[428]

Clement relates the concept of likeness to other metaphors for Christian *gnosis*. In at least one place, he makes it synonymous with the notion of

---

[425] *Strom.* 2.18:81.1; *FC*, 85: 212.

[426] *Strom.* 7.13:82.2; *ANF* 2: 547. The adjective θεῖος suggests qualitative divinity — i.e., divine-like or holy — not substantial deity. See Liddell & Scott, *Lexicon*, s.v. "θεῖος"

[427] See *Strom.* 4.13:90.3,4; *ANF*, 2: 425.

[428] *Strom.* 4.22:137.1; *ANF*, 2: 434.

perfection, writing: "Therefore, *likeness* to the divine Savior emerges for the [Christian] Gnostic, as far as is possible for human nature, since he becomes *perfect* 'as the Father,' he says 'who is in heaven.'"[429] In another place he distinguishes the perfection of a common believer from that of the Christian Gnostic, arguing that only the latter achieves true likeness to God. The perfection of common believers, he writes, consists of "abstinence from evil things."[430] This perfection is the normal expectation of all Christians. There is however a more perfect state (*hexis*) in which the believer progresses beyond passively resisting evil to a steadfast habit (*hexis*) of pursuing good. He writes: "And in whomsoever the increased force of righteousness advances to the doing of good, in his case perfection abides in the fixed habit of well-doing after the *likeness* of God."[431] Thus, it is clear that Clement admits degrees or stages of Christian Gnostic perfection and likeness to God.

What is important to see is that none of the ideas Clement associates with Christian Gnostic holiness is static or Platonic in derivation. Righteousness is forceful and energetic; it consists of actively avoiding evil and enthusiastically doing good. To be righteous is to manifest the quality of God's own character. Dynamic righteousness locked in the pursuit of good is what it means to be a Christian Gnostic for Clement.

Even though Clement may occasionally give the impression of arguing inappropriately that the Christian Gnostic anticipates becoming actually divine, a close reading in context proves that this is not the case. Anthropology is always governed by theology in Clement's system; humanity is never imagined as becoming divine in any substantive sense. This is especially evident in those few

---

[429] *Strom.* 6.12:104.2. Translation mine. An obvious allusion to Matthew 5:48.

[430] *Strom.* 6.7:60.2; *ANF,* 2: 494.

[431] *Strom.* 6.7.60.3; *ANF,* 2: 494. Italics mine.

168

places where Clement's consistently latent, but nonetheless strong element of aspiration comes into view. No better example exists than a petition found in the concluding prayer of *Paedagogos*:

> Give to us, who follow Thy command, to fulfill the *likeness of the image*, and to see, according to our strength, the God who is both a good God and a Judge who is not harsh. Do Thou Thyself bestow all things on us who dwell in Thy peace, who have been placed in Thy city, who sail the sea of sin unruffled, that we may be made tranquil and supported by the Holy Spirit . . . unto the perfect day, to sing eternal thanksgiving to the one only Father and Son, Son and Father, Educator and Teacher with the Holy Spirit.[432]

As we see, Clement maintains an appropriate tension between the proximate 'likeness' of life now and the perfect 'likeness' of life in the world to come. As far as existence on earth is concerned, the Christian Gnostic achieves through love-empowered faith all the likeness to the divine character that is possible for human beings to attain. The fulfillment of faith's destiny, which Clement intimates will consist of the full reunification of 'likeness' and 'image', is reserved for the eschatological future.

Apatheia

Clement's use of the term *apatheia* as a metaphor for Christian holiness is unique in the history of Christian thought, which may explain why it has caused so much difficulty for scholars. *Apatheia* translates as 'passionlessness, impassability' and, at first glance, appears entirely alien and irreconcilable to the Christian faith.[433]

Clement's use of the term has been criticized on at least two counts. First, he often describes both the Savior and the Christian Gnostic as dwelling in a state of *apatheia*. The idea of a passionless Savior, much less a passionless Christian is

---

[432] *Paed.* 3.13:101.1, 2; *FC*, 23: 275. Italics mine.

[433] See Liddell & Scott, s.v. ἀπάθεια. Tollington comments, *Clement of Alexandria*, 2: 86: "[Clement's] . . . fondness for the conception [*apatheia*] has laid him open to much criticism."

not only foreign, but also unappealing to the Western church, which is affected by Scholastic realism, reformation biblicism and pietistic reactionism. *Apatheia* as a metaphor for holiness is not just far removed from the theological formulations of the West; it appears internally inconsistent with other things Clement teaches, such as love-energized faith and the habituation of virtuous actions.

Second, *apatheia* is entirely incongruous with the thought and language of the New Testament. Neither Jesus of Nazareth nor his followers are ever portrayed as passionless. In fact, one of the most appealing portraits the New Testament presents is the Christ who is truly human, the one who bears the full range of emotions and sufferings common to all men and women. The issue is further complicated by the fact that the Apostle Paul never uses *apatheia* in his discussion of Christian faith and practice. Yet Clement, who so often quotes Paul, does not hesitate to employ it as a descriptive term for Christian Gnostic character and perfect love for God.

In order to reconcile these incongruities and hopefully redeem Clement from being further misunderstood, we shall begin by briefly examining the background of the term.

Background

The Stoic philosophers employed *apatheia* as an analogy of moral virtue. It gained important proponents among the later philosophical schools, including Middle Platonism and Neoplatonism. One noted proponent of *apatheia* was the Jewish philosopher Philo of Alexandria.[434] Within the classical divisions of philosophy, *apatheia* was considered under the category of *pathos* or 'passion'. Among post-Aristolians *pathos* emanates from an utterly irrational unruly

---

[434] Lilla, *Clement of Alexandria*, 84-106 has the best recent discussion of the probable sources of Clement's doctrine of *apatheia.*

appendage to the intellectual soul, the source of all moral ill.[435] Sensations introduced to the soul through the sensing faculties of the body produce passions, which create a volatile breach between body and soul. These internal ills work outwardly as evil acts and immoral behavior. The philosophers taught that one of the goals in gaining wisdom is the removal and abrogation of all passion. In therapeutic terms this was described as the healing of the passions. It was thought that through the healing of one's passions a true reconciliation of soul to body and a restoration of harmony between mind and flesh were possible. *Apatheia* was regarded as the means to this end. By renouncing passion, the individual would find freedom from the unsettling turmoil that perturbs the soul. If all passions, both the repugnant as well as the pleasurable, are diminished and eventually expunged, then true moral virtue can be achieved.

Although the logic of the philosophical argument is easily grasped, is *apatheia* an adequate description of Christian holiness? How can Clement legitimately apply the term both to the Christian believer and Christ? These are questions that we shall take up next.

Apatheia and the Christian Gnostic

If we recall that Clement's audience consisted of educated Greeks, his use of *apatheia* begins to make sense. He uses the term as a description of Christian Gnostic holiness in order to reconcile biblical and Greek notions of the virtuous person. *Apatheia* serves as a practical link, in Clement's estimation, between the Hellenistic thought-world and the Judeo-Christian Bible. Let us consider a few examples of what Clement has to say concerning *pathos* and *apatheia*.

---

[435] Not all post-Aristotelian philosophers agreed, not even all Stoics. Lilla notes that one of Stoicism's founders Chrysippus (ca 281-205 BC) viewed passion as the wrong use of the rational soul, in effect making passion an intrinsic part of the soul. Later philosophers, however, especially the Stoic Posidonius (ca. 135-51 BC) as well as the Middle Platonic and Neoplatonic schools, held that the passions are inevitably irrational and not indigenous to the soul. See Lilla, *Clement of Alexandria*, 86-87. Cf. also Coppleston's discussion of Chrysippus in *A History of Philosophy*, 1: 390-93.

First, Clement concedes the philosophical argument that the passions are irrational and are to be viewed as an illness of the soul.[436] In *Stromateis* he states:

> A *passion* is an overwhelming impulse, one that exceeds the bounds of reason, an impulse which is carried away and does not listen to reason. So the *passions* are an unnatural movement of the soul in disobedience to reason.[437]

The passions constitute a "rebellion," he writes, "[i]f anyone were to pursue each of the passions individually, he would find them all irrational desires."[438] Passions such as anger and lust "war against the reason."[439]

Clement's purpose is not to debate abstract philosophical issues; it is to articulate a philosophy of Christian living. In his evangelistic appeal to Gentiles, he points out the deleterious effects that *pathos* has inflicted upon morality in general. He accuses idol-worshipping Greeks of effacing the *imago Dei* by indulging their passions to the neglect of the right worship of God:

> You who have done violence to man, and erased by dishonour the divine image in which he was created, you are utter unbelievers in order that you may give way to your *passions.* You believe in the idols because you crave after their incontinence; you disbelieve in God because you cannot bear self-control.[440]

Clement calls on those who have grown up knowing only the mythic cults of Hellenistic culture to abandon their traditions. He argues that no tradition is

---

[436] Lilla notes that Clement owes his understanding of *pathos* to Posidonius and that this reliance also links the Alexandrian to Middle Platonism, Neoplatonism, and Philo. These schools and Philo all considered the passions to be irrational products of the soul rather than the consequences of the wrong use of reason. See S. Lilla, *Clement of Alexandria*, 87.

[437] *Strom.* 2.13:59.6; *FC*, 85: 199. Italics mine.

[438] Ibid.

[439] *Strom.* 4.6:40.2; *ANF*, 2: 416.

[440] *Protr.* 4:61.4; *LCL*, 92:139,41. Italics mine.

172

worth preserving that commends its followers to the domination of the passions and gives them over to wickedness.[441] Clement draws a sharp contrast between the doubtful worth of superstitious fetishes and the certainty of faith in Christ:

> Men who believe in wizards receive amulets and charms which are supposed to bring safety. Do you not rather desire to put on the heavenly amulet, the Word who truly saves, and, by trusting to God's enchantment, to be freed from *passions*, which are *diseases of the soul*, and to be torn away from sin? *For sin is eternal death.*[442]

To be governed by the pagan religious passions is tantamount to spiritual death.

Second, Clement embraces the philosophers' notion that the healing of *pathos* is therapy for the soul. However, the healing that Clement describes is not absence of ordinary emotion, but the absence of sin. *Apatheia,* as Clement employs it here, refers not to the Stoic ideal of passionlessness, but rather to the Christian ideal of sanctification and personal holiness.[443] It is important to note that Clement begins to develop this therapeutic model as early as *Paedagogus* where he invokes the healing of the passions as one of the chief benefits of salvation. At the very outset of the treatise Christ is identified as the healer of passion. Christ the Word, heal declares, "heals and counsels . . .[offering] a cure for. . . [the] passions."[444] Christ trains believers to form virtuous habits, to fulfill their obligations, to always choose the good and reject the bad. The result is the "healing of the passions."[445]

Third, although Clement is able to argue *apatheia* at the abstract philosophical level, he has it as the second part of his goal to employ it as a

---

[441] *Protr.* 10:89.2,3; *LCL,* 92: 197.

[442] *Protr.* 11:115.2-3; *LCL,* 92: 245,47. Italics mine.

[443] Lilla, Clement of Alexandria, 96, 98.

[444] *Paed.* 1.1:1.4; *FC,* 23: 4.

[445] *Paed.* 1.1:3.1; *FC,* 23: 4.

metaphor for Christian practice. Of particular note is his use of the teaching/learning model. *Paedagogus,* whose educational methodology lends itself well to practical discussions of self-control, provides Clement with an opportunity to instruct his readers in appropriate practices for the Christian. For instance, Clement rails against profligate behavior engendered by drunken revelry. Such "irrational passions," he declares, too often decline into gross promiscuity.[446] He condemns self-indulgent practices such as the use of erotic perfumes and nonessential ointments, arguing that "a luxury without any useful purpose . . . is a drug to excite the passions."[447]

Moral accountability is paramount in Clement's mind. In one place he points out the difference between a pagan Gnostic and a believer in pursuit of Christian *gnosis* by contrasting Basilides, a leading Gnostic teacher, and the Apostle Paul. Basilides taught that the passions are malevolent spirits that attach themselves to the human soul. These parasitic spirits mimic lower animals such as wolves, apes, lions and goats, which according to the Basilideans, cause human beings to take on irrational, animalistic traits. Clement rejects as preposterous such ideas. In St. Paul's well known discourse in Ephesians 6, where the apostle addresses the problem of "spiritual forces of evil, " Clement says that Paul is not referring to malevolent supernatural forces; rather he is illustrating the fallen human nature against which all believers must struggle.[448] Clement will have nothing to do with hellenistic Gnosticism and its superstitions; he lays the cause of moral evil where it belongs, upon fallen humanity. To attribute moral evil to

---

[446] *Paed.* 2.4:40.1. τὰ ἀλόγιστα πάθη. Translation mine.

[447] *Paed.* 2.8:68.4; *FC,* 23: 152.

[448] *Strom.* 2.20:110.1; *FC,* 85: 230. Cit. Ephesians 6:12.

supernatural spirits is nothing other than a faulty attempt to relieve individuals of their moral culpability.[449]

The educative, practical theme emerges again when Clement says that the very "nature of the soul" is to progress with regard to virtue.[450] Even though all human beings are "naturally constituted for the acquisition of virtue," not all acquire it; for, "one man applies less, one more, to learning and training."[451]

Fourth, although the discussion of *pathos* and *apatheia* may have their origins in Greek philosophy, Clement's use of these terms is biblically oriented. In the overwhelming majority of instances where Clement writes of *pathos* he associates the term with sin and the corruption of fallen humanity. In the instances where he discusses *apatheia* the meaning involves personal transformation and holy living. His description of the Christian Gnostic's likeness to God has drawn liberally on Pauline thought. Clement writes:

> For both the gospel and the apostle urge that they are "to take themselves prisoner" [2 Cor. 10:5] and slay themselves; they are to violently put to death "the old man who is corrupted through lusts" and raise "the new man" [Eph. 4:22, 24] from the death of his old twistedness, by putting away from themselves the *passions* and becoming sinless.[452]

We see in the above excerpt a good example of how Clement fills the philosophical *apatheia* with biblical meaning. He emphasizes the Apostle's admonitions concerning death to sin and the old life, and rising to a new life. The

---

[449] *Strom.* 2.20:112.1-118.7; *FC*, 85: 231-35. Against such folly, Clement cites the *Epistle of Barnabas* (which he regarded as authentic) to show that human moral evil cannot be attributed to the influence of evil spirits. Evil spirits do not inhabit the souls of unbelieving persons. If this were the case, then salvation would consist of the banishment of evil spirits. Rather, from a biblical perspective salvation consists of forgiveness and cleansing of an individual's sins.

[450] *Strom.* 6.12:96.2, 3; *ANF*, 2: 502.

[451] *Strom.* 6.12:96.3; *ANF*, 2: 502.

[452] *Strom.* 7.3:14.2. Translation and italics mine. The term rendered "sinless" (ἀναμαρτήτος) Clement likely derived from John 8:7.

passions are inextricably linked to the distorted nature of the believer's old way of living. "Putting away . . . the passions" — i.e., *apatheia* — becomes the philosophical equivalent of St. Paul's ideal 'new man.'

Fifth, Clement links *apatheia* to other terms that convey a biblical and distinctly Eastern way of speaking of sanctification. For instance, *apatheia* is linked to *exhomoiosis* ('likeness, assimilation'). The concept of 'likeness' to Christ as the expression of holy living now comes into view. In one place Clement exclaims: "Indeed, perseverance leads to *divine likeness* by harvesting *apatheia* through endurance."[453] In *Stromateis* 6 he writes that the Christian Gnostic "is constrained to become like the Teacher [Christ] in *apatheia*."[454] Clement takes up the connection between *exhomoiosis* and *apatheia* again in *Stromateis* 7. This time he links both terms with the concept of perfection, writing:

> And above all, concerning the *apatheia* of the Gnostic of whom we speak, the *perfection* of the believer advancing through *love* arrives "at perfect [*teleios*] manhood [and] the measure of the stature"[Eph. 4:13]; *being made like God* [*exhomoiosis*], he has become truly the equal of angels; and many other testimonies from Scripture can be additionally furnished. . . . [455]

Apatheia is synonymous with the mature character of the believer in Christ described by the Apostle Paul.

We find Clement exploring the relationship between *apatheia, exhomoiosis,* and *teleiosis* on the basis of a careful reading of St. Paul. In an interpretation of 1 Corinthians 6:9-11 Clement declares that the Christian Gnostic throws off "the passions of the soul in order to become assimilated [*exhomoiosis*] . . . to the

---

[453] *Strom.* 2.20:103.1. Translation and italics mine. Cf. *FC,* 85: 169.

[454] *Strom.* 6.9:71.5-72.2. Translation mine. Cf. *ANF,* 2: 496-97.

[455] *Strom.* 7.14:84.2. Translation and italics mine. Cf. *ANF,* 2: 547.

176

goodness of God's providence."[456] He [the Christian Gnostic] has been "sanctified
. . . falling into none of the passions in any way."[457] The one who is holy, Clement
writes, is also:

> passionless [*apathes*], gnostic [*gnostikos*], perfect [*teleios*], formed by
> the teaching of the Lord; in order that in deed, in word, and in spirit
> itself, being brought close to the Lord, he may receive the mansion
> that is due to him. . . .[458]

Even more telling is Clement's analysis of Matthew 5:48, which he
presents in the context of discussing the mystery of salvation, the church, and the
believer's holiness.[459] Clement issues an admonition that is clearly reminiscent of
St. Paul's covenantal language. He writes: "For he who behaves like a heathen in
the Church, whether in act or word or even merely in thought, commits
fornication against the Church and *against his own body*."[460] He says that it is
impossible for such a person to sin against God and yet hope in Christ. This
person contrasts with the one who is "*joined to the Lord* after a different kind of
union, in spirit. . . ."[461] Clement says of the one who is united to the Lord Jesus:

> He is wholly a son, a holy man, passionless [*apathes*], gnostic
> [*gnostikos*], perfect [*teleios*], being formed by the Lord's teaching, in
> order that he may be brought close to Him in deed and word and in
> his very spirit, and may receive that *mansion* which is due to one
> who has thus approved his manhood.[462]

---

[456] *Strom.* 7.14:86.5; *ANF*, 2: 548.

[457] *Strom.* 7.14:86.7; *ANF*, 2: 548.

[458] *Strom.* 7.14:88.3; *ANF*, 2: 549.

[459] See *Strom.* 7.14:88.1-7; *ANF*, 2: 549; Hort and Mayor, *Miscellanies Book VII*, 154-57.

[460] *Strom.* 7.14:88.1; Hort and Mayor, *Miscellanies Book VII*, 155. Hort and Mayor find a number
of references to the New Testament in sec. 88, which they indicate with italics. See their nn.
1-5.

[461] *Strom.* 7.14:88.2; Hort and Mayor, *Miscellanies Book VII*, 155.

[462] *Strom.* 7.14:88.3; Hort and Mayor, *Miscellanies Book VII*, 155.

The nature of the Christian Gnostic's intimate relationship with God is a mystery, but his moral character is not. Clement writes:

> For it is not necessary to disclose the mystery, but only to recall it to memory for those who are partakers of *gnosis*, who shall also understand that it was said by the Lord "Be perfect as your Father is perfect," perfectly forgiving and forgetting sins, and spending one's life in the *hexis* of *apatheia.*[463]

It is easy to see how one might read the prepositional phrase "*hexis* of *apatheia*" as a philosophical abstraction that is foreign to Christian perfection.[464] Yet if we remember that *hexis* for Clement always connotes activity, and that *apatheia* connotes freedom from willful sin, what emerges is a proto-Eastern Orthodox doctrine of sanctification. Christian Gnostic perfection consists of fulfilling Christ's command to be perfect as God is perfect, forgiving the grievances of others and living in *apatheia,* viz., free from sin — all of which relates to loving one's neighbor.

Even as he recalls the gospel injunction to be perfect, Clement declares the impossibility of becoming perfect as God is perfect: "[I]t is impracticable and impossible that any one should be as perfect as God is; . . ."[465] This is an important point theologically. Human beings do not aspire to divine perfection. Why? Clement explains: "For we do not agree in the impious opinion of the Stoics as to the identity of human and divine virtue."[466] Clement rejects the inherent pantheism of Stoic thought. Instead, he preserves the essence of Matthew 5:48 and the gospel command to be perfect. Clement continues: "[B]ut our Father wishes that we should arrive at an unimpeachable perfection by living

---

[463] *Strom.* 7.14:88.4,5. Translation mine.

[464] ἐν τῇ ἕξει τῆς ἀπαθείας — lit. "in the state/habit of passionlessness." "

[465] *Strom.* 7.14:88.6; Hort and Mayor, *Miscellanies Book VII,* 155.

[466] *Strom.* 7.14:88.5,6: Hort and Mayor, *Miscellanies Book VII,* 155.

178

according to the obedience of the Gospel."[467] Obedience to the gospel is the meaning of the command. To be perfect in the Christian sense is to live in proximate likeness to the perfect character of God. The gospel command to be perfect, he concludes, entails that "we shall know the will of God and shall conduct ourselves piously and at the same time generously according to the *moral value of the command.*"[468] The command to be perfect is a moral command. Christian Gnostic perfection is to live according to the moral demands of the gospel.

We have seen that for the Christian Gnostic, *apatheia*, like *teleios*, is a moral term; it is a euphemism for freedom from willful sin. By defining *apatheia* in therapeutic and practical terms, we discover that Clement's vision of the believer's holiness is biblical and Eastern orthodox in origin, not Stoic and Platonic.

Apatheia and Christ

Modern scholars have been puzzled by Clement's description of Christ as 'passionless'. Christ was "impassable" from the beginning, he declares.[469] As we stated earlier, such an assertion seems completely alien to the Jesus portrayed in the Gospels. However, a closer examination of the evidence reveals that Clement is making a dogmatic, not an exegetical claim. Theologically, *apatheia* functions to define the Son's unique combination of natures. On the one hand, the Son's *apatheia* speaks of his full deity and preincarnate existence. Christ the Son, who

---

[467] *Strom.* 7.14:88.6; Hort and Mayor, *Miscellanies Book VII*, 157.

[468] *Strom.* 7.14:88.7. Translation mine. See also Hort and Mayor, *Miscellanies Book VII*, 157: "[W]e shall both recognise the will of God and shall live a life of piety and aspiration, in a manner worthy of the commandment."

[469] *Strom.* 7.2:7.3; *ANF*, 2: 524. See Hort and Mayor, *Miscellanies Book VII*, 13: "[Christ is] eternally free from passion. . . ."

bears all the attributes of God, reveals God "the Father of the universe."[470] Christ is the "Word of the Father" to whom has been entrusted the "administration" (*oikonomia*) of all things.[471] On the other hand, *apatheia* supports the Son's perfect humanity and role as the only worthy Redeemer of humankind. The Son persuades all who are willing to listen. He is impassible — free from sinful passions of envy and impure pleasures.[472] The Son can never hate humanity; on the contrary, he exceedingly loves "human flesh," so much so that he took into himself all that is human in order to save humanity.[473] Clement says that the Son "assumed flesh, which by nature is susceptible of suffering, [and he] trained it [*paideuo*] to the condition [*hexis*] of impassability" — an obvious reference to the incarnation.[474]

Still, Clement's assertion of the impassability of the Son is susceptible to criticism. Has the Alexandrian gone too far in his use of philosophical language to articulate revealed truth? Did he actually think of Christ as 'passionless' in the way Stoics defined the term? Few would find the image of a Stoic Christ very appealing, to say nothing of that fact that one could scarcely make a biblical case for such a notion. Yet there is something about the Gospel portrait of the Son that

---

[470] *Strom.* 7.1:2.3; *ANF*, 2: 523. Clement writes here that among the teachings of "ancient philosophy and the most revered prophecies" Christ is "the timeless and unoriginated First Principle and Beginning of existences. . . ." This is a classic description of the idea of God. Translation in part mine.

[471] *Strom.* 7.2:5.6; *ANF*, 2: 524.

[472] *Strom.* 7.2:6.3; 7.1, 5; *ANF*, 2: 524, 25. The term "pleasure" translates ἡδονή from which English derives *hedonism* and etc. In Greek literature this term is typically associated with sensuality and lust. See Liddell & Scott, *Lexicon*, s.v. "ἡδονη".

[473] *Strom.* 7.2:8.1; *ANF*, 2: 525.

[474] *Strom.* 7.2:7.5; *ANF*, 2: 525. Clement is certainly representative of the Eastern Church's fondness for describing the Christian life as *paideia* — "instruction, training, education" — for eternal life in the presence of God. See Walter H. Wagner, "The Paideia Motif in the Theology of Clement of Alexandria" (Ph.D. diss., Drew University, 1968).

180

bespeaks of One who, though by no means without emotion, nonetheless encounters suffering and withstands the violence of the Cross without yielding confidence in his eventual vindication by his Father's mighty hand.

The idea of an eternal Son who took into his Being real humanity without relinquishing his Deity is at the heart of the Eastern Church's faith. All of the controversies that arose in the early church arguably revolved around the God-man mystery. On the one hand Christ is divine; he in some sense transcends the world of human sin and suffering. On the other he is human and has voluntarily entered into that same world. Even though he suffers the *pathos* of the Cross, because He is who He is and for the sake of the world's redemption, he is *apathetic* with regard to sin. And indeed, it is the notion of the incarnate Son who is passionless with regard to sin that governs Clement's discussion.[475]

If our reading of the evidence is correct, then for Christ the Son to be eternally passionless is analogous to the claim that he was without sin. The abundant evidence cited earlier in which Clement exhorts the Christian Gnostic to become like the Son seems to support to support this hypothesis. The Christian Gnostic, Clement asserts, "is compelled to become like his Teacher in impassability."[476] He is a "lover of God" (*theophilos*) who is developing the habit of "godliness" (*theoprepeia*) and in so doing is "being assimilated [*exhomoiosis*] to God."[477]

Clement's use of *apatheia* as a metaphor for Christ's sinlessness is conceptually no different than the teaching of Scripture and the later creeds. If this is the case,

---

[475] In many ways, Clement anticipates controversies occurring much later, including those that led to the Council of Chalcedon (451 A.D.) and the Council of Nicaea II (787 A.D.). See Leo Donald Davis, *The First Seven Ecumenical Councils (325-787): Their History and Theology* (Collegeville, MN: Liturgical Press, 1983.

[476] *Strom.* 6.9:72.1-2; *ANF*, 2: 496.

[477] *Strom.* 7.1:3.6-4.1; *ANF*, 2: 524.

then Clement must be considered one of the formative sources and fathers of classical orthodoxy.

Summary of Apatheia

Clement applies the concept of *apatheia* both to the believer and to the Son. The Son's *apatheia* is eternal; it is manifested in the incarnation. The believer's *apatheia* is acquired through salvation, which is marked by cleansing from sin and increasing likeness to the Son. When Clement says that the Son is passionless, he is not saying that he lacks love, concern, feeling for his creatures, or any other quality that is appropriate to one who is incarnate deity. Rather, he is saying that the Son is without sin. *Apatheia* is the absence of sin because it is the absence of *pathos*, which as we saw earlier, carried a negative moral connotation in Greek literature.

Whether Clement is talking about the essential *apatheia* of Christ, who bears all the attributes of God, or the acquired *apatheia* of the Gnostic Christian who has assumed the likeness of Christ, the term refers to moral character. While Clement has indeed borrowed philosophical terminology and at times appears to be inconsistent in his use of it, he has redefined its content in order to convey a biblical point of view.

Participation

The doctrine of participation is less prominent in Clement's thought than some of the others we have examined. The term participation translates the Greek nouns *methexis* and *metousia*; 'to participate, partake' conveys the action of the Greek verb *metecho*.[478] Plato employed participation as a metaphor to describe the relationship between the eternal forms (universals, ideals) and temporal sensible

---

[478] See Liddell & Scott, *Lexicon*, s.v. μέθεξις, μετουσία, μετέχω.

182

things (particulars, objects in the concrete world).[479] Forms are the basis of all material reality. Only as concrete objects participate in a 'form' do they exist. The forms have a separate eternal existence apart from the material world, an existence discernible only to the intellectual soul.[480]

Plato's doctrine of participation is primarily concerned with ontology, but it encompasses religious and ethical dimensions as well. Participation establishes, among other things, the proper relationship between God and the human soul.[481] In Plato's ethics, participation describes the relationship between 'being' and 'becoming'. For example, justice is an eternal ideal, perfect in every respect. Human beings, on the other hand, may become just by acting in a just manner. By 'participating' in justice they in some sense become just.[482]

Though Clement employs the 'participation' sparingly, it is clear that his interest in the concept lies in the moral and religious spheres, not ontological. In one place he writes: "Some things . . . are good in themselves, and others by participation in what is good."[483] In another he cites Plato to establish that an individual becomes virtuous "in . . . [the] proportion he will be a partaker [*methexis*] of it [virtue]."[484]

Clement also discovers a relationship between participation and *apatheia*. In a commentary on the fourth commandment, he states that by actively obeying

---

[479] For further background see Charles P. Bigger, *Participation: A Platonic Inquiry* (Baton Rouge, LA: Louisiana State University Press, 1968); Kenneth M. Sayre, *Plato's Late Ontology: A Riddle Resolved* (Princeton, NJ: Princeton University Press, 1983); Diogenes Allen, *Philosophy for Understanding Theology* (Atlanta, GA: John Knox Press, 1985), 15-37; F. Coppleston, *History of Philosophy*, 1: 163-206.

[480] Allen, *Philosophy*, 20-21.

[481] Bigger, *Participation*, x.

[482] See Sayre, *Plato's Late Ontology*, 20, 27.

[483] *Strom.* 4.6:39.3; *ANF*, 2: 416.

[484] *Strom.* 5.14:136.4; *ANF*, 2: 474.

God throughout life one appropriates wisdom and achieves *apatheia*. Through obedience one participates (*methexis*) in divine wisdom, which in turn instructs the individual in both divine and human things.[485] Clement appropriates Plato's notion of participation and applies it to the Christian Gnostic's *apatheia*. He writes:

> Whenever the one who *participates* via *gnosis* in a holy character spends time in *contemplation* of God and is conversing [with God] in purity, he enters more intimately into the habit of a *passionless* [*apathes*] identity, ...[486]

The Christian Gnostic becomes holy in two ways — by becoming passionlessness with regard to sin and by participating in the character of God.

There is also an eschatological aspect to Clement's view of participation. In one place he argues that by participating in the things of God the Christian Gnostic realizes in part the future blessings of salvation. He writes:

> [The Christian Gnostic] . . . rejoices in the good things present and he also rejoices in the things promised, as if they were already present. Indeed, this joy has not left him as though the things promised were still absent, for through these promises he has known in advance what sort of things they are. Therefore by this knowledge [*gnosis*] he has been persuaded that each of these future promises he has already acquired.[487]

The realization of future salvific blessings in the present is accomplished through gnostic wisdom. Clement continues:

> For abundance and poverty are measured according to what one has. Therefore, if . . . [the Christian Gnostic] has acquired wisdom and

---

[485] *Strom.* 6.16:138.3,4; *ANF*, 2: 512.

[486] *Strom.* 4.6:40.1. Translation mine.

[487] *Strom.* 7.7:47.4-5. Translation mine.

wisdom is divine, then the one who *participates* [*metecho*] in that which lacks nothing should himself lack nothing.[488]

By participating in the wisdom of God — especially, the moral nature of God — the Christian Gnostic is engaged in an ongoing process of moral and spiritual improvement. Clement concludes:

> Thus all things are potentially good things for our [Christian] Gnostic, but not yet actual, since he would otherwise be immutable throughout the remaining inspired moral process and administration [of divine grace].[489]

As with his use of other philosophical concepts, we see that Clement views 'participation' in biblical terms with the emphasis falling upon the process of the becoming holy.

Contemplation

Clement employs the doctrine of contemplation in combination with other metaphors to describe the virtue and holiness of the Christian Gnostic. The Greek term *theoria* and its cognates — *thea, theorema, theoremon, theoretikos,* etc. — are found frequently in Greek literature. Conceptually *theoria* connotes actions involving the gathering of empirical data such as viewing, investigation, consideration; but it also may involve philosophical speculation and contemplation.[490] Clement uses the term frequently in both ways depending on context.[491] It is the philosophical and theological usages of *theoria* that concern us here.

---

[488] *Strom.* 7.7:47.5. Translation mine.

[489] *Strom.* 7.7:47.7. Translation mine. I have left out a small portion of the text (47.6) because it is a digression.

[490] See Liddell & Scott, *Lexicon,* s.v. θεωρεῖον, θεωρία, *et al.*

[491] For example, see *Strom.* 2.2.5.1; *FC,* 85: 160: "study (θεωρίαν) of the natural world." In many other places, however, he adheres to a more abstract and reflective connotation of the term.

Background

For background we turn once again to Plato, who treated contemplation (*theoria*) under the rubric of his ontology of Forms, making it the *telos* of human spiritual existence. Plato's idea of the Good is based upon the disparity between the eternal world of Forms and the changeable world of material objects.[492] He argued that the highest human undertaking is the Good, the acquisition of which constitutes happiness; but since the Good is to be found only in the Forms, happiness requires retreat from the material world and participation in ideals such as goodness, justice, continence, and wisdom.[493] Since these eternal Forms, though not material themselves, are the sources of all their particular appearances in the material world, it can be said that temporal particulars reveal eternal reality of the Forms. Happiness, which as we noted is participation in the Good, is achieved through contemplating the particular appearances of the eternal realities, viz., the Forms. Contemplation therefore is truly the experience of the particulars of the temporal world leads the mind through contemplation to participation in the unchangeable world of the Forms. The goal of human existence is to achieve true happiness, and the means to that end is contemplation.

Plato saw that the idea of contemplation is particularly well suited for the discussion of aesthetics and religion because it stands in contradistinction to discourse.[494] Discourse is fundamentally an active intellectual movement to examine, investigate, discover, assess, and draw conclusions. Contemplation, on

---

[492] For summaries of Plato's moral theory see the following: Eduard Zeller, *Plato and The Older Academy*, trans. S. F. Alleyne and A. Goodwin (New York: Russell & Russell, Inc., 1962), 436-44; R. C. Lodge, *Plato's Theory of Ethics* (New York: Harcourt, Brace and Co., 1928), 126-27. On Plato's theory of forms see Coppleston, *History of Philosophy,* 1: 163-206. On the relation of Plato's theory of Forms to Christian theology in general see Diogenes Allen, *Philosophy,* 15-37.

[493] Lodge, Plato's Theory of Ethics, 127.

[494] J. A. Stewart, *Plato's Doctrine of Ideas* (New York: Russell & Russell, Inc., 1964), 132-34.

the other hand, has to do with passive experiences such as memory, gaze and love. Contemplation is best defined as focusing upon a thing for the sake of the thing itself. The individual experiences the uniquely single real presence of the object being contemplated.

The concept of contemplation has some important implications for Christian thought. Philosophical contemplation has to do with what a person desires or loves. [495] At its core, the Christian faith similarly has to do with desire and love — love for God, love for neighbor, desire to please and obey God, desire to serve God.

Clement's Use of Contemplation

Contemplation has been closely linked to the mystical theological tradition.[496] Although Clement arguably displays mystical tendencies, as an ante-Nicene apologist he cannot properly be classified as a mystical theologian.[497] Clement's doctrine of contemplation has to do with intellectual love, but it is also very much tied to practice.

In Clement's thought there is a strong connection between 'contemplation' (*theoria*) and Christian *gnosis* in that the former is one feature of the Christian Gnostic's character. He writes:

---

[495] E. Zeller, *Plato and The Older Academy*, 441.

[496] See *Catholic Encyclopedia*, s.v. "Contemplation" and "Contemplative Life" for a brief history of the contemplative Christian tradition.

[497] Some disagree. Coppleston wants to class Clement among the mystics. See *History of Philosophy*, 2: 26-27. So also does J. Quasten in *Patrology*, 2: 20. Charles Bigg provides a more accurate assessment in *The Christian Platonists of Alexandria: Eight Lectures Preached Before the University of Oxford in the Year 1866* (Oxford: Clarendon Press, 1886), 98. Bigg writes: "Though the father of all the mystics [Clement] . . . is no mystic himself. He did not enter the 'enchanted garden' which he opened for others. . . . The instrument to which he looks for growth in knowledge is not trance, but . . . disciplined reason." I agree. Clement's principal argument that faith's validity is established via faithful practices and actual moral improvement places the him more in the category of a practical and pastoral theologian than a mystic.

> Our philosopher [i.e., practitioner of Christianity] holds firmly to these three things: first *contemplation* [*theoria*]; second, fulfilling the commandments; third, the formation of people of virtue. When these come together they make the Gnostic Christian. If any one of them is missing, the state of Gnostic knowledge is crippled.[498]

While it sounds foreign to Protestant ears, Clement believes that contemplative holiness is implicitly taught in Scripture. In the following excerpt, he interprets a familiar Old Testament expression:

> Scripture often takes up the words "I am the Lord your God." It is entreating us to turn around, teaching us to follow the God who has given us the commandments. It is gently reminding us to search for God, and as far as possible to make an effort to know him. This is the highest form of *study* [*theoria*], the supreme revelation, real knowledge [*episteme*], not to be overthrown by reason. This has to be the only knowledge [*gnosis*] known to wisdom, and it is never separated from the practice of righteousness.[499]

Exegetical considerations aside, there is no mystical contemplation in view here; rather, we see that Clement links contemplation to practical righteousness. To truly know God is to obey God. For Clement, the Christian Gnostic contemplates God first and foremost through obedience.

The Christian Gnostic is called to become like Christ. Contemplation is an alignment of the Gnostic's will and practice with the will of God. Commenting on the words of Jesus in Matthew 10:24-25, he writes:

> "No disciple is above his master; it is enough if he is like his master." Not in essential being; [for,] it is impossible for that which is secondary to be equal to that which is naturally primary in respect of essential being. Rather, by virtue of having become eternal, of having come to know [*gignosko, gnosis*] the *contemplation* [*theoria*] of reality [i.e., God], of being called sons, of seeing the Father on his own on the basis of that which is related to him. In all this, the will

---

[498] *Strom.* 2.10:46.1; *FC*, 85: 190. Italics mine.

[499] *Strom.* 2.10:47.4; *FC*, 85: 191. Italics mine.

> leads the way; the powers of reason are naturally servants of the will. . . . For the Gnostic Christian, will, judgment, and praxis are one and the same.[500]

Again, we see the close association between *gnosis* and *theoria*; both are conceived in primarily moral terms. There is also a close identification of these concepts with the biblical notion of sonship. The regenerative effects of contemplation make it possible for the Gnostic Christian to both judge and act in accordance with what it means to be like Christ.

Though Clement often associates *theoria* with the present and practical aspects of life, this does not diminish the concept's eschatological implications. The soul that "is ever improving in the acquisition of virtue [*arete*] and the increase of righteousness" is assured a better place in the world to come, a world that consists of "the transcendent and continual *contemplation* of the Lord in eternity."[501]

In summary, contemplation is a large theme in the Alexandrian's thought. His utilization of *theoria* is but one more example of his apologetic method of defining Christian salvation in philosophical terms.

Stages of Christian Gnosis

Although we have already shown that there is a point in Clement's system where an individual passes from spiritual death to spiritual life through the exercise of simple faith, properly speaking salvation remains an eschatological concept in which it awaits completion at the end. Until then, as with rest of the Easter tradition, Clement views the salvation experience in time and history as process, not event. Having said this, we do not want to overlook the fact that within the temporally experienced process of salvation Clement identifies stages

---

[500] *Strom.* 2.17:77.4, 5; *FC,* 85: 209-10. Italics mine.

[501] *Strom.* 7.3:10.1-3; *ANF,* 2: 525 *passim.* Italics mine.

through which believers normally pass. For example, consider the following excerpt:

> [T]he all-loving Word, anxious to *perfect* [*teleioo*] us in a way that leads *progressively* to salvation, makes effective use of an order well adapted to our development; at first, He *persuades* us, then He *educates*, and after all this He *teaches*.[502]

The goal of Christ the Word is to perfect the believer (i.e., make him/her mature) that advances toward the goal of final salvation. Obviously, the emphasis falls upon the process of perfection, which is salvation experienced in time, toward final salvation, which is eschatological salvation or salvation completed at the end of time. What follows next is Clement's proposal for the education of the soul, which is not at all divorced from catechesis. Neither is it strictly confined to catechesis, for it is the "all-loving Word" at work beneath and through catechetical training and discipline.

First, he employs term *persuasion* has to do with the proclamation of the Gospel to non-believers. The use of this term is a conspicuous allusion to *Protrepticos*, the design of which (as we saw earlier) was to evangelize Greek-speaking Gentiles who had little or no acquaintance with Christianity. Second, the notion of *education* refers to the task of discipling converts, acquainting them with what it means to live as a Christian. Clement intended *Paedagogos* to embody the essence of Christ's instruction for such individuals. Finally, Clement refers to the task of *teaching*. Although as we noted earlier some have argued that this refers to a treatise [viz., *Didaskalos*] that Clement had intended to write but never did, we have proposed that *Stromateis* is the so-called teaching document, since its emphasis is upon Christian maturity. The ample discussion Clement

---

[502] *Paed.* 1.1:3.3 *FC,* 23: 5. Italics mine.

provides in *Stromateis* on the relationship between faith and the higher Gnostic life may very well be the planned culmination of the his theological system.

Summarizing thus far, we observe that from the starting point of exhortation (*Protrepticos*), to instruction (*Paedagogos*) and on to *gnosis* (*Stromateis*) we find in Clement's theology clearly defined stages of Christian experience. To put these in more familiar language, we are looking at repentance and faith, discipleship and Spirit-filled living, and personal holiness or sanctification. This can be regarded as nothing other than the classical Christian *ordo salutis*.

Two Lives

Charles Bigg in an early study of Christian Platonism at Alexandria proposed that Clement combined New Testament doctrines with the thought of the Jewish philosopher Philo. Bigg notes that Philo relegated all humanity into one of two classes: 1) the godless and immoral; and 2) the moral and spiritual.[503] The moral/spiritual class he further divided into a) the life of infancy and b) the life of perfection. Bigg argues that these latter two lives — infancy and perfection — originated in Greek philosophy as the *bios praktikos* and *bios theoria*, the 'practical' life and the 'contemplative' life. The practical life was further subdivided into *askesis* (discipline, practice), *mathesis* (learning, instruction) and *phusis* (principle of growth). The contemplative life was subdivided into *sophia* (wisdom) and *teleiosis* (perfection).

Bigg claims that Clement borrowed Philo's doctrines of the practical and the contemplative life, and then applied them to the New Testament. For example, he says that Clement found two stages of faith — spiritual infancy and perfection — implied in 1 Corinthians 3:2. Therein, St. Paul distinguishes between those he fed "milk" and those he gave "solid food."[504] Bigg concluded

---

[503] Bigg, *Christian Platonists of Alexandria*, 21, n. 1.

[504] Bigg, *Christian Platonists of Alexandria*, 86. This matter is not as clear as Bigg thinks. See *Strom.* 5.10:66.2,3; *ANF*, 2: 460.

from such observations that Clement's view of salvation must be hierarchical (a process of ascent) rather than linear (a process of maturation and growth).

We tend to disagree with Bigg on this matter. If Clement had viewed Christian spirituality in essentially hierarchical terms, then the argument would hold that he is more a Platonist than a Christian. However, there is evidence that Clement rejects Christian spirituality conceived in simple hierarchical terms.[505] Given other kinds of evidence, much of it already reviewed, we believe that Clement tends to view salvation moving along a continuum consisting of spiritual enlargement and ever-increasing intimacy with God — although as we have stated, sometimes he is inconsistent in this regard.

Earlier in this chapter we identified two kinds of faith, simple and scientific. We observed how Clement distinguishes between simple faith, which relates to the revelatory quality of Scripture, and scientific faith, which is based upon the demonstration of Scripture in the believer's experience. Let us now examine more specifically how he relates faith to the believer's spiritual progress. The relationships discussed below should be seen as parallel expressions of what is normally called progressive sanctification.

From Faith to Hope

In the following excerpt Clement describes the relationship between faith and hope. He writes:

> There are *two forms of faith* as there are two forms of time. . . .
> Memory has to do with the part of time which is past, *hope* with the part to come. It is faith which tells us that the past has existed and that the future will do so. Further, we show love [for God?] because

---

[505] See *Paed.* 1.6:31.2; *FC*, 23: 31: "It is not, then, that some are enlightened Gnostics and others are only less perfect Spirituals [*psuchikoi*] in the same Word, but all, putting aside their carnal desires, are equal and spiritual before the Lord." This is another good example of Clement taking over Gnostic terminology and refuting it with Christian content.

192

we are convinced by faith that the past has existed and that the future will continue to do so.[506]

There is a faith directed toward the past and a faith directed toward the future. Future-oriented faith is actually hope. One believes on the basis of Scripture that God has carried out good acts in the past. One is justified in believing that God will act similarly in the future. The believer's growth from simple faith to Gnostic love is advanced by hope. Because of God's merciful acts in the past, the believer hopes to receive his mercies in the future. Such hope in turn produces even greater love for God.

From Fear to Love

In Clement's system love is the highest motivation; it is the essence of Christian piety and the mark of Christian *gnosis*. The process leading to Gnostic love is therefore of some concern. In the following excerpt he explains how fear of God is a positive act that advances to love:

> [F]ear [*phobos*] is the beginning of love, and as it develops turns into faith and then love. My fear of a wild animal is different, being combined with hatred (remember there are two kinds of fear). [The fear I am talking about] . . . is more like my fear of my father, where fear is combined with love. . . . [I]n my fear of chastisement, I am showing self-love, and choose to feel fear. And anyone who fears to offend his father is showing love towards him.[507]

The beginning of salvation is fear. One obeys God because one fears divine punishment. Implied but not stated is the idea that God has already amply demonstrated in history that he judges sin and rewards righteousness. Fear is borne out of a desire for self-preservation, but it is obviously not the highest motive for serving God. Through fear the believer comes to realize that God is not essentially wrathful, but rather he is more like a loving parent. Fear then takes

---

[506] *Strom.* 2.12:53.1; *FC*, 85: 194-95. Italics mine.

[507] *Strom.* 2.12:53.3,4; *FC*, 85: 195.

on a new role. No longer does the believer obey simply because he fears punishment, but he obeys because he does not want to offend his loving Father. Love is the higher motive; it replaces fear as the impetus for continued faith and obedience. The Christian Gnostic no longer does the good because he fears divine punishment. Neither is abstaining from evil the struggle it once was; rather he does "good out of love [for God], and for the sake of its own excellence [*arete*]."[508] Even though fear of punishment is banished, fear as reverence mixed with love remains. Reverential love is the highest of all motivations for serving God; it is the basis upon which the virtue of the Christian Gnostics rests.

From Beginning Faith to Gnostic Maturity

As we have already seen, Clement differentiates between the initial experience of faith and mature Christian *gnosis*. In his opening remarks to *Stromateis* 6, he alludes to this distinction in the design of his writing:

> The Instructor [i.e., the treatise *Paedagogus*], divided by us into three books, has already exhibited the training and nurture up from the state of childhood, that is, the course of life which from elementary instruction grows by *faith*; [*Paedagogus*] . . . prepares beforehand the soul, endued with virtue, for the reception of *gnostic knowledge*.[509]

Clement views obedience to the divine commands as essential to spiritual progress. Faith works together with obedience to prepare the believer for the Gnostic stage. The "summit of faith," he writes, "is . . . knowledge (*gnosis*) itself."[510]

---

[508] *Strom.* 4.22:135.1, 4; *ANF*, 2: 434 passim.

[509] *Strom.* 6.1:3,4; *ANF*, 2: 480. Italics mine.

[510] *Strom.* 6.18:164.3; *ANF*, 2: 519.

194

    Stromateis chapter 7 is generally seen as the epitome of Clement's treatment of Christian *gnosis*. In the following excerpt, he traces the movement from initial faith to Gnostic contemplation.

> [The potential Gnostic Christian] . . . becomes an eager pupil of the Lord. Immediately, having heard both God and providence, he believed and worshipped because of these things. Consequently, being set in motion in every way, he *cooperates* [*sunergeo*] with the instruction, procuring all those things through which he is able to receive the *knowledge* [*gnosis*] of the things he desires (Desire combines with faith by a process of growth and seeks to be increased), which is to become worthy of such great and important *contemplation* [*theoria*]. Thus the Gnostic will taste the will of God; for he does not offer his ears but his soul to the realities being revealed by the spoken words.[511]

Although a bit convoluted, the above excerpt demonstrates movement from initial faith to Gnostic contemplation through a process marked by instruction, cooperation (*sunergos*), and obedience. Several lines later, Clement states that the Christian Gnostic trains himself in "scientific contemplation" (*epistemonike theoria*), that is, contemplative knowledge proven by experience.[512] This latter comment occurs within the context of a discussion of the Mosaic commands, which would seem to indicate that Clement has in mind a contemplative *gnosis* achieved through ordinary moral obedience.

From Metriopatheia to Apatheia

    The distinction between *metriopatheia* and *apatheia* is a prime example of Clement's attempt to present biblical concepts couched in philosophical language. *Metriopatheia* has to do with the restraint or moderation of passion; it is a concept that, like *apatheia*, originates with classical Greek philosophy.[513] In Clement's

---

[511] *Strom.* 7.11:60.1.4-3.1. Translation mine. Cf. *ANF*, 2: 540.

[512] *Strom.* 7.11:61.1.

[513] See Lilla, *Clement of Alexandria*, 99-103.

system *metriopatheia* is analogous to initial faith and obedience to God. Though salvific, *metriopatheia* is not the end; it is preparation for *apatheia* and Christian Gnostic perfection. Clement writes:

> The one who has first moderated his passions [*metriopatheia*] and [then] trained himself in *apatheia*, and as a result increased in gnostic perfection, is therefore surely like an angel."[514]

There is a pedagogical relationship between *metriopatheia* and obedience to the divine law. Clement explains:

> Therefore, if . . . the absence of fear is the absence of evils, which the fear of the Lord produces, then fear is a good thing, and the fear of the law is not only just but it is also good because it annuls evil; but just because absence of fear is produced by fear does not mean that passionlessness [*apatheia*] is produced by passion [*pathos*]. Rather, fear of the law produces moderation of passion [*metriopatheia*] through instruction [*paideia*].[515]

Clement actually bases the above argument on a reading of Galatians 3:24: "Therefore the law was our disciplinarian [*paedagogos*] until Christ came, ..." *Metriopatheia* is analogous to the reverence for God engendered by the moral law given to Moses on Mt. Sinai. As we already discussed, obedience to the law stemming from fear of punishment, or even fear of God himself, is not the highest possible motive for being moral. Nonetheless, such fear is effective in establishing moral behavior at the beginning of one's walk in faith. Again as we saw earlier, the highest cause for serving and obeying God is love, as both the Gospels and St. Paul argue. *Metriopatheia* is to virtue based in fear what *apatheia*

---

[514] *Strom.* 6.13:105.1. Translation mine. Cf. *ANF*, 2: 504.

[515] *Strom.* 2.8:39.4,5. Translation mine. Cf. also *FC*, 85: 185, though I believe that Father Ferguson's translation misses the mark here.

is to virtue based in love.[516] This seems to be the sum of the analogy that Clement attempts to draw.

From Immaturity to Perfection

Finally, Clement distinguishes those who are yet immature believers from those who have attained Gnostic perfection. There are some who are saved but are less than adult in terms of their spiritual and moral maturity. He writes:

> For those that endure from love of glory, or from fear of some severer punishment, or with a view to any joys or pleasures after death, these are mere children in faith, blessed indeed, but not yet having attained to manhood, like the gnostic, in their love to God, — for the Church too has its crowns both for men and for boys, just as the gymnasium has, — but love is to be chosen for its own sake, not for any other reason.[517]

Those who persevere in faith, though motivated by fear of punishment, are still saved; yet they have not achieved the adult faith of the Christian Gnostic who obeys God for the sake of love. As we see have seen here and previously, the highest motivation for obeying God is love.

3. Happiness

One of the more prominent themes in Clement's theology is happiness, *eudaimonia*, which he largely views as synonymous with virtue. Plato said that happiness is to possess the Good, which is why all human beings desire to be happy.[518] He also said that the highest good of all is intellectual knowledge

---

[516] That *apatheia* is the ultimate ground of the believer's experience of and service to God we have already seen. Gnostic *apatheia* is nothing other than "the perfection of the believer advancing through love" until he arrives at "perfect manhood" and likeness to God. *Strom.* 7.14:84.2. Translation mine.

[517] *Strom.* 7.11:67.2-5; Hort and Mayor, *Miscellanies Book VII*, 115,117. Cf. *ANF*, 2: 542.

[518] On Plato's doctrine of the highest good see Zeller, *Plato and the Older Academy*, 436-41 and Coppleston, *History of Philosophy*, 1: 216-18. On happiness in Plato's thought see Lodge, *Plato's Theory of Ethics*, 383-93.

grounded in contemplation of the eternal Forms. To contemplate the Forms is to participate in, or become like God. Plato recognized that a good life must admit a certain amount of sensual pleasure, though only in strict proportion to intellectual knowledge. He excluded all illicit acts because the pleasure derived from such things is antithetical to virtue. Happiness for Plato is becoming like God intellectually through contemplation and actually through virtue. Only by living virtuously may one achieve true happiness.[519]

We have already discussed Aristotle's doctrine of the good, which we will now relate more directly to the concept of happiness. Aristotle links happiness to virtue from a teleological perspective.[520] For Aristotle, happiness is the *telos* of a life spent in virtuous activity.[521] Happiness cannot therefore be passive, because then it would be possible to be virtuous without doing good.[522] Neither does happiness consist in achieving only transitory good, for life without perpetual happiness is incomplete. In order for a life to be both good and happy, it must be spent both in contemplation of virtue and in virtuous activity.[523]

Clement unambiguously follows Aristotle's notion that virtuous activity is the highest good. He agrees that happiness is the proper *telos* of life. He also affirms Aristotle's notion that the virtue practiced over a lifetime is the only way

---

[519] See Zeller, *Plato and the Older Academy,* 444-46.

[520] On Aristotle's ethics see Coppleston, *History of Philosophy,* 1: 332-50.

[521] For an interesting take on *eudaimonia* see John M. Cooper, *Reason and Human Good in Aristotle* (Cambridge, MA: Harvard University Press, 1975), 89-92, esp. n. 1. Cooper argues that Aristotle employed the term *eudaimonia* in a way which does not fit the usual English translation "happiness" (which derives from the Latin *felicitas*). The happy life for Aristotle, according to Cooper, is much more concerned with the attainment and actualization of mature abilities over the course of life ("flourishing") than with the achievement of a state of blessedness.

[522] *EN.* 1099a.1 ff.

[523] *EN.* 1100b.18-21.

198

to arrive at happiness.[524] Though happiness is life's single *telos,* the virtues that lead to it are many. Clement observes: "Blessedness [*eudaimonia*] is a *single thing,* its causes, the virtues, are multiple."[525]

Having stated the obvious, he elaborates that the whole range of virtues collectively constitute a single potential:

> Consider this, *virtue is single in power,* but the fact is that when it is realized in one form of action it is called practical wisdom, in another, disciplined moderation, in others, courage or justice.[526]

So, virtue is much like truth. Though truth is one, it is realized in the concrete world in any number of particulars. All recognize that diverse aspects of truth appear in various fields of inquiry such as geometry, music and philosophy. In the same way, there are a number of actions human beings perform that may be called virtuous, but all pertain to one notion that we call virtue. Happiness then, for Clement, is the *telos* of the person who actualizes virtue through the practice of virtuous acts.[527] In this regard, Clement makes the teleological goal of happiness the equivalent of virtue.

Clement believes that Plato anticipated New Testament teaching relative to moral character. In Plato's notions of perfection, likeness to God, justice, holiness and wisdom Clement finds analogues to the thought of the Apostle Paul, the writer of Hebrews, and the Old Testament prophets Ezekiel and Isaiah.[528] However, as he points out, the chief difference between the happy life of the philosophers and the blessedness of the Christian is the way one achieves the

---

[524] *Strom.* 2.21.128.3,4; *FC,* 85: 241.

[525] *Strom.* 1.20:97.2; *FC,* 85: 96. Italics mine.

[526] *Strom.* 1.20:97.3; *FC,* 85: 96. N.B.: Clement follows Plato's classification of the virtues for the most part, but his insistence that they are actualized only through activity derives from Aristotle.

[527] *Strom.* 1.20:98.2, 3: *FC,* 85: 97.

[528] See *Strom.* 2.22:134.2-136.6; *FC,* 85: 247-49 for references to same.

desired happy end. For the philosophers, happiness is a product either of contemplation or simply doing virtuous acts. For the Christian Gnostic, happiness is the product of faith made tangible through loving obedience. Clement observes:

> [Paul] establishes a target for faith in "the likeness to God so far as possible in the justice [*dikaios*="righteousness"] and holiness combined with practical wisdom," and the goal [*telos*] in the actualization of the promise on the basis of faith.[529]

Clement's synthesis of Platonic and Aristotelian ethics provides a useful analogue to the essential meaning of Scripture concerning the development of character and the proper *telos* of faith. Faith, which operates through virtuous loving actions, is the essence of the Christian life.[530]

Though Clement agrees with the Platonic and Aristotelian schools on many issues, he also departs from them by making two crucial moves that affect the landscape of his thought and place him squarely within the boundaries of Christian orthodoxy. The first is to link Plato's notion of likeness to the divine with the biblical doctrine of the *imitatio Christi*. Citing the philosopher, Clement writes: "It is essential that the person who hopes to find God's approval should be so far as possible *like* God."[531] In Plato's concept of likeness to God Clement discovers an appropriate analogue of the believer's imitation of Christ. He writes:

> We have the promise of reaching a goal that never comes to an end if we obey the commandments and live in their light faultlessly in full understanding derived from the revealed knowledge of God's will. The greatest possible *likeness* to the true Logos, the hope of being established fully as adopted sons through the Son — this is

---

[529] *Strom.* 2.22:136.6; *FC*, 85: 249. Ferguson indicates that the citation is taken from Plato's *Theaetetus*, 176 B.

[530] Galatians 5:6.

[531] *Strom.* 2.22:132.4; *FC*, 85: 246. Cit. *Theaetetus*, 176 B. Italics mine.

our *goal*, a sonship which constantly glorifies the Father through the "great high priest" who deigned to call us "brothers" and "fellow heirs."[532]

By invoking Plato's doctrine of the highest good and then setting it in an allusion to Scripture, Clement's doctrine of the higher Christian life would have had universal appeal among his Hellenistic readers. Virtuous happiness (*eudaimonia*) becomes the content of what it means to be an imitator of Christ.

The second move Clement makes is to link Plato's likeness doctrine and Aristotle's happy *telos* with St. Paul's understanding of faith and eschatology. He writes:

> The Apostle [Paul] in his Letter to the Romans writes a summary sketch of our *end* or *goal* [*telos*]: "Now that you have been set free from sin, and have become God's slaves, you have your harvest in *sanctification*, and your *end* is eternal life." He knows that the *hope* is of two kinds — one presently experienced, one in the future. He teaches that the *goal* is presently the establishment for which we hope. "Patience," he says, "produces character; character produces hope. Hope does not bring disillusion, because the love of God has been poured out in our hearts through the Holy Spirit he has given to us." Through this love we find ourselves established in hope, which Scripture says elsewhere is given to us as a rest.[533]

Freedom from sin, sanctification, is the realized aspect of eschatological salvation. The consistent and future end is eternal life. The distinction between a realized and consistent eschatology is further emphasized by a twofold hope. One the one hand, hope is presently experienced as a *telos* consisting of moral character and love. On the other hand, hope is directed to a future *telos* consisting of eternal life.

---

[532] *Strom.* 2.22:134.1,2; *FC*, 85: 247. Italics mine.

[533] *Strom.* 2.22:134.3,4; *FC*, 85: 247. N.B. the emphasis on two forms of hope. Italics mine. Cf. also *Strom.* 2.5:22.5,6; *FC*, 85: 172 where Clement alludes to Romans 7:14: "Everyone who commits sin is a slave. The slave does not continue in the house forever. If the Son [through faith] frees you, you will be free, and the truth will free you."

Together, these moves give Clement's doctrine of Christian holiness several important characteristics. First, we see again that *gnosis* conceived Christianly is ethical in nature. Clement believes that it is important for the Gnostic Christian to be actually holy. Unlike the desert fathers of later generations, Clement knows of no holiness achieved through ascetic separation. Faith must be lived out dynamically in virtuous activity. Second, holiness consists essentially of happiness; it is the *telos* of the Christian life. Finally, holiness is realized through love. As we have demonstrated, Clement finds in virtuous love the earthly realization of both Greek and Judeo-Christian aspirations. Love toward God and neighbor is the prime cause of the Christian Gnostic's superior moral character.

4. Gnostic Character

The term which best describes Clement's approach to character is *paideia* or 'instruction'. As we observed in our discussion of *Paedagogos,* traditional *paideia* centered upon training in virtue and the development of character. Even though it was primarily of Graeco-Roman origin, analogues of the concept appeared in the Old Testament and Jewish wisdom traditions. Early Christian *paideia* came about as a synthesis of the Graeco-Roman and Old Testament forms.[534] *Paideia* governs the structure of Clement's theology and, in particular, his discussion of Christian character.

Although Clement deals with character issues in both *Protrepticos* and *Paedagogos,* he gives more systematic attention to the theme as a whole in *Stromateis* under the rubric of the Christian Gnostic. In his spiraling way, Clement weaves a portrait of Christian Gnostic holiness in *Stromateis* that culminates in book 7. Ordinarily, he speaks of his ideal Gnostic in the third

---

[534] For a detailed discussion of this background see W. Wagner, "The Paideia Motif in the Theology of Clement of Alexandria," 23-126.

202

person — e.g., "The Gnostic . . . ." This format allows Clement considerable freedom in pursuing collateral concerns (which he quite often does) while still moving toward a conclusion.

The image of the true or ideal Christian Gnostic underlies all discussions of character in *Stromateis*. Clement puts together a collection of character traits that he believes ought to mark the life and practice of the Christian Gnostic. For instance, in *Stromateis* 2 he states that "[faith] is essential to the *true Gnostic,* as essential as breath is to life for anyone living in this world."[535] Later in the same book Clement discourses on the twofold nature of faith and attempts to show the vital connection between faith and love. He writes: "Throughout, love has been the companion of *the Gnostic,* because he knows that there is one God. . . . and that everything he had made was very good."[536] Such statements are typical.

As we have already seen, Clement's portrait of Gnostic character includes a strong emphasis upon personal holiness. The Christian Gnostic has left sin behind to become pure in body and soul.[537] Clement declares that "we shall find the divine likeness and the holy image" because the Gnostic is "being purified and performing blessed deeds."[538] The Gnostic Christian is of great value and worth in the sight of God because the divine presence indwells him and the *gnosis* of God *establishes* him as a holy individual.[539] He does not simply fear God; he loves God.

---

[535] *Strom.* 2.6:31.3; *FC,* 85: 179.

[536] *Strom.* 2.12:53.2; *FC,* 85: 195.

[537] *Strom.* 4.25:159.2,3; *ANF,* 2: 438.

[538] *Strom.* 7.5:29.5-7; *ANF,* 2: 530.

[539] Ibid. Italics mine. Clement uses the verb καθιερόω (*to dedicate, establish as sacred*) in the passive voice, indicating that the subject is the recipient of the verb's action. God makes the Christian Gnostic holy.

He follows God and wants to serve Him only. In short, the Christian Gnostic "as far as is possible, imitate[s] God."[540]

Clement says that while on earth the Christian Gnostic will not attain the perfection of Christ; yet he will achieve a certain "gnostic perfection," consisting of proficiency in the Gospel.[541] To achieve such competence involves both abstention from evil and active promotion of good. Nowhere is perfection more in evidence than in the Christian Gnostic who forgives others. In fact, Clement illustrates Christ's command to be perfect as God is perfect (Mt. 6:12; Lk. 11:4) by the Gnostic believer's readiness to forgive those who have sinned against him.[542]

Finally in this synopsis, we should note that Clement's portrait of Christian Gnostic character is derived from his own study of Scripture and his personal knowledge of how Scripture was being employed in his day. In fact, one thing that distinguishes Clement's Christian Gnosticism as utterly other than and separate from Hellenistic Gnosticism is his absolute reliance upon the teachings of Christ communicated through Scripture and interpreted by the church. Clement writes:

> We find that the [Christian] [G]nostic alone, having grown old in the study of the *actual Scriptures*, guards the orthodox doctrine of the Apostles and the Church and lives a life of perfect rectitude in accordance with the *Gospel*, being aided by the Lord to discover the proofs he is in search of both from the *law* and the *prophets*. For the life of the [Christian G]nostic, as it seems to me, is nothing else than deeds and words agreeable to the tradition of the Lord.[543]

---

[540]   *Strom.* 4.26:170.4, 171.4; *ANF*, 2: 441.

[541]   *Strom.* 4.21:180.2,3; *ANF*, 2: 433.

[542]   *Strom.* 7.13:81.1-3; *ANF*, 2: 546.

[543]   *Strom.* 7.16:104.1-2; Hort and Mayor, *Miscellanies Book VII*, 183. Cf. *ANF*, 2: 554. Italics mine.

Clement believed that he was not adding anything new to the Christian revelation, rather he was teaching the apostolic faith. If he were present to defend his approach, one would think Clement would argue that his only innovation was to attempt a systematic analysis of the *ordo salutis* using the language and learning of classical philosophy.

Chapter 5
Arguments

Having examined Wesley's references to Clemens Alexandrinus in chapter three and having undertaken an analysis of Clement's soteriology in chapter four, we are now ready to argue the ways in which Wesley may have been influenced by the thought and theology of this important early Christian writer. Our discussion will proceed on the basis of four arguments, which we categorize according to the type of evidence each represents:

A. Textual Evidence
B.. Thematic Similarities
C. Stylistic Similarity
D. Doctrinal Development

Our working hypothesis is simply as follows: John Wesley read the works of Clement of Alexandria (or significant portions thereof); he appropriated certain aspects of Clement's soteriology which he understood to be paradigmatic of scriptural Christianity; and he incorporated those insights into his own teaching on Christian faith and practice.

A. Argument from Textual Evidence

In chapter three we examined the direct references that John Wesley made to Clement. There is other evidence, however, which is of a more indirect nature. This evidence is textual in nature; and in two cases it derives from secondary sources. The inferences to be drawn from this material are logical and therefore fairly clear.

1. Two Charles Wesley Hymns

'Jesu' Lover of My Soul'

The first piece of evidence was brought to light in a 1994 article that appeared in the *Proceedings of the Wesley Historical Society,* where James Dale notes similarities between portions of two hymns authored by Charles Wesley and several lines found in Clement's *Protrepticos.*[544] Dale suggests that certain lines in *Protrepticos* bear a striking resemblance to a strophe of Charles' *Jesu, Lover of my soul.*[545] Even more interesting is that Clement had borrowed the lines from an ancient Greek classic, Homer's *Odyssey.*[546]

In *Protrepticos* 12 Clement recalls brave Odysseus' struggle against the tempting call of the mythical sirens. He employs this image as a metaphor by which he appeals to his Greek audience to abandon the siren song of idol worship. To succumb to temptation's call leads to destruction; to resist and flee to the cross of Christ leads to the safe harbor of heaven. Clement exhorts:

> Sail past the [sirens'] song; it works death. Exert your will only, and
> you have overcome ruin; bound to the wood of the cross, thou shalt

---

[544] James Dale, "Charles Wesley, The Odyssey, and Clement of Alexandria," *Proceedings of the Wesley Historical Society* 48 (May, 1992): 150-52.

[545] Ibid., 150-51.

[546] Ibid.

be freed from destruction: the word of God will be thy pilot, and the Holy Spirit will bring thee to anchor in heaven.[547]

Jaroslav Pelikan notes that Clement "made the most effective and profound use [among the early fathers] of the image of Odysseus at the mast as a foreshadowing of Jesus [sacrificial death upon the cross]."[548]

Dale argues that the following strophe from *Jesu, Lover of my soul* is reminiscent of the citation from *Protrepticos*:

> Hide me, O my Saviour, hide,
> Till the storm of life is past;
> Safe into the haven guide;
> O, receive my soul at last.

He observes that the original title of the hymn was not *Jesu, Lover of My Soul*, but was instead *In Temptation*. Dale believes that the warning to avoid temptation, which we find in the excerpt cited from *Protrepticos* and which we know was based upon the *Odyssey*, provides the nautical setting for Wesley's hymn. He comments:

> Here, Clement and Charles Wesley are both seeing things from the standpoint of the individual — a hypothetical 'Greek' or 'heathen' in Clement's case, a believer undergoing temptation in 'Jesu, Lover of my soul.'[549]

Indeed, both Wesley and Clement employ a nautical theme to teach and encourage endurance in the midst of temptation. Both show that salvation comes to the one who endures. Wesley's Christ, who leads the believer into the safe haven, is reminiscent of the Holy Spirit, who delivers the believer to safe

---

[547] *Protr.* 12: 118.4; *ANF* 2: 205. Cf. also *LCL*, 92: 253.

[548] Dale, "Charles Wesley, The 'Odyssey,' and Clement of Alexandria," 150. Cit. Jaroslav Pelikan, *Jesus Through the Centuries* (New Haven: Yale University Press, 1985), 42.

[549] Ibid., 151.

208

anchorage. Might Charles have borrowed from Clement this same idea and adapted for *Jesu, Lover of My Soul,* a hymn of comfort for Christians undergoing trials, as Dale suggests? The argument is plausible.

'Rejoice for a Brother Deceased!'

Dale continues the same line of investigation with a second Charles Wesley hymn, *Rejoice for a Brother Deceased!,* which also carries a nautical theme. This hymn was written on the occasion of the premature death of one of the Wesleys' friends. It appeared initially in *Funeral Hymns* (1746), though it may have been composed as early as 1744.[550] The poignant image of a departed friend who finally attains safe harbor is again reminiscent of Clement's appeal to his audience that they trust the Savior and the Holy Spirit to guide them into eternal rest. Dale suggests that the image of the "haven of heaven" in *Protrepticos* may very well have served as Charles' inspiration for both hymns.[551]

2. Edward Welchman

David Tripp, who re-examined evidence presented three decades earlier by V. H. H. Green, followed another line of investigation.[552] Green had found in his examination of the *Oxford Diaries* that in 1731 Wesley noted having read Archdeacon Edward Welchman's *XXXIX Ariticuli Ecclesiae Anglicanae, Textibus Sacrae Scripturae et patrum primaevorum Testimoniis confirmati.* Published in 1713 at Oxford, the treatise contains the text of the *Thirty-Nine Articles* along with supporting passages from Scripture and the church fathers.

---

[550] Franz Hildebrand and Oliver A. Beckerlegge, eds., *A Collection of Hymns for the Use of the People Called Methodists,* vol. 7 of *The Works of John Wesley,* (Nashville: Abingdon, 1983), 139, n. 48.

[551] James Dale, "Charles Wesley, The Odyssey, and Clement of Alexandria," 152.

[552] David H. Tripp, "Clement of Alexandria and The Wesley Brothers," *Proceedings of the Wesley Historical Society* 49 (Feb., 1994): 113-16.

Tripp observes that Welchman included six citations from Clement of Alexandria in support of six of the *Thirty-Nine Articles*. Five of the six are quotations from Clement's *Quis Dives Salvetur*, the sixth is taken from *Stromateis* 7.[553] Tripp states that Welchman's citations of *Quis Dives* collectively "show the human personality as a locus of divine action," and that the same insights show up later in Wesley's soteriology.[554]

It is important to note that Welchman had based his citations of Clement on the English translation of *Quis Dives* published by Bishop John Fell in 1683. Fell (1625-86) is remembered as a consummate scholar, who a year earlier in 1682, had published a critical edition of the works of Cyprian (d. 258 AD). His knowledge of the church fathers was extensive. Fell had benefited from the revival of Anglicanism that occurred after the Restoration of the monarchy. [555] One of Fell's main contributions was to reform the academic curriculum along conservative lines and to reestablish Anglicanism in light of the liberalizing tendency represented by Richard Baxter and post-Tridentine Catholicism.[556] Fell articulated a broad vision of how Christ Church College and Oxford should serve

---

[553] Tripp, "Clement of Alexandria and the Wesley Brothers," 115-16

[554] Ibid., 116.

[555] See *ODCC*, s.v. "Fell, John." In 1660 Fell was appointed Dean of Christ Church, then sixteen years later ascended to the bishopric of Oxford in 1676 (which he held concurrently with the Deanery).

[556] See G. V. Bennett, "Loyalist Oxford and the Revolution," in *The History of the University of Oxford,* eds. L. S. Sutherland and L. G. Mitchell (Oxford: Clarendon Press, 1986), 10: "At Oxford John Fell, dean of Christ Church, was the leading figure in a patristic revival which sought to confound Bellarmine and Baxter by demonstrating that Anglican Church order conformed closely to the pattern of primitive Christianity."

the church. That vision included the preparation of a generation of scholars who would be thoroughly Anglican in terms of their theology and allegiance.[557]

One of the young scholars to benefit indirectly (through Welchman) from Bishop Fell's work was John Wesley, who matriculated at Christ Church in 1725.[558] Though Fell had passed from the scene long before Wesley's day, and though there is no evidence that Wesley had read Fell's edition of *Quis Dives*, it is interesting that Wesley came in contact with the bishop's work indirectly by reading Welchman's *Thirty-Nine Articles* in the college where Fell had served.

3. Alexander Knox

Background

Alexander Knox (1757-1831) was a younger contemporary and friend of John Wesley.[559] Even though they differed greatly in age (Wesley was sixty-two, Knox was eight when they first met) Knox developed a lasting interest in the Methodist movement.[560] Wesley met young Alex during a 1765 visit to the Knox family home in Londonderry. Sometime later, the two began a correspondence that continued until Wesley's death.[561] Knox had a chronic nervous disorder that

---

[557] Bennett, "Loyalist Oxford and the Revolution," 11-12: "Fell . . . did not doubt that he was creating the future leadership of a ruling class which would be firmly attached to the church and which would see its own security in the defence of the Anglican cause."

[558] Outler, *John Wesley*, 6.

[559] For additional biographical material on Knox see L. Stephen and S. Lee, eds., *The Dictionary of National Biography* (London: Oxford University Press, 1917), 11: 304-05.

[560] For vitae on Alexander Knox see Telford, *Letters of John Wesley*, 6: 203-204 ; Charles Forster, ed., *Thirty Years Correspondence between John Jebb and Alexander Knox*, 2nd ed., 2 vols. (London: Duncan and Cochran, 1836), 2: 25. The first published letter posted by Wesley to Knox is dated Jan. 27, 1776 (Telford, *Letters of John Wesley*, 6: 204-05).

[561] This correspondence was more extensive than indicated by Wesley's published letters. See Knox's "Remarks on the Life and Character of John Wesley" in Robert Southey, *The Life of Wesley and the Rise and Progress of Methodism*, M. Fitzgerald, ed., 2 vols. (London: Longman, Brown, Green, and Longmans, 1846; reprint, London: Oxford University Press, H. Milford, 1925), 2: 338: "I have between forty and fifty letters [from John Wesley], the last written

caused him to suffer bouts of depression, which in turn may explain the nature of their relationship. Wesley had always been a gifted pastor when it came to dealing with individuals who suffered emotional and spiritual anxiety. It is not at all surprising that Knox found in the much older Wesley a spiritual guide and mentor who was willing to give him the time and friendship that few others would.

In spite of Knox's emotional difficulties, he was no shallow individual by any means. Though largely self-taught, he is remembered as an engaging conversationalist and political analyst who possessed a keen intellect. Knox became an apologist for the Church of England, whose self-appointed task was to defend historic Anglicanism was the true middle way between Protestantism and Roman Catholicism.[562] Toward this end he read broadly, studying church history and doctrinal theology.

Though Alex Knox always stood on the periphery of Methodism, never counting himself a member of the movement, he remained a friendly critic and admirer of Wesley and the Methodists. Through their friendship, Knox gained acquaintance with some of the influences that had earlier shaped Wesley's thought. Following Wesley's death in 1791, Knox spoke candidly with other friends about Wesley.

Evidence

One of Knox's closest friends later in life was Bishop John Jebb (1775-1833) with whom he shared an exchange of correspondence. In an 1804 letter Knox recalls some of the more significant theological influences upon Wesley:

---

about nine months before his death. I myself account them invaluable; as they still, in the most forcible and interesting way, bring the good old man before me; . . ."

[562] See *ODCC*, s.v. "Knox, Alexander."

> In John Wesley's views of *Christian perfection*, are combined, in
> substance, *all the sublime morality of the Greek fathers*, the spirituality
> of the mystics and the divine philosophy of our favourite Platonists.
> Macarius, Fenelon, Lucas, and all of their respective classes, have
> been consulted and digested by him; and his ideas are, essentially,
> theirs. But his [Wesley's] merit is . . . , that *he has popularized these
> sublime lessons*, in such a manner, *in his and his brother's hymns*, that
> he . . . . [text unfinished in original][563]

By linking Wesley's doctrine of Christian perfection to the early Eastern writers,
among them Macarius the Egyptian (d. 390 A.D.), Knox confirms what Wesley
himself had either stated directly or alluded to on various occasions. He credits
Wesley with a kind of practical genius in having assimilated a wide body of
learning, then popularizing it in his and Charles' hymns.

Seventeen years later in 1821, Knox again writes to Jebb concerning
Wesley:

> Great minds are not vain: and his [John Wesley's] was a great mind,
> if any mind can be made great, by disinterested benevolence,
> spotless purity, and simple devotedness to that one supreme Good,
> in whom, with the united αισθησις [*perception, knowledge*] of the
> *philosopher* and the *saint*, he saw, and loved, and adored, all that was
> infinitely amiable, true, sublime, and beatific.[564]

Based upon an intimate acquaintance over several decades, Knox assesses John
Wesley as having combined the qualities of a keen philosophical mind with an
incontrovertibly pure character.

Although some of Knox's reminiscences of Wesley are clearly
hagiographic in nature, in others he provides a more critical assessment. For
example, in a doctrinal tome to Hannah More on the subject of divine providence,
Knox writes:

---

[563] Charles Forster, ed., *Thirty Years Correspondence between John Jebb and Alexander Knox*, 2nd
edition, 2 vols. (London: Duncan and Cochran, 1836), 1: 145. Italics mine.

[564] Ibid., 2: 460. Italics mine.

John Wesley had, naturally, more acuteness in thought and ardency in action, than warmth of affection. To the study of our best authors he had added the severities of an ascetic life, and, had he continued within the shelter of a college, he might have never suspected his want of any Christian feature.[565]

Perhaps more than any of Wesley's younger contemporaries, Knox recognized the place of Methodism within the larger scheme of church history. He writes:

Wesleyan Methodism, [is] not as a field of wheat, whose value depends upon its present produce, but . . . [it is] a nursery of stock in which a new and important kind of engrafture has been, probably, for the first time, experimented, ...[566]

Knox believed that one of Wesley's chief achievements was to synthesize the Augustinian doctrine of effectual grace and peace with God with Eastern Christianity's doctrine of inward experience resulting in moral purity.[567]

The general improvement in moral character he observed among Methodists deeply impressed Knox, so much so that his recollection was still vivid even near the end of his life. In his "Remarks on the Life and Character of John Wesley," published posthumously, he observes:

Whatever may have been the defects or excesses of Wesleyan Methodism, it has certainly been the most moral of all similar associations; and the ruling claim which held so many thousands in adherence to a standard so much above their original frame of mind and habits of life was the exemplary virtue of their leader.[568]

---

[565] Alexander Knox, "Letter to Mrs. Hannah-More on the Design of Providence Respecting The Christian Church," *The Remains of Alexander Knox,* (London: Duncan and Malcolm, 1844), 3: 135-36.

[566] Ibid., 3: 153.

[567] Ibid., 3: 153-72 *passim.* Knox concludes that Wesley in effect united Chrysostom with Augustine (p. 170).

[568] Knox, "Remarks on the Life and Character of John Wesley," Southey, *Life of Wesley,* 2: 342.

214

Methodism was known by the moral character it produced in the lives of members — a character comparable to that possessed by the movement's founder. Knox says of Wesley:

> [W]e sometimes meet persons who, in their very mien and aspect, as well as in the whole habit of life, manifest such a stamp and signature of virtue as to make our judgement of them a matter of intuition rather than a result of continued examination. I never met a human being who came more perfectly within this description than John Wesley.[569]

Two pages later Knox makes a very important observation:

> From his first years of serious reflection, [John Wesley's] . . . standard of Christian virtue was pure and exalted. He formed his views in the school of the *Greek Fathers*, and in that of their closest modern followers, the Platonic divines of the Church of England . . . . The ardour of Mr. Wesley's soul was fired by the spirit which he thus inhaled: and to realize in himself the *perfect Christian of Clemens Alexandrinus* was the object of his heart.[570]

Knox says that Wesley's chief personal aim was to actualize the portrait of Christian character depicted by Clement of Alexandria.

As we noted earlier, Knox was a student of church history and Christian doctrine. He read widely among the Latin and Greek church fathers. One of his special interests was the doctrinal difference between Anglicanism and the Lutheran/Reformed branch of Protestantism. Luther and the Reformers had taught a primarily forensic view of justification. By emphasizing the change in the believer's standing before God, they tended to neglect the regenerative effects upon character that accompany faith. On the other side of the question, while the Roman Church never lost sight of the moral effects of salvation, through its

---

[569] Ibid., 2: 343.

[570] Ibid., 2: 345. Italics mine.

doctrine of infused faith it had conflated works with faith, making righteous acts a prerequisite for saving grace.[571]

Knox recognized that Anglicanism addressed these problems theologically by following a *via media* between Protestant justification and Catholic good works. But Anglicanism had failed in the translation of theology into the Christian experience of ordinary of believers. Wesley, in Knox's view, had overcome this failure by articulating vis-à-vis the believer's experience the relationship between grace, faith, assurance, regeneration and perfection.

As we saw earlier, Clement of Alexandria taught a stage of Christian maturity, *gnosis*, in which the soul has overcome internal conflict and achieved a state of peace with God. Knox was evidently familiar with Clement's theology. He writes:

> The attainableness of such a state [of maturity] was maintained, by all the earlier fathers. The first that made it the subject of direct description, was *Clemens Alexandrinus*, in the 6th and 7th books of the *Stromata*; his [Christian] gnostic being identically the mystic of a later period.[572]

Knox argues that Clement's Christian Gnostic was based upon the teachings of Jesus and Paul, both of whom had distinguished "between a mere state of grace, and . . . [the] advance upon it."[573]

It turns out however that Knox was both an admirer and critic of Clement. He writes: "Clement's portraiture of the perfect Christian is one of the noblest things of the kind that the world ever saw: yet the assertions cannot always be defended."[574] Though he fails to explain the challenge implied by this remark,

---

[571] See Knox, "Letter to Mr. Parken on Justification," *Remains,* 1: 281-317.

[572] Knox, "Letter to D. Parken, Esq. on the Character of Mysticism," *Remains,* 1: 350.

[573] Ibid., 1: 349.

[574] Ibid., 1: 351.

Knox goes on to reaffirm the Alexandrian and his importance for the larger church.

> That the ancient spiritualists taught a most important truth, when they asserted a settled, unclouded serenity of soul, to be the inheritance of the perfect Christian, I cannot but believe; . . . I cannot otherwise understand St. John's "perfect love," which casteth "out fear". . . . *Had Clemens Alexandrinus, Macarius, and others of like soaring minds, been wanting, the very idea of mature Christianity, as distinguished from weak and struggling piety, might have been, at this day, lost and forgotten.*[575]

Either Knox came to these conclusions on his own, or he gleaned them from Wesley or someone else. Given his facility with Greek and Latin, we believe that Knox probably read Clement for himself. Whether he did so with Wesley's encouragement or guidance remains unknown.

Alexander Knox gives every indication of having been a reliable source on certain aspects of Wesley's life and thought. As we have demonstrated, he decisively linked Wesley to the Eastern church writers in general, and to Clement of Alexandria in particular. Unless further written evidence emerges, it is not possible to determine with greater certainty how Knox came to know Wesley's thinking on this matter. All the circumstantial evidence, however, suggests that it came to him from Wesley himself.

4. Bishop John Potter

Relationship with the Wesleys

John Potter (1674-1747) was an older contemporary of and mentor to John and Charles Wesley during their time at Oxford. As both a scholar and churchman, Potter's credentials were superb. In 1707 he was given a regius appointment to Oxford as professor of divinity, which he ended up holding until his death in 1747. In 1715 he was elected to the episcopate of Oxford, and in

---

[575] Ibid., 1: 352-53. Italics mine.

1737 he was elevated to serve as Archbishop of Canterbury. L.W. Barnard notes that Potter was drawn more toward pastoral ministry than he was the functional and administrative aspects of his office.[576]

Both John and Charles were ordained by Archbishop Potter — John as deacon in 1725, then as priest in 1728. Potter and John formed a mentor-protégé relationship that began at least as early as 1725 when John was but twenty-two years of age.[577] For the young Wesley, Potter modeled the kind of intellectual commitment and personal integrity demanded of an ecclesiastical leader. Potter was the quintessential Church of England bishop — learned, well read in Christian antiquity and above all, one who almost effortlessly combined the offices of scholar and pastor.

Unlike other contemporaries, Potter from the beginning assumed a congenial attitude toward the Holy Club.[578] His characteristically gentle and irenic manner favorably inclined him toward the Wesleys and the Methodist movement, whom Potter saw as wanting nothing more than to live holy lives.[579] Barnard is correct in assessing Potter as "a man of his age" who was firmly grounded in the past with a tolerant and open attitude toward the present.[580]

Many years later, John reminisced about his friendship with Bishop Potter, recalling an incident that occurred during the early days of the Methodist

---

[576] L.W. Barnard, *John Potter An Eighteenth Century Archbishop* (Elms Court, G.B.: Arthur H. Stockwell Ltd., 1989), 61, 62. Barnard notes that Potter was "methodical in persevering in his care of the parishes . . . . Potter much preferred pastoral work in his diocese and in Oxford to sojourns at the Court in London."

[577] Noted in the *Oxford Diaries* for August 25, 1725.

[578] Ibid., 98: "There is nothing to suggest that Potter, during his Oxford episcopate, had been troubled by the activity of the Wesleys or the 'Holy Club'."

[579] See Telford, *Letters,* 8: 267: "Archbishop Potter had told Charles Wesley. . . that if the Methodists were attached to the Church they might 'leaven the whole,' . . . ."

[580] Barnard, *John Potter,* 120.

movement. Around 1743 or 44 John and Charles accepted responsibility for two churches that had once been part of a ministry to French Huguenots.[581] Potter was among the few Anglican clergy aware of the situation who, though they were temporarily serving outside the Anglican communion, did not question the Wesleys' fundamental loyalty to the Church of England. Wesley fondly recalls how Potter publicly stood by them: "Those gentlemen are irregular; but they have done good, and I pray God to bless them."[582]

The Methodists' emphasis upon holy living impressed Potter, for he also had similar leanings. It would not have passed by his attention that the attempt by the Methodists to create a community life based upon holy charity shared much in common with the early church. Near the end of his own life, Wesley paid homage to his long-deceased friend and mentor, recalling a conversation that took place not long after Aldersgate:

> Near fifty years ago, a great and good man, Dr. Potter, then Archbishop of Canterbury, gave me an advice for which I have ever since had occasion to bless God: "If you desire to be extensively useful, do not spend your time and strength in contending for or against such things as are of a disputable nature; but in testifying against open, notorious vice, and in promoting real, essential holiness."[583]

A certain irony accompanies the sermon from which the above citation has come. Even as Wesley had always affirmed his loyalty to the Anglican communion, especially during the early days when Potter had encouraged these 'irregular' Methodists, Wesley would soon have to accept the inevitable split between Methodism and the Church of England.

Potter as Scholar

---

[581] Ward and Heitzenrater, *Journals and Diaries*, II, 19: 326, n. 12.

[582] Telford, *Letters*, 8: 141.

[583] "On Attending the Church Service," Outler, *Sermons*, III, 3: 478.

Given their friendship early in Wesley's career, it is likely that Potter's mentoring in ecclesiastical matters carried over into academics as well. He was in fact a consummate scholar whose contributions to the fields of history, philosophy, and theology endured well beyond his own lifetime.[584] Potter was especially interested in ancient Greece, so much so that he published critical editions of select works by the Middle Platonist Plutarch (*Variantes Lectiones,* 1694) as well as the obscure rhetorician Lycophron (*Lycophronis Chalcidiensis Alexandra,* 1697). More notable, however, was his *Archaeologia Graeca,* a history of Greek culture and thought, that was published in two volumes (1697, 1699) and went through a number of reprints. Wesley included a revised edition in the curriculum at Kingswood School, though he admitted that it was a "a dry, dull, heavy book."[585] Potter's theological works, which disclose much more of his pastoral and ecclesiological interests, were collected after his death in three volumes.[586]

Critical Edition of The Works of Clemens Alexandrinus

Of all Potter's scholarly output, nothing has been more valuable and resilient than his critical edition of the works of Clement of Alexandria. Potter published *Clementis Alexandrini opera, quae extant recognita & illustrata par*

---

[584] Barnard, *John Potter,* 21: "[Potter] . . . was eminent in classical studies from an early age."

[585] Ward and Heitzenrater, *Journals and Diaries, III,* 20: 363 and esp. nn. 90-92. Wesley was working on three different manuscripts in October of 1750. These included a revision of *Archaeologia Graeca* by John Potter, a revision of *Origines Hebraeae* by Thomas Lewis, and an abridgment of *Primitive Christianity* by William Cave. All three were employed in the curriculum at Kingswood. He also was not thrilled with Cave's approach to the church fathers, but apparently thought its content sufficiently worthwhile to keep it in the curriculum.

[586] *The Theological Works of the Most Reverend Dr. John Potter, Late Lord Archbishop of Canterbury, Containing His Sermons, Charges, Discourse of Church Government and Divinity Lectures,* 3. vols., (Oxford: Printed at the Theatre, 1753, 54). Much of this material was composed and delivered in English, but the divinity lectures remain untranslated in Latin.

Johannem Potterum in two volumes in 1715.[587] We noted in chapter four that Stählin's edition of Clement was based largely upon Migne's *Patrologia Graeca*. Barnard observes that Potter's edition varies little from Migne.[588] In point of fact, Migne is actually based on Potter's version.

Potter undertook an exhaustive researching of parallels and citations to known works, especially Philo. The result was a critical edition that was better than anything produced previously.[589] This is evidenced by the fact that *Clementis Alexandrini Opera* remained unsurpassed for nearly two hundred years until Stählin's edition appeared at the beginning of the twentieth century. The editing task was monumental. Potter was assisted in part by William Lowth (1660-1732). Lowth was a capable theologian and scholar who is remembered for having read and annotated almost every known Greek and Latin writer. His work on Clement of Alexandria proved invaluable to Potter's effort.[590]

Wesley, Potter, Clement Connection

The close mentoring relationship that Potter had with John Wesley increases the likelihood that the two had at various times discussed theological issues. It may well be that Wesley derived a good deal of his fascination with the early church from the good bishop. Wesley notes in his diary that he read Potter's *A Discourse on Church Government* while in the Georgia colony.[591] The treatise is

---

[587] John Potter, ed., *Clementis Alexandrini opera, quae extant recognita & illustrata par Johannem Potterum, Episcopum Oxoniensen* (Oxford, 1715).

[588] Barnard, *John Potter*, 140.

[589] So states Stählin in *Clemens Alexandrinus zweiter Band: Stromata Buch I-VI*, vol. 15, GCS (Berlin: Akademie-Verlag, 1985), xii, d.

[590] See *Dictionary of National Biography*, s.v. "Lowth, William D.D. (1660-1732)". William was the father of Robert Lowth (1710-87), bishop of London, who was a contemporary and friend of John Wesley.

[591] Ward and Heitzenrater, *Journals and Diaries, I*, 18: 418, 419.

a comprehensive defense of Anglican ecclesiology supported entirely by early church writers.[592]

Wesley not only attempted to model Potter's churchmanship, but his interest may also have been kindled to pursue issues in which Potter was the leading authority of his day — viz., Clement of Alexandria. Wesley states unequivocally that he read Clement while at Oxford. It was almost certainly a copy of Potter's 1715 edition of Clement that he read. It leaves little to speculation to suggest that Wesley was formally if not initially introduced to Clemens Alexandrinus by Archbishop Potter.

B. Argument from Thematic Similarities

Wesley stated unequivocally that he was influenced by Clement's ideal of Christian virtue and character. In these introductory comments we first want to address briefly the question of methodological approach. Then secondly and in more detail we want to set forth some reasonable criticisms of the inquiry we are undertaking here.

First, in the explorations that follow we have taken a modified inductive approach. The basic question before us at all times is, "What principal theological concerns and emphases for Wesley are also major theological issues in the extant writings of Clement of Alexandria?" We shall identify themes or topics that are common to both Clement and Wesley, present evidence from both writers' literary remains, and then let the reader decide. Obviously, not all occurrences in either thinker nor all the nuances of either's thought can be

---

[592] Ward and Heitzenrater, *Journals and Diaries, I*, 18: 212-213, n. 95. By January, 1738 Wesley had begun to recognize that part of the reason for his sense of failure in the Georgia mission was because he had accorded too much authority to certain practices commended in the holy tradition. He now realized that some early church observances and decretals were necessitated solely by their historical context; they were not meant to be observed for all time. Yet he continues to affirm Vincent of Lerin's *consensus veterum* for the proper interpretation of Scripture.

presented in full detail. This is one of the unavoidable weaknesses of a broad study. Nonetheless, we have attempted to avoid in every way possible obscure comments, particularly by Clement since it is assumed that he is not as familiar or accessible to most readers of this study as is Wesley, in order to present a fair and accurate representation of each writer's positions.

Second, we admit that our methodological approach is not foolproof. One of the difficulties is that one or even a number of similarities do not substantiate the generalization that there is an actual dependence or influence at work. Perhaps, what is being observed is simply coincidence. Another difficulty is that perhaps any apparent similarities are nothing more than general concerns held by Christian thinkers over the centuries, making it not surprising in the least that they would be concerns held by Clement and Wesley as well. Finally, perhaps Wesley did read Clement; but we know that he also read other fathers as well from both the East and West. Are we to grant equal weight to the familiarity he had with the works of these writers? Was he as familiar with the works of Ephrem Syrus as he was with Cyprian, or with Clement or Rome, or with Ignatius, etc.? Were any of these claims exaggerated at all, made in the midst of a heated argument? In fairness to Wesley, the comments he makes concerning these writers does suggest that he knew the essence of what these writers were about, but did he know the nuances? If the answer to any of these questions creates doubt, then why should one believe *ex cathedra* his statement about Clement?

By now, it should be obvious that any argument from thematic similarities is only going to be able to accumulate so much weight. Whether it is decisive enough to tip the scales, the reader will have to judge. However, let us not forget one thing: it was Wesley himself who established the link between Clement's portrait of ideal Christian character and his own *Character of a Methodist*. Furthermore, on the basis of the other evidence already assembled — especially Wesley's relationship to the foremost scholar of the day Bishop John Potter —

there is more than sufficient justification to undertake a serious, open-minded investigation of the evidence.

1. Salvation

There are two issues that Wesley and Clement emphasize, which bear a striking resemblance to one another and may indicate some kind of dependence or influence. The one is salvation viewed as personal transformation and various categories pertaining thereto; the other is allowance for stages of faith in one spiritual pilgrimage. Apart from the fact that these concepts can be traced back to the classical Eastern Christian tradition, it is interesting that they show up in the theology of one of Wesley's few specifically named sources.

a. *Personal transformation*

Both Wesley and refer to salvation using transformational language, arguing that salvation is a lifelong process advanced by faithful obedience and characterized by an ever-increasing holiness of heart and life.

Wesley

(1) Experience of Faith

The concept of faith experience is quite apparent in Wesley's *Character of a Methodist:*

> By salvation [the Methodist] . . . means holiness of heart and life.
> And this he affirms to spring from true *faith alone.* Can even a
> nominal Christian deny it?"[593]

There are two concepts embedded in excerpt that contrast with notions characteristically held by the Reformed thinkers of Wesley's day. First, he says that, at its essence, salvation is holiness of heart and life. The reformers had

---

[593]   "Character of a Methodist," Davies, *The Methodist Societies,* 9:35.

tended to view salvation as mainly a legal or positional change before God: the believer, through faith alone *(sola fide)*, is judged righteous on the basis of Christ's righteousness. Wesley affirms *sola fide*, but he departs from the reformers' views by stressing the actual regenerative effects that occur in the heart.

Second, by calling attention to 'nominal' Christianity Wesley sets up an important distinction. Nominal Christianity is marked by individuals for whom faith is little more than a confession made with the mouth, unsupported by actions. Genuine Christianity, on the other hand, is faith demonstrated through moral character and good deeds. Faith alone, unproven by good works, is nominal Christianity in Wesley's view.

In *Character of a Methodist* Wesley identifies what he later argued consistently is the real danger of an unreflective acceptance of *sola fide* — antinomianism. Citing the Apostle Paul, he observes: "'Do we then make void the law through faith? God forbid! Yea, we *establish* the law.'"[594] Wesley insists that a Methodist is marked by the "fruits of a living faith" consisting primarily of heart and life holiness. The caution against a rigidly forensic view of salvation is echoed and reinforced throughout Wesley's writing.[595]

Heartfelt religion is also a distinguishing characteristic of Methodism. Wesley argues that saving faith is felt deeply within the heart. He writes:

> "[A] Methodist is . . . one who 'loves the Lord his God with all his heart, and with all his soul, and with all his mind, and with all his strength'. God is the joy of his heart, and the desire of his soul, . . . "[596]

In the sermon *Salvation by Faith* (1738), he clarifies:

---

[594] Ibid. Cit. Rom. 3:31. Italics mine.

[595] See for example "The Law Established through Faith, Discourse I and II," Outler, *Sermons II*, 2: 20-43.

[596] "Character of a Methodist," Davies, *The Methodist Societies*, 9:35.

What faith is it then through which we are saved? It may be answered: first, in general, it is a faith in Christ — Christ, and God through Christ, are the proper objects of it. Herein, therefore, it is sufficiently, absolutely distinguished from the faith either of ancient or modern Heathens. And from the faith of a devil it is fully distinguished by this, — *it is not barely a speculative, rational thing, a cold, lifeless assent, a train of ideas in the head; but also a disposition of the heart.* For thus saith the Scripture, "With the heart man believeth unto righteousness;" and, "If thou shalt confess with thy mouth the Lord Jesus, and shalt believe with thy heart, that God hath raised him from the dead, thou shalt be saved."[597]

Wesley knows of no salvation that does not engage the whole being of the believer. While he does not deny that saving faith properly involves intellectual assent, he does deny that it is only that. There is something deeply personal and transformational about saving faith.

(2) Heart Purity

One of Wesley's recurring transformational metaphors is heart purity. Recalling the *Sermon on the Mount*, he observes:

"The pure in heart" are they whose hearts God hath "purified even as He is pure;" who are purified, through faith in the blood of Jesus, from every unholy affection; who, being "cleansed from all filthiness of flesh and spirit, perfect holiness in the" loving "fear of God."[598]

Salvation, for Wesley, is in effect purity of heart-motivation. Those whose hearts God has purified experience the reality of God: "The pure in heart see all things full of God," Wesley declares.[599]

---

[597] "Salvation by Faith," Outler, *Sermons I*, 1: 120. Italics mine.

[598] "Sermon on the Mount, III," Outler, *Sermons I*, 1: 510.

[599] Ibid., 1: 513.

226

The believer's inward experience of transformation is not the sole evidence of heart purity. Purity of heart must necessarily result in a transformed way of life. Wesley explains:

> [I]t is most true that the root of religion lies in the heart, in the inmost soul; that this is the *union of the soul with God,* the life of God in the soul of man. But if this root be really in the heart it cannot but put forth branches. And these are the several instances of *outward obedience,* which partake of the same nature with the root, and consequently are not only marks or signs, but substantial parts of religion.[600]

We see that, for Wesley, transformed living will always point back to its inward point of origin. He writes:

> [B]are outside religion, which has no root in the heart, is [worth nothing]; . . . God delighteth not in such outward services, no more than in Jewish burnt-offerings . . . .[601]

Wesley admits no doctrine of faith that does not link inward purity to outward holiness. The sacrifices of true religion arise from the heart and result in holy actions.

(3) Holiness

We saw earlier that another of Wesley's favorite metaphors for transformation is holiness. He writes in *Character of a Methodist*:

> All that is in the [Methodist's] soul is holiness to the Lord. . . . [The Methodist] continually presents his soul and body a living sacrifice, holy, acceptable to God.[602]

Wesley pinned the distinctiveness of Methodism conceptually on personal holiness. Several years after the publication of *Character,* he wrote a similarly

---

[600] "Sermon on the Mount, IV," Outler, *Sermons, I,* 1: 542. Italics mine.

[601] Ibid.

[602] "Character of a Methodist," Davies, *The Methodist Societies,* 9:38, 39.

minded treatise entitled *Advice to the People Called Methodists* (1745) in which he states:

> By Methodists I mean a people who profess to pursue *(in whatsoever measure they have attained) holiness of heart and life,* inward and outward conformity in all things to the revealed will of God; who place religion in an uniform resemblance of the great Object of it; in a steady *imitation* of him they worship in all his imitable perfections; more particularly in justice, mercy, and truth, or universal love filling the heart and governing the life.[603]

'Holiness of heart and life' represents the entire sanctification of one's existence — inner and outer, spiritual and ethical. It is not holiness in absolute or static terms, but rather holiness touching every aspect of one's life — every arena in which one reflects, makes moral decisions, and acts.

Despite frequent misunderstandings, Wesley consistently said that the believers are made progressively holy and that it is normal for various individuals to achieve holiness in varying degrees. He is clear on this issue in *Advice to the People Called Methodists.* Holiness must be considered "in whatsoever measure they have attained."[604] By protecting the term 'holiness' from the danger of static conceptualization, Wesley can reasonably argue that Methodism is the essence of New Testament religion without falling into dry moralism or, even worse, a modern version of Phariseeism.[605]

In a 1773 letter, Wesley recalls the principles upon which he and Charles had originally organized the Methodist movement:

---

[603] "Advice to the People Called Methodists," Davies, *The Methodist Societies,* 9: 123-24. Italics mine.

[604] Ibid., 123.

[605] See "Thoughts upon Methodism," Davies, *The Methodist Societies,* 9: 529: "From this short sketch of Methodism (so called) any man of understanding may easily discern that [Methodism] . . . is only plain scriptural religion, guarded by a few prudential regulations. The essence of it is *holiness of heart and life,* the circumstantials all point to this." Italics mine.

228

> We set out upon two principles: (1) None go to heaven without *holiness of heart and life*; (2) whosoever follows after this (whatever his opinions be) is my "brother and sister and mother." And we have not swerved an hair's breadth from either one or the other of these to this day.[606]

Wesley was convinced that holiness is the essence of salvation and therefore a prerequisite for heaven. On many other issues, he allowed room for disagreement among Christians of good will, but from this he never budged.

Clement

Given our analysis in chapter four, there should be little doubt that salvation, for Clement, essentially involves personal transformation. On this, there is no question that Clement and Wesley agree. However, given the vast differences in historical location and language, the nature of their agreement is too often obscured. Nonetheless, some important similarities can be identified.

(1) Experience of Faith

Clement attests to the priority of faith for salvation: "[Faith] . . . is essential to the true Gnostic, as essential as breath is to life for anyone living in this world."[607] Implicit in these words is a distinction between the true and the false believer. What sets the two apart is not the intellectual grasp of doctrine; it is heartfelt experience of faith. The argument develops gradually in Clement's thought. For example, in *Protrepticos* he writes:

> [L]et us repent with our whole heart, that with our whole heart we may be able to contain God. . . . Believe Him who is man and God, who suffered and is adored. . . . Believe, and receive salvation as your reward. Seek God, and your soul shall live.[608]

---

[606] Telford, *Letters*, 6: 61. Italics mine.

[607] *Strom.* 2.2:31.1,3; *FC* 85: 179.

[608] *Protr.* 10.106:4,4; *ANF* 2: 201.

The involvement of repentance and faith at the heart level comes into view. Saving faith is not just intellectual assent (though it is that); but it is more a matter of the heart.

Clement continues this theme on a more sophisticated level, in his opening remarks to *Stromateis* Book 1. He writes:

> When anyone elects out of faith to go to the banquet, he has *faith* as a reasonable criterion of judgment, and is strong to receive the *words of God*. From that point, *conviction* pursues him out of his superfluity. This is the real meaning of the prophet's words: "If you do not have faith, you cannot understand.[609]

Though clothed in allegory, his argument is really quite simple. Salvation can never be attained through intellectual investigation alone. The "words of God" (i.e., the gospel) demand faith in order to be grasped. Without faith, salvation is impossible.

The personal aspect of saving faith is illustrated by Clement in a lengthy discussion of epistemology, wherein he observes that there is an intrinsic relationship between experience and knowledge:

> *Scientific knowledge* [*episteme*] is constituted by reason and cannot be overthrown by any other form of reasoning. At this point, it is constantly involved with *revealed knowledge.*[610]

Personal experience produces a kind of knowledge which speculation, rationalization, and abstract reasoning cannot overturn. Conversely, the lack of personal experience renders knowledge of God incomplete at best. Clement applies these epistemological insights to saving faith. When the believer experiences the salvation that is spoken of Christianity's "revealed knowledge" — viz., Scripture — the scientific knowledge *(episteme)* produced by that experience

---

[609] *Strom.* 1.1:8.2; *FC* 85: 28. Italics mine.

[610] *Strom.* 2.17:76.1-77.6; *FC* 85: 209. Italics mine.

the believer that Scripture's record of revelation is true.[611] For Clement, personal experience is as much an essential aspect of faith as is practice. Clement declares: "Faith shall lead you, *experience* shall teach you, the Scripture shall train you."[612] Like Wesley, Clement argues that experience properly follows faith. The believer must believe in order to experience the blessedness of believing.

(2) Heart Purity

Clement employs the metaphor of heart purity in his transformational view of salvation. "Living with his Lord," he writes, "[the Christian Gnostic] . . . will remain his 'associate' and table-companion in the spirit, *pure in body and heart*, sanctified in this thought."[613] Purity of heart-motivation is essential to salvation.[614] What Clement means by purity of heart is very similar to the notion held by Wesley. Both take the concept from the *Sermon on the Mount.* However, like Wesley, Clement recognizes that purity has really to do with intention and motivation:

> Pure then as respects corporeal lusts, and pure in respect of *holy thoughts*, . . . [are those] who attain to the knowledge of God, when the chief faculty of the soul has nothing spurious to stand in the way of its power.[615]

---

[611] See above n.

[612] *Protr.* 9:88.1; *LCL*, 92: 195. Italics mine.

[613] *Strom.* 2.20:104.2; *FC* 85: 226. Italics mine.

[614] Wesley agrees. See for example "Sermon on the Mount, III," Outler, *Sermons, I,* 1: 510: "'The pure in heart' are they whose hearts God hath 'purified even as He is pure;' who are purified, through faith in the blood of Jesus, from every unholy affection."

[615] *Strom.* 4.6:39.4; *ANF* 2: 416. Italics mine. The soul's principal faculty is the intellect, wherein lies the capacity to reason and to know God.

Clement regards purity of heart — viz., *holy thoughts* — intention as the deciding factor in producing moral behavior. Purity is perfect only when, beginning with the thoughts of the heart, it is reflected in one's deeds and words.[616]

(3) Holiness

Holiness is a major theme for Clement and an oft-employed metaphor for Christian Gnostic character. Clement defines holiness in several ways, beginning with some foundational remarks in *Stromateis* 2:

> It is the Christian Gnostic who is "in the image and likeness," who *imitates* God so far as possible, leaving out none of the things which lead to the possible likeness, displaying continence, patience, righteous living, sovereignty over the passions, sharing his possessions so far as he can, doing good in word and deed.[617]

Clement's Christian Gnostic, who imitates God "so far as possible," is analogous to Wesley's Methodist, who strives to conform to God's will and to resemble God in "steady imitation."[618] Holiness for Clement's Christian Gnostic involves a renunciation and avoidance of sin and produces "purity of body and soul."[619] Like Wesley, Clement believes that heart intention is the principal issue in holiness. He declares, "purity is to think holy thoughts."[620] In *Protrepticos,* the evangelical appeal to learned Greeks, Clement speaks of God's "holy and blessed power" that makes it possible for human beings to serve God by imitating Christ. "Holy

---

[616] *Strom.* 4.22:142.4. Paraphrase of Greek text mine.

[617] *Strom.* 2.19:97.1; *FC* 85: 221. Italics mine.

[618] See esp. "Advice to the People Called Methodists," Davies, *The Methodist Societies,* 9: 123-24. Cf. also *Strom.* 4.26:171.4; *ANF* 2: 441: "For the [Christian] gnostic must, as far as is possible, *imitate* God." Italics mine.

[619] *Strom.* 4.25:161.1; *ANF* 2: 439.

[620] *Strom.* 4.22:142.1; *ANF* 2: 435.

service" is the irrefutable evidence that the spark of divine love has "burst forth into flame" within the soul.[621]

Summary

Clement and Wesley agree that holiness is unmistakable evidence of Christian conversion and faith. Lacking holiness, both would question whether salvation has actually occurred. Both believe that personal transformation the very essence of Christian salvation. Although wide differences in culture, language, and polemical concerns tend to obscure these similarities, other evidence should make them clearer.

B. Stages of Faith

Though the idea that salvation involves personal transformation is noteworthy in the attempt to link Wesley to Clement, more significant is that both are strongly committed to a development model of Christian existence, which is grounded in the observation that it is normal for a believer to pass through stages of faith on the way to spiritual maturity. This model has a number of advantages, not the least of which is its open-endedness. No believer ever achieves in this life an ability to trust God that admits no further increase. Every Christian may strive for and achieve even greater likeness to God.

Wesley

Always the keen observer of religious experience, John Wesley noted that among diverse individuals personal faith tends to vary qualitatively and quantitatively. The faith of some seems to increase at a quick rate of maturity and magnitude, while the faith of others remains immature for a longer period of time. Wesley found that these disparities were not infrequent, but on the contrary were quite common. As a result, he drew two important conclusions: (1) it is both

---

[621] *Protr.* 11:117,1-3; *ANF* 2: 204.

normal and expected that there will be degrees of faith among believers; (2) the faith of every believer is capable of increasing in both maturity and extent.[622]

(1) Passive versus Active Faith

The doctrine of stages or degrees of faith became more than just an abstraction for Wesley when it gained public prominence during the Moravian 'stillness' controversy. Wesley's chief protagonist was Philip Molther (1714-1780), a Moravian missionary from Herrnhut. Molther was first introduced to the Fetter Lane Society in 1739.[623] The Wesleys and Moravian missionary Peter Böhler had founded the society in 1738 shortly before Böhler left for America.[624] Meetings involved intense times of prayer, and emotions often ran high. Molther detested what he perceived to be a lack of proper worship restraint during these meetings, and as Zinzendorf's official emissary saw it as his duty to bring order into the situation.[625] The core theological issue was not so much emotionalism per se; it was the evangelical doctrine of assurance — i.e., inner heart certainty that one has believed and truly been saved. The controversy erupted over the proper

---

[622] See "Christian Perfection," Outler, *Sermons II*, 2: 105: "But it should be premised that there are several stages in Christian life as well as in natural."

[623] See Ward and Heitzenrater, *Journals and Diaries, II*, 19: 119, n. 2. For additional background see Rack, *Reasonable Enthusiast*, 202-03 and Rupp, *Religion in England 1688-1791*, 363-64.

[624] It has been debated what kind of society Fetter Lane was. See Rack, *Reasonable Enthusiast*, 141. Although Böhler's involvement should not be minimized, it is clear that the concerns of the society, coupled with the fact that John and Charles were its acknowledged leaders, make it Methodist in character. It is therefore all the more ironic that in the end, the Wesleys would be forced to depart and Fetter Lane would become entirely a Moravian work.

[625] On Nikolaus Ludwig Graf von Zinzendorf see *ODCC*, s.v. Molther's influence was apparent not long after his arrival. See Ward and Heitzenrater, *Journals and Diaries, II*, 19: 119-20: "In the evening I met the women of our society at Fetter Lane, where some of our brethren strongly intimated that none of them had any true faith; and then asserted in plan terms (1) that till they had true faith, they ought to be *still*, that is (as they explained themselves) 'to abstain from "the means of grace", as they are called — the Lord's Supper *in particular*'; (2) 'that *the ordinances are not means of grace,* there being no other means than Christ'."

way to achieving assurance, and it was on this issue that Wesley and the Moravians, Molther in particular, disagreed.

Molther was Protestant Quietist by both upbringing and preference, who subscribed to the Moravian notion of 'stillness' — that is, ceasing from all outward acts of piety, including partaking of the sacrament — as the only path to assurance. 'Stillness' required a posture of utter quietude and passivity before God. Molther advised penitents to refrain church attendance, holy communion, fasting, prayer and Scripture reading.[626] Only by passively waiting upon God, he insisted, could one hope to receive the heartfelt assurance of faith.

The Wesleys, following longstanding Anglican practice, had been teaching the Fetter Lane members to seek assurance of faith by actively pursuing the means of grace, which included private prayer, Bible reading, and partaking of the Lord's Supper. Participation in the ordained means by which God normally conveys grace, not passive waiting is the way to assurance of salvation.[627] In no uncertain terms Wesley denounced Molther's stillness doctrine, arguing that it was flawed, having no support either in Scripture or church fathers. Molther's apophatic approach to assurance bordered on mysticism.

As part of his polemical attack, Wesley took as his paradigm the faithful soul who progresses through the stages of faith to perfection. He writes:

> I believe, . . . [t]here are *degrees of faith,* and that a man may have *some degree* of it before all things in him are become new; before he has the full assurance of faith, the abiding witness of the Spirit, or the clear perception that Christ dwelleth in him. . . Accordingly I believe that there is *a degree of justifying faith* (and consequently a state of justification) short of, and commonly antecedent to, . . . [assurance].[628]

---

[626] Wesley enumerates a list of stillness doctrine proscriptions in Ward and Heitzenrater, *Journal and Diaries, II,* 19: 132.

[627] Cf. "The Means of Grace," Outler, *Sermons I,* BE 1: 378-97.

[628] Ward and Heitzenrater, *Journal and Diaries, II,* 19: 132.

235

Wesley insists that the absence of assurance is not by itself evidence that an individual necessarily lacks justifying faith. Although he affirms evangelical piety and the reception of a subjective assurance of faith, he refuses to make it the decisive factor. Instead, he resorts to the ancient catholic idea that saving faith begins with assent, and then is followed by assurance. An individual may believe and therefore be saved without having yet received the assurance of salvation.

(2) Weak Faith versus Saving Faith

In addition to his radical insistence upon 'stillness', Molther said that faith which is weak or accompanied by doubts is the equivalent of no faith at all. Wesley again reacted strongly, writing:

> By 'weak faith' I understand, (1) That which is mixed with fear, particularly of not enduring to the end; (2) that which is mixed with doubt, whether we have not deceived ourselves, and whether our sins be *indeed* forgiven; (3) That which has not yet *purified the heart,* at least not from all its idols. And thus *weak* I find the *faith* of almost all believers to be, within a short time after they have first 'peace with God'.[629]

Wesley admits that doubt, fear and even sin may characterize the person whose faith is weak and immature. He cites as an example the Apostle Peter for whom Jesus had prayed that his faith might remain strong. Yet on the night of the Lord's arrest Peter not only doubted and feared for his own life, he sinned by denying his master. In spite of Peter's miserable failure, Wesley observes:

> Nevertheless he was 'clean, by the word Christ had spoken to him', i.e., *justified,* though 'tis plain he had not *a clean heart.* Therefore, there are *degrees in faith,* and *weak faith* may yet be *true faith.*"[630]

---

[629] Ibid., 19: 154.

[630] Ibid., 19: 155.

Would Molther deny that Peter was saved, even though his faith proved entirely weak and inadequate at that moment in time? Wesley thinks not.

Faith of a Servant versus Faith of a Son

One of Wesley's clearest expositions of the developmental faith paradigm was produced shortly before his death. In his 1788 sermon *On the Discoveries of Faith,* Wesley argues from Scripture that there is a clear distinction between the "faith of a servant" and the "faith of a son."[631] The faith of a servant is rudimentary in nature. It is genuine yet servile, founded upon a cringing fear of divine punishment. Such faith is efficacious, though, because it produces obedience to God and moral transformation.

Filial faith, the faith of a son, also produces obedience, but for different reasons, which makes it qualitatively better and quantitatively greater. The faith of a son is free "from the spirit of bondage unto fear"; it exists in "the spirit of childlike love."[632] Filial faith is the product of an intimate and loving relationship between the believer and God. Such faith is both mature and still maturing. There is no earthly limit to its increase and growth. Both the faith of a servant and the faith of a son produce actual righteousness, but Wesley clearly regards the latter as a higher and better sort.

To summarize, Wesley views the life of faith as progressively active, normally passing through stages as it matures. There are degrees of faith. Weak faith is still faith; it justifies and therefore saves, even though it is immature and incomplete. The mature faith of a son is superior because it is based upon a profound love and depth of intimacy. Such faith imparts a dynamic inward

---

[631] "On the Discoveries of Faith," Outler, *Sermons, IV,* 4: 35. See esp. n. 52 for a brief account of the two faiths in Wesley's thought.

[632] Ibid.

consciousness of God's presence and heartfelt knowledge of God as "Abba, Father."[633]

Clement

Again, our analysis in chapter four should leave little doubt that Clement views faith in terms of progressive degrees or stages. We observed there how Clement measures the difference between lesser and greater faith by the believer's motives for obeying God. The one who obeys the moral commands out of a puerile fear of retribution, or simply as an expression of reverence lives at a lower stage of faith. Mature faith is achieved only when the believer obeys from a heart filled with love for God.

Clement remarks that it is normal for one to believe initially with a certain amount of fear or timidity. Faith grounded in fear is efficacious because it is exercised through repentance and hope; it is part of a larger soteriological pedagogy whose outcome is love. He writes:

> [F]aith is exercised in relation to repentance and hope, *caution* in connection with faith, and . . . the patient practice of all these combines with a *process of learning* to have its outcome in *love.*[634]

Fear plays a facilitative and intermediate role within Clement's soteriological framework. As he explains:

> So just as the days are a part of our ongoing life, so *fear* is the beginning of *love*, and as it develops, [fear] turns into faith and then love. My *fear* of a wild animal is different, being combined with hatred (remember that there are two kinds of *fear*). [Fear of God]. . . is more like my fear of my father, where the *fear* is combined with love. Again, in my fear of chastisement, I am showing self-love,

---

[633] Ibid., 4: 36. See also "The Witness of the Spirit I and II," Outler, *Sermons, I,* 1: 270-298 *passim.*

[634] *Strom.* 2.9:45.1; *FC* 85: 189. Italics mine. On the meaning of "caution" see Liddell & Scott, *Lexicon*, s.v. εὐλάβεια. The term indicates *reverence, piety, timidity.* Wilson translates "fear" for εὐλάβεια in the same pericope. See *ANF* 2: 357.

and choose to feel fear. And anyone who *fears* to offend his father is showing love towards him. How blessed is the person who finds faith, being compounded of *love* and *fear.* Faith is a force leading to salvation, a power leading to eternal life.[635]

Clement affirms fear as a valid, even essential stage of faith. It is a stage of faith that is useful in establishing a saving relationship with God and fostering spiritual growth. Though perhaps, Clement does not draw the kind of sharp contrast that Wesley does, it is clear that both writers distinguish relationship with God based on fear from relationship based on love. The former is the initial stage that one passes through on the way to the latter.

Love, of course, is the superior motivation for serving God. Clement recalls the Apostle Paul's statement in Romans 13 concerning love when he writes:

"*Love* is," then, "the fulfilling of the law;" like as Christ, that is in the presence of the Lord who loves us; and our loving teaching of, and discipline according to Christ. By *love*, then, the commands not to commit adultery, and not to covet one's neighbour's wife, are fulfilled, [these sins being] formerly prohibited by *fear.*[636]

In practice, fear and love produce the same moral result, obedience. But the benefits attached to these motives have different kinds of rewards. Clement continues:

The same work, . . . [i.e., obedience to the commands], presents a difference, according as it is done by *fear* or accomplished by *love*, and is wrought by faith or by knowledge. Rightly, therefore, their rewards are different."[637]

---

[635] *Strom.* 2.12:53.3-5; *FC* 85: 195. Here, we find a remarkably clear statement (for Clement) of how the term 'fear' may be used. He uses the more usual term for fear, φόβος, as opposed to εὐλάβεια. The effect is the same.

[636] *Strom.* 4.18:113.5,6; *ANF* 2: 430. Cit. Romans 13:10. Italics mine.

[637] *Strom.* 4.18:113.6, 114.1; *ANF* 2: 430. Italics mine.

Clement takes the position that the motivation behind an act is at least as significant as the act itself, if not more so. Again, this corresponds well with Wesley's insistence that purity of intention and motivation are more important than action.

In his description of the Christian Gnostic in *Stromateis* 7, Clement discusses the difference that motivation makes in the degree of holiness achieved. Holiness produced by fear and that produced by love are both salvific, but they differ qualitatively. Again, there is correspondence with Wesley. Clement observes:

> [R]ighteousness is twofold, the one caused by *love*, the other by *fear*. . . . [T]hey who turn to faith and righteousness from fear endure forever. . . . *[F]ear* brings about abstinence from evil . . . [but] *love* prompts us to do good, building us up to a willing mind, in order that one may hear from the Lord the words, "No longer do I call you servants, but friends," and may thenceforward join with confidence in the prayers.[638]

While the righteousness achieved through fear and that gained through love appear externally the same, the *quality* of life produced through each is not. Faith guided by fear is salvific; but fear-founded faith in and of itself is not the *telos* of Christian living. Righteousness produced by love manifests a more intimate relationship with God, which in turn is marked by confidence with regard to prayers. However, whether the product of fear or love, Clement knows no righteousness that is not actual. As we noted in chapter four, there is virtually no consideration of imputed righteousness in Clement's soteriology.

Conclusions

We find several places where the thought of Wesley and Clement intersect with respect to degrees or stages of faith. First, both recognize that the degree of

---

[638] *Strom.* 7.12.78.7–79.1; Hort and Mayor, *Miscellanies Book VII*, 137. Italics mine.

faith normally varies among believers and is contingent upon whether an individual's faith springs from fear or from love. Both admit that faith arising from either motive is efficacious and therefore salvific. Second, the quality of the believer's relationship with God is entirely dependent upon the motivation for which the individual believes and obeys God. The one whose obedience is motivated by love experiences a fuller, more meaningful relationship with God. Finally, faith arising from fear is only the initial stage in the spiritual pedagogy of the believer. The *telos* is faith grounded in love, which is an anticipation of eternal blessedness and the life to come.

Although the evidence is not conclusive, there is strong circumstantial warrant for suggesting that Wesley and Clement were guided by similar ideas. Again, recalling that it is Wesley himself who establishes the link between himself and Clement, we believe that Wesley was indeed aware of Clement's notions of salvation as personal transformation and faith development. If so, he found in Clement an affirmation of the implicit teachings of Scripture as well as something of his own spiritual pilgrimage.

2. Love

Wesley

There is no better evidence of faith than, says Wesley, than love. In *Character of a Methodist* he writes:

> [A] Methodist is one who has '*the love of God* shed abroad in his heart by the Holy Ghost given unto him'; one who '*loves the Lord* his God with all his heart, and with all his soul and with all his mind, and with all his strength'.[639]

The Methodist possesses "perfect love," which replaces fear of judgment with profound joy in the believer's relationship to God.[640]

---

[639] "Character of a Methodist," Davies, *The Methodist Societies*, 9: 35. Italics mine.

[640] Ibid.

To love perfectly, however, entails love for neighbor as well. Wesley frequently associates the idea of loving neighbor as self with command language. He writes of the Methodist:

> And while . . . [the Methodist] thus always exercises his love to God, by prayer without ceasing, rejoicing evermore, and in everything giving thanks, *this commandment is written in his heart,* that 'he who loveth God, loves his brother also.' And . . . [the Methodist] according 'loves his neighbour as himself'; he loves every man as his own soul. His heart is full of love to all mankind, to every child of 'the Father of the spirits of all flesh'.[641]

Wesley follows the Apostle Paul's exhortation in Romans 13: Love for one another fulfills the righteous demands of the law. [642] Unquestionably, this is one of Wesley's favorites themes. It can be said without fear of contradiction that Wesley's grasp of holiness was based upon an understanding of love as the fulfillment of the law. In his now famous sermon *The Circumcision of the Heart*, delivered January 1, 1733, he exhorts:

> "Love is the fulfilling of the law," "the end of the commandment". Very excellent things are spoken of love; it is the essence, the spirit, the life of all virtue. It is not only the first and great command, but it is all the commandments in one.[643]

---

[641] Ibid., 9: 37. Italics mine.

[642] Cit. Romans 13:8-10: "Owe no one anything, except to love one another; for the one who loves another has fulfilled the law. The commandments, 'You shall not commit adultery; You shall not murder; You shall not steal; You shall not covet'; and any other commandment, are summed up in this word, 'Love your neighbor as yourself. Love does no wrong to a neighbor; therefore, love is the fulfilling of the law."

[643] "The Circumcision of the Heart," Outler, *Sermons, I*, 1: 407. Cit. Romans 13:10; 1 Timothy 1:5.

This important sermon sets forth with clarity what Wesley believed and taught with respect to the virtuous life. Love is the only true fulfilling of the law open to human beings.[644]

At the height of the 'stillness' controversy, Wesley examined the Moravian claim that the sole duty of every Christian is simply "to believe."[645] He counters by arguing that the believer's duty is not only to believe, but also to prove the genuineness of one's faith by keeping the commands.[646] Faith by itself does not motivate one to Christian service, but faith motivated by love creates a genuine desire to serve. He writes:

> As glorious and honourable as [faith] . . . is, it is not the end of the commandment. God hath given this honour to love alone: Love is the end of all the commandments of God. Love is the end, the sole end, of every dispensation of God, from the beginning of the world to the consummation of all things.[647]

There are few other themes appearing with more frequency across the breadth of Wesley's writing than faith expressed through love.

Clement

Like Wesley, Clement grounds his doctrine of love in the levitical command "you shall love your neighbor as yourself" — which he views as the heart and soul of the Mosaic Law.[648] Clement is well aware of the significance of the command, especially in light of the affirmation accorded it by Jesus in the Matthean tradition. In the parable of the rich young ruler Jesus is asked,

---

[644] What is remarkable about this sermon, in addition to its clarity concerning Wesley's views, is that it was written and delivered over five years before Wesley's Aldersgate experience. For a helpful introduction, see Outler, *Sermons I*, 1: 389-400.

[645] Ward and Heitzenrater, *Journals and Diaries, II*, 19: 154.

[646] Ibid., 19:155.

[647] "The Law Established through Faith," II, Outler, *Sermons, II*, 2: 38.

[648] Leviticus 19:18.

"Teacher, what good deed must I do to have eternal life?" Jesus replies that one must keep the Mosaic prohibitions regarding murder, adultery, theft, and bearing false testimony. He then connects these connects to their underlying principle: "You [also] shall love your neighbor as yourself."[649] Clement, like Wesley, interprets love as the essential virtue upon which the entire edifice of the Mosaic law rests.

The perfection of the Christian, for Clement, depends on fulfilling the command to love. In *Paedagogus* he reprimands those who desire wealth, arguing that it is better to possess the invisible treasure of God's kingdom. He writes:

> For such an one — one who fulfils the command, 'Thou shalt *love* thy neighbour as thyself' — is *perfect*. For this is the luxury — the treasured wealth.[650]

In the kingdom of God, the one who is wealthy is the one who possesses the sublime treasure of love.

Love takes many forms including "gentleness, goodness, patience, freedom from jealousy or envy, freedom from hatred, no holding of grudges."[651] The Christian Gnostic is required "to love strangers for their own sake, enemies for the sake of peace, our neighbor for the sake of mutual happiness."[652] In every instance, fulfilling the command to love benefits both the one who loves and the one who is loved. For Clement, love is a grace. He writes: "It is God who grants us gifts of good things, [therefore] . . . we ought as servants of the grace of God to sow God's gracious gifts and enable our neighbors to become people of honor."[653]

---

[649] Matthew 19:16-22 and v. 19b.

[650] *Protr.* 2.12:120.4,5; *ANF* 2: 268. Italics mine.

[651] *Strom.* 2.18:87.2; *FC* 85: 216.

[652] *Strom.* 2.18:88.1-90.3; *FC* 85: 216-18 *passim*.

[653] *Strom.* 2.18:96.4: *FC* 85: 221.

As with Wesley, Clement sees a crucial relationship between the law and love. In *Stromateis* 1 he discusses the law's function:

> The Law cares for its subjects; it *educates* them in reverence for God; it tells them what they ought to do; it keeps them from offences; it sets a penalty for a modest offence; when it sees a person in a seemingly incurable state, plunged up to his neck in crime, then in concern that the others may be infected by him, as if it were amputating a limb of the body, it executes him for the greatest health of all.[654]

The law functions as a tutor in righteousness; it educates concerning what is good and just, in part by identifying what is evil and unjust. The right use of the law, however, includes more than just the ability to distinguish good from bad or the righteous from the unrighteous. Clement recalls Paul's warning to young Timothy concerning those who would instruct others in the moral demands of the law. The law is good, but the right use of the law does not reside in natural understanding. Rather, "[t]he aim of our charge [i.e., instruction] is love proceeding from a pure heart, a good conscience and a sincere faith."[655]

Summary

Both Clement and Wesley stress the doctrine of love as the only possible fulfillment on earth of the righteousness demanded by the law. Both regard love as commensurate with personal holiness. Love is the irrefutable evidence of the holiness that constitutes salvation. As with most matters, Wesley and Clement come at this issue from different perspectives; but these differences were probably shaped more by historical and social location than content. Clement writes to an audience whose worldview was shaped by classical Greek philosophy. As an apologetic tactic, he empties idealistic, aesthetic love of its abstract sterility and fills it with Christian meaning and purpose. Love is not a virtue to be

---

[654] *Strom.* 1.27:171.4; *FC* 85: 149. Italics mine. See also *Strom.* 2.18:91.1; *FC* 85: 218: "[T]he Law is good and human, a 'tutor leading us to Christ.'"

[655] *Strom.* 1.27:175.2; *FC* 85: 151. Cit. 1 Timothy 1:3-7.

contemplated; it is a state of active obedience to God and service to neighbor. Wesley's audience was shaped by Lockean experimentalism. He emphasizes the practical and experiential aspects of love, which frees the individual to love as Christ loved. If one is at least willing make some allowance for differences caused by historical separation, Wesley and Clement are notably in agreement concerning the Christian's empowerment and obligation to love.

3. Perfection

The concept and language of perfection is a large theme shared by both writers. Since this is a diverse topic, we will examine it in under three subheadings: progress, love, and regeneration.

A. Perfection as Progress

Wesley

As we have seen, John Wesley views salvation generally in a dynamic sense. This is also the case when it comes to his discussion of the believer's perfection. For Wesley, the Christian life is a linear process that begins with saving faith and progresses until death, when the soul achieves absolute holiness and happiness. In the present, however, one may expect to be made holy in heart and life (hence, perfect) according to the demands of the gospel. This perfection, as we saw above, consists of love for God and neighbor.

In concert with classical Lutheran and Reformed thought, Wesley makes a distinction between justification and sanctification. The one has to do with forensic pardon, the other with actual righteousness and moral renewal. But Wesley departs from the Reformers, Luther especially, by rejecting the notion that only upon death is the believer made actually righteous. For Luther, the believer does not really die to the power of sin until he physically dies and is resurrected. Perfection has do with dying with Christ now and looking forward to physical death when the problem of sin is finally vanquished. [656] For Wesley, perfection has to do with holiness of heart and life now. It is the temporal *telos* of the sanctifying process begun at justification that admits of continual increase until death.

Wesley produced a series of thirteen addresses based on the *Sermon on the Mount* that serve well to illustrate his view of Christian perfectability. Although there were many published interpretations of the *Sermon* available in Wesley's day, his is important for understanding Christian perfection and spiritual progress. In the *Sermon on the Mount I* Wesley writes concerning the *Beatitudes*:

> Some have supposed that he [our Lord] designed in these to point out the several *stages of the Christian course*, the steps which a Christian successively takes in his journey to the promised land; others, that all the *particulars* here set down belong at all times to every Christian. [657]

Some see the Christian *Beatitudes* as stages of progress, others as particulars along the way. In the end, it does not matter. He continues:

> It is undoubtedly true that both 'poverty of spirit' and every other temper which is here mentioned are at all times found in a greater or less degree in every *real Christian*. And it is equally true that real Christianity always begins in poverty of spirit, and goes on in the order here set down till 'the man of God' is made *'perfect'*. [658]

Wesley does not identify those who viewed the *Beatitudes* as stages of Christian progress, but as will be seen momentarily, Clement is one who indeed had done so. Whether as stages or particulars, the Christian life is a pilgrimage in which

---

[656] Luther is somewhat inconsistent here. On the one hand, he suggests that the when the justified believer has the Spirit; the process of sanctification has begun. On the other, he denies that the believer may become actually righteous until death. For a concise treatment of these matters see Paul Althaus, *The Theology of Martin Luther,* trans. Robert C. Schultz (Philadelphia: Fortress Press, 1966), esp. 269-71, 408.

[657] "Sermon on the Mount, I," Outler, *Sermons, I,* 1: 475. Italics mine.

[658] Ibid. Italics mine.

the "real Christian," according to Wesley, is expected to acquire and increase in virtue along way.[659]

Wesley must have recognized that primitive Christianity, especially in the East, had conceptualized spiritual growth on a neo-platonic model of soul ascent. He also seems aware of the limitations of that model in his day, not the least of which would have been its Roman Catholic mystical connotations.[660] Instead of a vertical model of ascent to perfection, Wesley adopted a linear model of spiritual growth that both set him apart from the mystical tradition and also better reflected a biblical view of time and history. The theological content found in both structures, however, is essentially the same. The Christian life begins with repentance and justification, which are accompanied by spiritual and moral regeneration. Faith extends its reach over time to bring about the transformation of every part of life until finally, the believer becomes mature or perfect.

Wesley was convinced that perfection is a realizable goal. Individuals who witnessed to having experienced it reinforced this conviction. Moreover, he found that those who reported having been made perfect shared some traits in common. For example, in his journal entry for March 6, 1760 Wesley records the testimonies of two women. Both had experienced a progression from initial faith marked by fear and uneasiness to expansive love for God and hatred of sin. He comments:

> I observe, the spirit and experience of these two run exactly parallel. *Constant communion* with God the Father and Son *fills* their hearts with *humble love.* Now this is what I always did and do now mean by *'perfection'.*[661]

---

[659] Ibid.

[660] Wesley had no desire to speculate concerning invisible reality. He was an empiricist philosophically and a traditionalist theologically. See *Of the Gradual Improvement of Natural Philosophy,* Jackson, *Works,* 13: 482-87.

[661] Ward and Heitzenrater, *Journal and Diaries, IV,* 21: 245.

248

Wesley emphasizes the efficaciousness of faith in saving from sin the one who believes. Although justification brings pardon for sins and the justified individual is no longer bound to commit sin as a consequence of the fall, he/she will likely still struggle with sin. The indisputable sign of perfected faith, according to Wesley, is deliverance from all sin. In the sermon *On Christian Perfection* (1741), he writes:

> It remains, then, that Christians are saved in this world from all sin, from all unrighteousness; that they are now in such a sense *perfect as not to commit sin,* and to be freed from evil thoughts and evil tempers.[662]

Wesley states unequivocally that believers are made perfect such that they no longer are liable to commit sin. At face value this seems to be a rather strong statement, yet it is a recurring theme in his thought.[663]

We find that Wesley set forth the implications and offered support for his position in two later sermons. In the earlier of the two, *On Sin in Believers* (1763), he writes that the one who believes has "power both over outward and inward sin" from the moment of justification.[664] Those who are justified do not normally as a matter of course continue in sin; they keep God's commands. However, Wesley admits that following justification, believers normally experience an ongoing struggle between two opposing principles, nature and grace — i.e., the fallen nature of one's humanity and the uplifting power of justifying grace.[665] On the one

---

[662] "Christian Perfection," Outler, *Sermons, II*, 2: 120. Italics mine.

[663] See also: "A Dialogue Between An Antinomian and His Friend," Jackson, *Works*, 10: 273: "And whoso are thus made pure and perfect are delivered from the dominion of sin. They do also bear forth the fruits of righteousness, not in order to become more holy, but because they are perfectly holy, through faith"; and, "A Farther Appeal to Men of Reason and Religion, Part II," Cragg, *Appeals to Men of Reason and Religion,* 11: 259: "Art thou thus led by the Spirit to every good word and work, till God hath thereby made thy faith perfect?"

[664] "On Sin in Believers," Outler, *Sermons, I,* 1: 321.

[665] Ibid., 1: 321-22.

hand, the believer is delivered, set free from the power of sin. On the other, the believer struggles with a latent inclination toward sin.

In the sermon *The Repentance of Believers* (1767) Wesley resolves the dilemma. He states that after justification the struggle between nature and grace ensues in some believers until death.[666] Within the divine economy, however, there is hope for a "second change" in which, through another impartation of grace, the struggle between nature and grace abates and the soul is cleansed. This perfecting grace, like justifying grace, is received through repentance and faith.[667] The believer is enabled to perfectly love God and to live in holiness from that point on until death.[668]

Clement

We saw in chapter four that Clement views the Christian life in terms of a progressive advance through stages. We can now show how this relates to his view of perfection. In order to highlight the similarity of Clement's thinking to Wesley's, we shall examine a pericope in which the Alexandrian discusses the *ordo salutis.*

In *Stromateis* 4.6 Clement examines the Matthean *Beatitudes.* He interprets Jesus' sayings as analogues of the soul's ascent to perfect blessedness. In every material circumstance — poverty, mourning, meekness, thirst, etc. — a spiritual

---

[666] "The Repentance of Believers," Outler, *Sermons, I,* 1: 346.

[667] "The Repentance of Believers," Outler, *Sermons, I,* 1: 346-47. See also n. 81. Wesley leans toward Luther's dialectical *simul justus et peccator* position with regard to the justified believer in whom nature and grace struggle. What sets Wesley apart from Luther, as Outler notes, is the possibility of a "second change" in which the "carnal mind" is extinguished. This "second change," Wesley consistently argues elsewhere, does not imply absolute or sinless perfection.

[668] Ibid., 1: 348-50. These ideas are echoed in "The Law Established through Faith, II" (Outler, *Sermons, II,* 2: 42) where Wesley says that faith not only purifies the heart from "all vile affections", but "if it have its perfect work, it fills him with all goodness, righteousness, and truth. It brings all heaven into his soul, and causes him to walk in the light, even as God is in the light."

lesson is taught and the possibility of spiritual growth is presented. The goal is Christian *gnosis,* mature knowledge of God, which he identifies as "the communication of immortality," viz., eternal life.[669] Clement's task then, is to describe the soul's progress from ignorance to *gnosis,* i.e., from immaturity to perfection, in terms his Hellenistic audience can understand.

First, Clement notes that spiritual progress is impossible without a fundamental alteration of the soul's disposition. Before the soul can turn to God and the good, it must turn from what is sinful and evil. Even the Stoics and Plato recognized that a decisive turning from what has kept the soul in darkness must precede any degree of enlightenment.[670] This turning Clement calls "conversion."[671]

Next, he applies these philosophical insights to the Christian concept of salvation. Since conversion and justification are inward realities, they are by definition invisible. The relation between them is similar to cause and effect. Conversion produces justification, which Clement supports with Matthew 10:39: "Those who find their life will lose it, and those who lose their life for my sake will find it." 'Losing' necessarily and logically precedes 'gaining'. Although by nature invisible, justification is marked outwardly by abstinence from evil. Clement has made a significant move here: justification, which by definition constitutes salvation, is manifested by an outward change in ethical behavior. Salvation therefore will always be apparent in the moral life of the believer.

As important as justification is, it does not constitute the *telos* of a Christian's life on earth. Perfection is demanded. Whereas justification is

---

[669] *Strom.* 4.6:27.2; *ANF* 2: 414. Gr., κοινωνία ἀφθαρσίας — "communion" or "sharing of immortality." This phrase combines St. Paul's common uses of κοινωνία and ἀφθαρσίας and is designed to emphasize that true *gnosis* of God guarantees eternal life.

[670] *Strom.* 4.6:28.1,2; *ANF* 2: 414.

[671] μεταστροφή — *turning from one thing to another.* Liddell & Scott, *Lexicon,* s.v.

primarily abstinence from evil, perfection is defined positively as "Christlike beneficence," i.e., intentional well doing.[672]

Although he comes at the issue in a slightly different way, Clement, like Wesley, envisions the Christian life as marked by two aspects of the same salvific reality. Genuine conversion and justification will produce abstinence from moral evil and wrongdoing. Perfection will be marked by doing moral good as Christ did good, motivated and sustained by love. Clement explains: [I]t is by *beneficence* that the *love*, which is according to the [Christian] gnostic ascending scale, ... *proclaims itself.*"[673]

Summary

Both Wesley and Clement view perfection as part of the process of salvation, and both see it as a higher level of Christian existence. We already observed in chapter four that Clement views St. Paul's words in Romans 1:17 as referring to two levels of faith, one which "lies beneath as a foundation", the other "which admits of growth and perfection."[674] Wesley echoes this interpretation in many places. One of the better examples is found in the sermon *Salvation by Faith*, when he writes that the Christian proceeds in divine strength "'faith to faith,' 'grace to grace' until at length he comes unto a perfect man, unto the measure of the stature of the fullness of Christ.'"[675]

Though Wesley never abandons a progressive model of perfection, he will come to admit a second decisive work of grace which perfects the believer's faith, ends the struggle between nature and grace, and enables the believer to actively

---

[672] *Strom.* 4.6:29.3; *ANF* 2: 414. Εὐποιία ("beneficence") connotes active well-doing and is synonymous with εὐεργεσία.

[673] *Strom.* 4.6:29.3,4; *ANF* 2: 414. Italics mine.

[674] See ch. 4, n. 127. Cf. *Strom.* 5.1:2.4-6; *ANF* 2: 444.

[675] "Salvation by Faith," Outler, *Sermons, I,* 1: 124-25.

carry out the good that the gospel demands. Clement, on the other hand, does not speak of a decisive second change. Instead, he sees the progress of the believer accomplished in stages of ever-increasing virtue. Clement's vertical ascent from justification to Christian gnostic perfection differs conceptually from Wesley's linear model, but the meaning and implications are the same. Those who are justified should expect to progress on to perfection in this life in order that their being and acting should take on the character of Christ.

B. Perfection and Love

Wesley

Love is the most commonly employed definition of perfection in the thought of John Wesley. In this respect Wesley consistently argued two points: (1) the law of God demands obedience that is perfect in scope, degree, and extent; (2) the only perfection attainable by the Christian on earth is perfection in love, which in turn fulfills the righteousness demanded by the law. The first point Wesley makes in *The Righteousness of Faith* (1746):

> [The] . . . law or [first] covenant (usually called the covenant of *works*) given by God to man in paradise, required an obedience perfect in all its parts, entire and wanting in nothing, as the condition of his eternal continuance in the holiness and happiness wherein he was created.[676]

Flawless obedience was required by the first covenant in order that Adam might remain in the state of blessedness in which he was originally created. Wesley states that this requirement has not been abrogated, either by time or by the fall. Perfect obedience is still righteous demand of the law.[677] The problem is that the

---

[676] "The Righteousness of Faith," Outler, *Sermons, I,* 1: 204.

[677] See also "Sermon on the Mount, I," Outler, *Sermons, I,* 1: 479 where Wesley argues that the first stage of repentance is the recognition that perfect obedience is the divine requirement, but that our fallen humanity prevents us from achieving it. He writes: "How shall he pay him that he oweth? Were he [hypothetically] from this moment to perform the most perfect obedience to every command of God, this would make no amends for a single sin, for any one act of past

fall produced an inability to render the perfect obedience required to satisfy the law's demand. If perfect obedience is no longer a real possibility for human beings, then salvation also is impossible — unless somehow the righteous demand of the law can be met.

Wesley argues that in such a fallen world as this where perfect obedience is not possible, perfect motivation is, and that perfect love (which is the equivalent theologically of perfect motivation or attitude) fulfills the righteousness demanded by the law. Now of course, this view would be theological liberalism in a fairly extreme form were it not for the fact that Wesley is able to base his views on holy Scripture. In his sermon *On Perfection* (1766), he writes:

> What is then the perfection of which man is capable while he dwells in a corruptible body? It is the complying with that kind command, 'My son, give me thy heart.' It is the 'loving the Lord his God with all his heart, and with all his soul, and with all his mind'. This is the sum of *Christian perfection:* it is all comprised in that one word, *love.*[678]

Love is the earthly *telos* of salvation, the realizable goal that God demands of all believers in Christ. Wesley writes in another place:

> *Love is the end of all the commandments of God.* Love is the end, the sole end, of every dispensation of God, from the beginning of the world to the consummation of all things.[679]

---

disobedience; seeing he owes God all the service he is able to perform, from this moment to all eternity: Could he pay this, it would make no manner of amends for what he ought to have done before. He sees himself therefore utterly helpless with regard to atoning for his past sins; utterly unable to make any amends to God, to pay any ransom for his own soul."

[678] "On Perfection," Outler, *Sermons, III,* 3: 74. Italics mine. Note Outler's discussion of the dating of this sermon, pp. 70-71.

[679] "The Law Established through Faith, II," Outler, *Sermons, II,* 2: 38. Italics mine. Actually, Wesley suggests that righteousness, whether under the Adamic covenant of works or the post-Adamic covenant of grace, is defined by love. See "The Doctrine of Original Sin, Part III,"

254

The grace of God that justifies the believer through faith produces an aspiring love for God, which in turn enables the believer to fulfill the righteous demands of the law. The sum of perfection is love.

Other biblical images of perfection — the "mind of Christ" of Philippians 2:5 ff., the "new self" created in "true righteousness and holiness of Ephesians 4:24, the wholly sanctified believer of 1 Thessalonians 5:23, and the gospel portrait of one saved from sin[680] — all fall logically under the aegis of perfect love. Wesley believed that Christian perfection is best defined in terms of motivation and aspiration; that is, what one loves will determine what one does.

Wesley consistently taught that perfect love is attainable in this life and that it is the ground of all inward and outward holiness. He illustrates this point in *The Scripture Way of Salvation* (1765):

> [A]t the same that we are justified, yea, in that very moment *sanctification* begins. . . . There is a *real* as well as a *relative* change. We are inwardly renewed by the power of God. We feel the '*love of God* shed abroad in our heart by the Holy Ghost which is given unto us', *producing love to all mankind,* and more especially to the children of God; expelling the love of the world, the love of pleasure, of ease, of honour, of money; together with pride, anger, self-will, and every other evil temper — in a word, changing the 'earthly sensual, devilish' mind into 'the mind which was in Christ Jesus'.[681]

Perfect love is essential to personal holiness. Without the twofold love of God and neighbor, all attempts to live righteously degenerate into perfectionism. Wesley well understood the inherent dangers of a misconceived, static doctrine of

---

Jackson, *Works*, 9: 344): "The love of God is righteousness, the moment it exists in any soul; and it must exist before it can be applied to action. Accordingly, it was righteousness in Adam the moment he was created. And yet he had a power either to follow the dictates of that love, (in which case his righteousness would have endured for ever,) or to act contrary thereto; but love was righteousness still, though it was not irresistible."

[680] See e.g., Luke 7:37-50.

[681] "The Scripture Way of Salvation," Outler, *Sermons, II,* 2: 158. Some italics mine.

perfection, which in part is why he regarded Methodism's chief task as the promotion of perfect love, the essence of biblical holiness.

Clement

Christian perfection defined as love is a recurrent theme in Clement's thought. The concept first emerges in *Protrepticos,* where he cites the Old Testament and Gospel command to love God and neighbor.[682] Subsequently, he shows that these two dimensions of love fulfill the divine commands.[683] He makes the same point in key portions of *Stromateis* 4, especially when he writes that love for God and neighbor are essential for the Christian Gnostic who aspires to live according to the example set by the apostles. To confess salvation with the mouth is one thing, but to "ascend also to love" is the mark of the perfect Christian.[684] Love is the "bond of perfection" whereby all virtues subsist in the heart and life of the Christian Gnostic.[685]

Clement's insight regarding perfection as love, though similar to Wesley's, follows a course tied more to the historical situation of his day when he says that ultimate love for God may very well result in martyrdom. He explains: "We call martyrdom perfection, not because the man comes to the end of his life as others, but because he has exhibited the perfect work of love."[686] Aside from the metaphorical use of perfection for martyrdom, the phrase phrase 'perfect love'

---

[682] *Protr.* 10:108.5; *LCL,* 92: 233.

[683] *Protr.* 11:115.5; *LCL,* 92: 247: "He who obeys Him gains in all things. He follows God, he obeys the Father; when erring he came to know Him; he loved God; he loved his neighbour; he fulfilled God's commandment; he seeks after the prize; he claims the promise."

[684] *Strom.* 4.9:75.2,3; *ANF* 2: 422.

[685] *Strom.* 4.7:55.3; *ANF* 2: 419.

[686] *Strom.* 4.3:14.3,4; *ANF* 2: 411.

is used rarely by Clement, appearing only three times in the entire corpus.[687] Of these, two are direct citations of 1 John 4:18: "perfect love casts out fear." The concept of 'perfect love' however is apparent everywhere. "The *perfect man*," Clement writes, "ought therefore to practise love, and thence to haste to the divine friendship, fulfilling the commandments from love."[688]

Clement devotes an entire chapter in *Stromateis* 4 to the concept of perfect love. Citing extensively from the Old and New Testaments as well as the Epistle of 1 Clement, he writes: "This is love, to love God and our neighbour."[689] Several chapters later he states that the Christian is characterized not merely by "abstinence from what is evil" (for this is but a preliminary stage in the process), nor is it "doing good out of fear," nor is it for "hope of recompense." But the believer is the one who does "good out of love, and for the sake of its own excellence."[690] In other words, the perfect is the one who does good because he loves the author of all goodness, God. Such love cannot help but be manifested toward neighbor as well, who has been created by the good God. All of the preceding are obvious allusions to Scripture, but more importantly, all point to pericopae that have particularly to do with discussions of what it means to be a perfect Christian or to be made perfect in love.

Clement agrees with Scripture and tradition that human beings are fallen creatures whose sinful nature prevents them from flawlessly obeying God. He writes:

> Certainly, though the number of human actions is infinite, it may be
> said that there are only two causes of all failure [*hamartia*[691]], both of

---

[687] *Strom.* 4.16:100..5,6; *ANF* 2: 427 and *Quis Dives*, 38.2; *ANF* 2: 602, which are merely quotations of 1 John 4:18; and *Strom.* 7.16:102.1,2; *ANF* 2: 553.

[688] *Strom.* 4.13:93.2,3; *ANF* 2: 426. Italics mine.

[689] *Strom.* 4.18:111.2; *ANF* 2: 429.

[690] *Strom.* 4.22:135.1-136.1; *ANF* 2: 434.

[691] Liddell-Scott, s.v. Often translated, "sin."

> which are in our own power, viz. ignorance and weakness on the part of the those who are neither willing to learn nor to gain the mastery over their desires. The former makes men judge wrongly, the latter prevents them from following out right judgments; for neither could any one act rightly if he were deceived in his judgment, even though he were perfectly able to carry out his determinations; nor on the other hand would he show himself blameless if he were a weakling in act, whatever might be his capacity to discern what was right.[692]

Note that according to Clement, sin is attributable either to ignorance or moral weakness. The former makes one liable to errors in judgment. The latter inhibits one from doing the good even though one knows what is right. Wesley agrees with this line of thought, when he observes that a great many sins are attributable to ignorance and infirmity.[693] According to Clement and Wesley, perfect performance cannot be the standard by which believers are judged perfect.

Clement, like Wesley, recognizes that the question of whether one has been made perfect in love is ultimately disclosed in the practical matter of loving one's neighbor. In *Stromateis* 2 he observes that human beings naturally love their family, friends, and those with whom they share common concerns. Such "natural wisdom" comes from God.[694] Christians, however, have a higher responsibility. They are to demonstrate love for all human beings in practical ways. He writes:

> The expression, . . . "I own something and have more than enough; why should I not enjoy it?" is not worthy of man nor does it indicate any community feeling. The other expression does, however: "I have something, why should I not share it with those in need?"

---

692 *Strom.* 7.16:101.6; Hort and Mayor, *Miscellanies Book VII,* 179.

693 See *Christian Perfection*, Outler, *Sermons, II,* 2: 104: "Christian perfection . . . does not imply . . . an exemption either from ignorance or mistake, or infirmities or temptations."

694 *Strom.* 2.9:41.6-42.2; *FC* 85: 187 and *Strom.* 2.9:45.1,2; *FC* 85: 189.

258

Such a one is *perfect*, and fulfills the command: 'Thou shalt love thy neighbor as thyself.'[695]

The perfect Christian will even love his enemies.[696] He writes:

> Corresponding to these [failures caused by ignorance and weakness] there are also two kinds of discipline provided, suitable for either class of failings [*hamartia*]; for the one, knowledge and plain proof derived from the witness of the Scriptures; for the other, training according to reason controlled by faith and fear: and both of these grow up into *perfect love*.[697]

In his typically sublime way, Clement is saying that love is made perfect through the disciplines of Scripture reading and faithful obedience — perfect love being the *telos* of the Christian's life on earth.

Summary

Both Wesley and Clement are realists with regard to the human condition. Human nature has been impaired by sin. Even if one possessed the perfect ability to do right, his damaged perception would mislead him. Should he possess the perfect ability to judge the good, his damaged will would prevent him from perfectly carrying it out. If both the perceptual and volitional faculties are damaged, then the only way that righteousness can be actualized is a transformation of one's core existence through a redirection of desire and motivation. Such transformation does not prevent further liability to commit sins borne from mistakes and weakness, but as time goes on it does make the recurrence of sins gradually less likely. When the primary object of desire has been redirected from the unrighteous self to God, and when righted desire is habituated through right actions over time, consistent moral behavior is the result. Both Clement and Wesley find a connection between perfection and love.

---

[695] *Protr.* 2.12:120.3-5: *FC* 23: 192. Italics mine.

[696] See *Strom.* 4.14; *ANF* 2: 426.

[697] *Strom.* 7.16:102.1,2; Hort and Mayor, *Miscellanies Book VII*, 179. Italics mine.

Ultimately, the manifestation of outwardly loving acts settles the question of whether one has been made perfect.

C. Perfection and Regeneration

Wesley

Although he was always careful to distinguish justification from sanctification, and initial faith from perfection, Wesley, as we have seen, viewed these concepts as points along a continuum rather than mutually exclusive ideas. Justification, he often argued, is not the same as sanctification, yet it is not unrelated to increasing holiness. The link connecting saving faith to perfection, and justification to sanctification is the concept of regeneration.

Wesley consistently argued from 1738 on that properly defined, regeneration is a supernatural work of moral renewal that takes place in the soul. It is the beginning of the spiritual life that takes place the moment one believes.[698] On this issue, Wesley was in near total agreement with the ancient Christian writers who argued that regeneration takes place by the infusion of divine grace in a moment of time. Over the centuries, infused grace came to be associated with good works leading to justification, not proceeding from it. By Wesley's day many Anglicans had come to view regeneration as a gradual process of moral improvement marked by good works, eventually resulting in justification.

Wesley however returned to the classical and biblical formulations of regeneration, arguing that it is an instantaneous inward renewal granted at the moment one believes, from which proceed virtuous work and moral piety. That moment, Wesley argued, is best illustrated in the gospel account of the 'new birth' (John 3:1-7). He faced opposition in some quarters by tying together so closely the concept of the new birth and the doctrine of regeneration, for some

---

[698] *A Letter to the Reverend Mr. Downes,* Jackson, *Works,* 9: 104.

argued that it implies regeneration is complete at the moment of justification and therefore perfect in the biblical sense.[699]

Wesley's instantaneous regeneration conceptualization set him at odds with the continental reformers. Martin Luther taught that regeneration is a gradual work that begins at baptism and continues throughout life until death.[700] Similarly, John Calvin viewed regeneration as a state of repentance that normally follows justification. He said that regeneration is gradual and should be defined in terms of 'mortification', the denial of one's fallen predisposition, and 'vivification', the active pursuit of righteousness.[701] Both Luther and Calvin had said that regeneration is a gradual renewal of the soul, which proceeds throughout life and is never complete; but the life of faith must still be conceived as a lifelong struggle with a proclivity toward sin until the very moment of death.

Among Wesley's Anglican contemporaries, William Law viewed regeneration as a gradual process, not an instantaneous event. Law in effect made regeneration synonymous with sanctification. Even though he admired Law's general understanding of holiness, in response to Law Wesley wrote that regeneration "is only the threshold of sanctification — the first entrance upon

---

[699] See Wesley's sermon "The New Birth," Outler, *Sermons II*, 2: 193-94: "[The new birth] . . . is that great change which God works in the soul when he brings it into life: when he raises it from the death of sin to the life of righteousness. It is the change wrought in the whole soul by the almighty Spirit of God when it is 'created anew in Christ', when it is 'renewed after the image of God', 'in righteousness and true holiness', when the love of the world is changed into the love of God, pride into humility, passion into meekness; hatred, envy, malice, into a sincere, tender, disinterested love for all mankind. In a word, it is that change whereby the 'earthly, sensual, devilish' mind is turned into 'the mind which was in Christ.' This is the nature of the new birth. 'So is everyone that is born of the Spirit.'"

[700] See Seeberg, *History of Doctrines*, 2: 283-84.

[701] See John Calvin, *Institutes of the Christian Religion*, 3.8 and esp. 9: "I interpret repentance as regeneration, whose sole end is to restore in us the image of God that had been disfigured and all but obliterated through Adam's transgression." Cit. from J. T. McNeill, ed., *Institutes of the Christian Religion*, vols. 20, 21, *The Library of Christian Classics* (Philadelphia: Westminster Press, 1960).

it."[702] Wesley insisted that regeneration is an instantaneous, supernatural, and complete work which "in plain English, [is] the new birth."[703] He rejected out of hand the notion of gradual regeneration.

Wesley reflected more accurately than William Law the historic teaching of the Church of England. Anglicans had always held a fundamentally more optimistic view of human perfectibility than continental Protestants. Instantaneous regeneration was not a sectarian opinion; it was embedded in the Church of England's articles of faith. Article XXVII *Of Baptism* compares regeneration to the new birth:

> Baptism is not only a sign of profession, and mark of difference, whereby Christian men are discerned from others that be not christened: *but is also a sign of regeneration or new birth*, whereby as by an instrument, they that receive baptism rightly, are grafted into the Church: . . . [704]

Wesley recognized that Article XXVII states that there is equivalence between the concept of regeneration and the event of the new birth. He also recognized that among the church fathers, the new birth represented a decisive conversion of the will to God and an actual improvement of the soul. So in reality, Wesley simply recovered and made explicit the implicit teaching of the Church of England's *Thirty-Nine Articles* and the older patristic tradition.

---

[702] "On God's Vineyard," Outler, *Sermons, III,* 3: 507.

[703] "A Letter to the Reverend Mr. Downes," Jackson, *Works,* 9: 104. See also "The Doctrine of Original Sin, Part II," Jackson, *Works,* 9: 310: "[R]regeneration is not 'gaining habits of holiness;' it is quite a different thing. It is not a natural, but a supernatural, change; and is just as different from the gradual 'gaining habits,' as a child's being born into the world is from his growing up into a man."

[704] "The Thirty-Nine Articles of the Church of England," Schaff, *Creeds of Christendom,* 3: 504. Italics mine.

In the sermon *Salvation by Faith* Wesley states that justification is to be understood as "salvation from sin and the consequences of sin."[705]   Justification, he writes, "implies a deliverance from the power of sin, . . . So that he who is thus justified or saved by faith is indeed 'born again'."[706]   The new birth is essential to salvation because it marks the beginning of a process whereby the believer grows "until at length he comes unto a *perfect* man, unto the measure of the stature of the fullness of Christ."[707]   We see clearly that for Wesley, regeneration forms the bridge between the event of formal justification and the ongoing process of sanctification. On the one hand, regeneration is perfect; it is a complete renewal of the soul and conversion of the will. On the other hand, it begins the process of perfection, which is otherwise called sanctification.

Nearly fifty years later in a sermon entitled *On God's Vineyard* (1787) Wesley clarifies his view of regeneration. Therein, he acknowledges that Martin Luther well understood justification; but the great Reformer did not do justice to the doctrine of sanctification. Likewise, he commends Roman Catholics such as Francis de Sales and Juan de Castaniza who spoke eloquently about sanctification, but who were effectively ignorant of the doctrine of justification.[708]   Wesley felt that the tendency in the past had been to fall prey to error by failing to keep in balance the two doctrines. He believed that Methodism was specially raised up by God to demonstrate the relationship between justification and sanctification without slighting one or the other. He explains:

> [Methodists] . . . know, indeed, that at the same time a man is *justified sanctification* properly begins. For when he is *justified* he is *'born again'*, *'born from above'*, 'born of the Spirit'; which although it

---

[705]   "Salvation by Faith," Outler, *Sermons, I*, 1: 124.

[706]   Ibid.

[707]   Ibid., 1: 124, 125. Italics mine.

[708]   "On God's Vineyard," Outler, *Sermons, III*, 3: 505-06.

is not (as some suppose) the whole process of *sanctification*, [it] is doubtless the gate of it.[709]

The difference between regeneration and Christian perfection/sanctification is analogous to the difference between a single moment in time when a substantial change occurs and successive moments in which ongoing changes occur. Wesley held unequivocally that regeneration and Christian perfection/sanctification are not the same, though they are related.

Clement

Clement, like Wesley, associates regeneration with the new birth experience. The new birth accomplishes a complete regeneration of the soul, so it must in that sense be regarded as perfect. He explains:

> When we were *reborn*, we straightway received the *perfection* for which we strive. For we were enlightened, that is, we came to the knowledge of God. Certainly, he who possesses knowledge of the Perfect Being is not imperfect.[710]

Typical of the early church fathers, Clement views the new birth, regeneration, justification, and sanctification as a salvific process that begins with baptism.[711] He writes:

---

[709] Ibid., 3: 506. Italics mine.

[710] *Paed.* 1.6:25.1,2; *FC* 23: 24, 25. Italics mine.

[711] See "The Marks of the New Birth,' Outler, *Sermons, I,* 1: 417, 430 esp. Wesley agrees with the historic Anglican position that the "privileges" of the child of God conveyed by the new birth "are ordinarily annexed to baptism." By Wesley's day, however, the act of baptism had been reduced to a mere social convention administered at birth. Many who had been baptized as infants now as adults were devoid of the regenerative effects of the new birth. They had come to rely on their baptism, even though they lacked any of the regenerative effects thereof; and thus, possessed of false sense of confidence. Wesley argues that for those baptized persons, who had failed to appropriate by faith the baptismal grace and been born again, their baptism is ineffectual. To these persons Wesley admonishes: "Lean no more on the staff of that broken reed, that ye *were* born again in baptism."

264

> When we are baptized, we are enlightened; being enlightened, we
> become adopted sons; becoming adopted sons, we are made *perfect*;
> and becoming *perfect*, we are made divine . . . . This ceremony is
> often called. . . "cleansing". . . because through it we are completely
> *purified* of our sins; . . .[712]

So the sacrament of baptism signifies the substance of the new birth experience,

which as Clement observes, has to do with perfection.

However, Clement does not regard the regeneration accompanying the

new birth as the culmination of perfection. He writes:

> The release from evil is only the beginning of salvation. Only those
> who have first reached the end of life, therefore, are those we can
> call already perfect.[713]

The 'perfect' aspect of regeneration, for Clement, is really the supernatural and

instantaneous effect that the new birth produces. In the moment of his "rebirth,"

the individual is "enlightened . . . [and] straightway rid of darkness."[714]

When attempting to reconcile how one may be perfect now, yet still aspire

to perfection, Clement like Wesley, appeals to St. Paul's illustration of the 'mind

of Christ' in Philippians 3:12 ff.[715] He writes:

> [Paul] . . . considers himself *perfect* in the sense that he has changed
> his old way of life and follows a better one, but not in the sense that
> he is *perfect* in knowledge [*gnosis*]. He only desires what is *perfect*.
> That is why he adds: 'Let us then, as many as are *perfect*, be of this
> mind,' meaning simply that *perfection* is turning away from sin and
> being *reborn*, after we have forgotten the sins that are behind, to faith
> in the only *Perfect One*.[716]

---

[712] *Paed.* 1.6:26.1,2; *FC* 23: 26. Italics mine.

[713] *Paed.* 1.6:26.3-27.1; *FC* 23: 26.

[714] *Paed.* 1.6:27.3; *FC* 23: 26.

[715] See "Character of a Methodist," Davies, *The Methodist Societies,* 9: 32.

[716] *Paed.* 1.6:52.3; *FC* 23: 48, 49. Italics mine.

Regeneration describes the complete (and therefore perfect) event of salvation; but it also points to the gradual increase of perfection that Wesley commonly referred to as sanctification. The idea is the same: regeneration is not identical to perfection, but it is vitally related to it.

Summary

As we have seen, neither Wesley nor Clement view regeneration as the equivalent of justification or sanctification. Rather, it is the bridge that connects the two along the continuum of God's salvific work in the life of the believer. Wesley undoubtedly has drawn his ideas on this subject more directly from the older Anglican Divines, but his reading of Clement in particular, should not be ruled out as an important influence. Both he and Clement support their views by appealing to St. Paul's statement in Philippians 3:12. While their sharing of opinion on this matter does not necessarily set them apart from other Christian thinkers, it nonetheless highlights one more aspect of Clement's thought that appealed to Wesley many centuries later.

4. Happiness

Wesley

We noted in chapter three that Wesley listed happiness as one of the chief traits of a Methodist, and that following ancient precedents, he linked happiness to holy living. Wesley believed that happiness and holiness are the inevitable products of an energetic faith.[717] This is seen in the fact that he often treats them in tandem as complimentary ideas. Note the following:

---

[717] For example, see Wesley's journal account of a meeting with Peter Böhler in Ward and Heitzenrater, *Journals and Diaries, I,* 18: 232 (March 23, 1738): "I met Peter Böhler again, who now amazed me more and more, by the account he gave of the fruits of living faith, — the holiness and happiness which he affirmed to attend it."

Such, then, was the state of man in Paradise. By the free, unmerited love of God, he was *holy* and *happy*: He knew, loved, enjoyed God, which is, in substance, life everlasting.[718]

This law, or covenant, (usually called the covenant of *works*,) given by God to man in Paradise, required an obedience perfect in all its parts, entire and wanting nothing, as the condition of his eternal continuance in the *holiness* and *happiness* wherein he was created.[719]

The essential, unchangeable difference [between the righteousness of the law and the righteousness of faith] is this: the one supposes him to whom it is given to be already *holy* and *happy*, created in the image and enjoying the favour of God; and prescribes the condition whereon he may continue therein, in love and joy, life and immortality: The other supposes him to whom it is given to be now *unholy* and *unhappy*, fallen short of the glorious image of God, having the wrath of God abiding on him, and hastening, through sin, whereby his soul is dead, to bodily death, and death everlasting; . . . .[720]

But true religion, or a heart right toward God and man, implies *happiness* as well as *holiness*.[721]

This *holiness* and *happiness*, joined in one, are sometimes styled, in the inspired writings, "the kingdom of God," (as by our Lord in the text,) and sometimes, "the kingdom of heaven." It is termed "the kingdom of God," because it is the immediate fruit of God's reigning in the soul.[722]

---

[718] "Justification by Faith," Outler, *Sermons, I,* 1: 184-85. Italics mine.

[719] "The Righteousness of Faith," Outler, *Sermons, I,* 1: 204. Italics mine

[720] Ibid., 1: 208-09. Italics mine. Note the contrast between holiness/happiness and unholiness/unhappiness.

[721] "The Way to the Kingdom," Outler, *Sermons, I,* 1: 223. Italics mine.

[722] Ibid., 1: 224. Italics mine.

[The natural man] . . . has no conception of that evangelical *holiness*, without which no man shall see the Lord; nor of the *happiness* which they only find whose "life is hid with Christ in God."[723]

But we rejoice in walking according to the covenant of grace, in *holy love* and *happy obedience.*[724]

For the same reason, except he be born again, none can be happy even in this world. For it is not possible, in the nature of things, that a man should be *happy* who is not *holy.*[725]

As the more *holy* we are upon earth the more *happy* we must be; (seeing there is an inseparable connexion between *holiness* and *happiness*;)[726]

"[B]eing justified by faith," we taste of the heaven to which we are going; we are *holy* and *happy*; we tread down sin and fear, and "sit in heavenly places with Christ Jesus."[727]

Wesley believes that holy living produces happiness. Holiness is an eternal vocation consisting of intimate fellowship with the Triune God. He declares:

One *happiness* shall ye propose to your souls, even an union with Him that made them; the having "fellowship with the Father and the Son;" the being joined to the Lord in one Spirit. One design you are

[723] "The Spirit of Bondage and of Adoption," Outler, *Sermons, I,* 1: 251. Italics mine.

[724] "The Witness of Our Own Spirit," Outler, *Sermons, I,* 1: 312. Italics mine.

[725] "The New Birth," Outler, *Sermons, II,* 2: 195. Italics mine.

[726] "God's Love to Fallen Man," Outler, *Sermons, II,* 2: 431. Italics mine.

[727] "A Plain Account of the People called Methodists," Davies, *The Methodist Societies,* 9: 255. Italics mine.

to pursue to the end of time, — the *enjoyment of God* in time and in eternity. Desire other things, so far as they tend to this.[728]

Wesley argues that such happiness is not possible unless all earthly and temporal desires are subordinated to the love of God:

Love the creature as it leads to the Creator. But in every step you take, be this the glorious point that terminates your view. Let every affection, and thought, and word, and work, be subordinate to this. Whatever ye desire or fear, whatever ye seek or shun, whatever ye think, speak, or do, be it in order to your *happiness* in God, the sole End, as well as Source, of your being.[729]

Although he would in no wise contend that happiness could be found apart from God, Wesley nonetheless recognizes that true happiness depends upon the free choice of the one who seeks it.

During his Oxford years, Wesley read a treatise that deeply influenced his thinking with regard to the necessity of human moral freedom. Published by William King (1650-1729) in 1702, *De Origine Mali* attempts to reconcile the moral evil with the idea of a good God on the basis of human freedom of choice.[730] Wesley follows King's argument that human beings, like God, possess the power to choose. God's choosing produces happiness because it necessarily defines happiness. The choices human beings makes are of course are contingent in nature — they may or may not result in happiness — but one thing is certain, the act of choosing contributes to their happiness, even when the results of those choices are undesirable. Minus the ability to choose, true happiness remains out of reach. The failure to accurately perceive the issues at stake, when confronted by the choice concerning God, may lead a person to miss the obvious, viz., that

---

[728] "The Circumcision of the Heart," Outler, *Sermons, I,* 1: 408. Italics mine. "The enjoyment of God . . ." is an allusion to the *Westminster Catechism* (1647), Question 1: "What is the chief end of man?" A: "Man's chief end is to glorify God, and to enjoy him forever."

[729] Ibid. Italics mine.

[730] See "To the Rev'd Samuel Wesley," Baker, *Letters, I,* 25: 264-67, n. 1.

God is the source of all temporal and eternal happiness. Wesley rightly concludes that the choice one makes to live a "life of religion" is not misery on earth and happiness in heaven; but it is happiness with "a foretaste of heaven now, and then heaven for ever [sic]."[731]

Clement

Wesley's insistent linking of happiness and holiness bears some similarity to Clement's thought. We observed in chapter four how Clement describes happiness as the idea of the good, as moral virtue, and as the culminating *telos* of life. We also noted that Clement identifies a correspondence between the happy life envisioned by the philosophers and the holy life described in the New Testament. Clement relies on the philosophers to provide an understanding of the essential nature and ground of happiness. He appeals to Plato to draw the intrinsic connection between moral virtue and happiness.[732] Human beings must pursue virtue and become like God so far as they are able.[733] Aristotle likewise taught that "happiness is [achieved in] the practise of the virtues."[734] There is no question in Clement's mind that the philosophers were right in identifying happiness as the universal end of human life.[735]

As a Christian, however, Clement recognizes that all attempts to define happiness via philosophical reasoning are inadequate because they fail to recognize the ultimate source and nature of happiness.[736] Plato came closest to the

---

[731] "The Important Question," Outler, *Sermons, III,* 3: 197.

[732] *Paed.* 1.9:82.3,4; *FC* 23: 74.

[733] Coppleston, *History of Philosophy,* 1: 218.

[734] *Paed.* 2.1:15.1; *FC* 23: 107.

[735] See *Strom.* 2.21:127-22:133.

[736] See *Strom.* 6.15:123.1,2; *ANF* 2: 508: "[T]he things which co-operate in the discovery of truth are not to be rejected. Philosophy, accordingly, which proclaims a Providence, and the

truth when he said that happiness is "likeness to God, defining likeness as 'justice and holiness combined with practical wisdom'."[737] Cleanthes the Stoic similarly wrote "that the just man and the happy man . . . [are] one in the same."[738] The majority of philosophers however, mistook the content of happiness for its source. True happiness, argues Clement, derives "from the revealed knowledge of God's will" and is accompanied by "the promise of reaching a goal that never comes to an end."[739] Happiness is the "greatest possible likeness to the true Logos, the hope of being established fully as adopted sons through the Son."[740] In other words, happiness is salvation.

Clement, like Wesley, sees an inexorable connection between happiness and holiness. He writes: "[I]f we live throughout holily and righteously, we are happy here, and shall be happier after our departure hence; not possessing happiness for a time, but enabled to rest in eternity."[741] "Happiness," he writes, "is proven in the practice of virtue."[742] The reward of a good life, a life marked by the avoidance of evil and the doing of good, is eternal blessedness.[743]

The Christian Gnostic does not base his confidence on the assurance of any acquired virtue or happiness derived therefrom. The Gnostic's "happiness and

---

recompense of a life of felicity [εὐδαίμονος], and the punishment, on the other hand, of a life of misery, teaches theology comprehensively; but it does not preserve accuracy and particular points; for neither respecting the Son of God, nor respecting the economy of Providence, does it treat similarly with us; for it did not know the worship of God."

[737] *Strom.* 2.22:131.5,6; *FC* 85: 245.

[738] *Strom.* 2.22:131.3; *FC* 85: 245.

[739] *Strom.* 2.22:134.1; *FC* 85: 247.

[740] *Strom.* 2.22:134.2; *FC* 85: 247.

[741] *Strom.* 5.14:122.3; *ANF* 2: 472.

[742] *Paed.* 2.1:15.4. Translation mine.

[743] *Paed.* 1.10:95.2; *FC* 23: 84.

blessedness consist in being a royal friend of God."[744] Clement rules out salvation by meritorious works. The profound happiness that accompanies salvation is entirely the product of a personal relationship with God. Such happiness is marked by "freedom and a dominant love for God."[745]

Summary

It can scarcely be debated that Wesley was optimistic concerning the redemptive possibilities of human nature. He consistently argued that personal happiness is inextricably linked to personal holiness. The Greek philosophers two millennia before had witnessed to the same connection; happiness is the by-product of personal virtue and a life directed toward the infinite realm of the ideal. Clement was one of the earliest Christian writers to draw the parallels between the philosophical view of happiness and the happiness of the believer in Christ. In essence, Clement Christianized the ancient secular ideal and related it to the holy character of a Christian. Wesley would have found in Clement an approach that confirmed his own experience of saving faith. His holy and happy Methodist is at the very least related analogously to Clement's holy and happy Christian Gnostic. Since both the Methodist and the Christian Gnostic are in some sense images designed to defend what both writers believed to be nothing other than true biblical Christianity, it is reasonable to at least entertain the notion that what we are seeing here is the influence of an ancient Christian writer upon one far removed in historical location.

C. Argument from Style

Wesley

---

[744] *Strom.* 4.7:52.2, 3. Translation mine. See also *ANF* 2: 481.

[745] *Strom.* 4.7:52.3. Translation mine.

An important but easily overlooked feature of *Character of a Methodist* is Wesley's use of third person descriptions of what a Methodist is. A few examples follow:

> He [the Methodist] cannot but rejoice whenever he looks on the state wherein he now is, 'being justified freely', and 'having peace with God through our Lord Jesus Christ'.[746]

> Who is a Methodist . . . ? I answer: a Methodist is one who has "the love of God shed abroad in his heart by the Holy Ghost given unto him"; one who "loves the Lord his God with all his heart, and with all his soul, and with all his mind, and with all his strength."[747]

> For he [the Methodist] is "pure in heart." The love of God has purified his heart from all revengeful passions, from envy, malice, and wrath, from every unkind temper or malign affection.[748]

> For as he [the Methodist] loves God, so 'he keeps his commandments.' Not only some, or most of them, but all, from the least to the greatest. He is not content to 'keep the whole law, and offend in one point', but has in all points 'a conscience void of offence towards God and towards man'.[749]

> For indeed he [the Methodist] 'prays without ceasing'. It is given him 'always to pray, and not to faint'. Not that he is always in the house of prayer—though he neglects no opportunity of being there. Neither is he always on his knees, although he often is, or on his face, before the Lord his God. Nor yet is he always crying aloud to God, or calling upon him in words. For many times 'the Spirit maketh intercession for him, with groans that cannot be uttered.' But at all times the language of his heart is this: 'Thou brightness of the eternal glory, unto thee is my mouth, though without a voice,

---

[746] "Character of a Methodist," Davies, *The Methodist Societies,* 9: 36.

[747] Ibid., 9: 35.

[748] Ibid., 9: 38.

[749] Ibid., 9: 39.

and my silence speaketh unto thee.' And this is true prayer, the lifting up the heart to God.[750]

The evidence is abundant, but what is its significance? A little later in 1742, the same year *Character of a Methodist* appeared, Wesley published *The Principles of a Methodist.* [751] Although the occasion differs, the aim is the same — to defend Methodists and Methodism from false accusations. In spite of it similarity to *Character,* the third person stylistic structure is missing, which begs the question, "Why?"

We suggest that Wesley's purpose in using the third person in *Character* was to describe in objective and non-defensive language what Methodism was. Methodists are not practitioners of an obscure or aberrant form of Christianity. We discussed in chapter three how Wesley employed the term 'sect', suggesting that it may reflect accusations of sectarianism. Wesley believed that Methodism was anything but sectarian. His use of the third person as a rhetorical device allowed him the freedom to describe the faith and practice of Methodism without appearing to be defensive. It also would have allowed him to speak in general terms about Methodists without having to answer for particular individuals who had not lived up to the ideal. Indeed, later controversies that arose from within the movement would show this to have been a wise choice.

There is a second, more significant reason why Wesley may have employed this third person stylistic form: it is the very same way that Clement chose to portray his ideal Christian Gnostic.

Clement

We already observed in chapter four how Clement frequently describes the Christian Gnostic in the third person, a convention found in the ancient *paideia*

---

[750] Ibid., 9: 37.

[751] "The Principles of a Methodist," Davies, *The Methodist Societies,* 9: 47-66.

tradition. His use of this form is intended to convey in objective language the character traits of the higher Christian life. Note the following examples:

The Christian Gnostic is rooted in faith.[752]

It is the Christian Gnostic who is "in the image and likeness," who imitates God so far as possible, leaving out none of the things which lead to the possible likeness, displaying continence, patience, righteous living, sovereignty over the passions, sharing his possessions so far as he can, doing good in word and deed.[753]

For the [Christian] Gnostic must, as far as is possible, imitate God.[754]

He [the Christian Gnostic], all day and night, speaking and doing the Lord's commands, rejoices exceedingly, not only on rising in the morning and at noon, but also when walking about, when asleep, when dressing and undressing; . . . ."[755]

Therefore the [Christian] Gnostic prays in thought during every hour, being by love allied to God. And first he will ask forgiveness of sins; and after, that he may sin no more; and further, the power of well-doing and of comprehending the whole creation and administration by the Lord, that, becoming pure in heart through the knowledge, which is by the Son of God, he may be initiated into the beatific vision face to face, having heard the Scripture which says, "Fasting with prayer is a good thing."[756]

There are numerous such examples. It is significant that the majority of third person references are concentrated in Books 2, 4, 6, and 7 of *Stromateis*—all loci where Clement describes the disciplines and practices of the Christian Gnostic's life. Perhaps the meaning lies in why Clement wrote in the first place:

---

[752] *Strom.* 2.11:50.3; *FC* 85: 193.

[753] *Strom.* 2.19:97.1; *FC* 85: 221-22.

[754] *Strom.* 4.26:171.4; *ANF* 2: 441.

[755] *Strom.* 7.12:80.3-4; *ANF* 2: 546.

[756] *Strom.* 6.12:102.1-3; *ANF* 2: 503.

> [I]t is our purpose at present to describe the *life* of the Gnostic, not to present the system of dogmas, which we shall afterwards explain at the fitting time, preserving the order of topics.[757]

Clement essentially says that he has written a theology of Christian practice, not a systematic treatment of doctrine. It is character that concerns him. Christian holiness is intensely practical for Clement, as it is for Wesley.

Summary

Although not decisive in and of itself, this shared stylistic feature suggests that Wesley was not overstating the case when he said that Clement's portrayal of Christian Gnostic character prompted him to write *Character of a Methodist.* Although certain aspects of Clement's theology — e.g., *apatheia* — Wesley may have rejected without fully recognizing the Alexandrian's aim, Wesley would not have missed Clement's use of the third person as a rhetorical device.

D. Argument from Doctrinal Development

One of the more perplexing problems encountered in attempting to understand John Wesley's appropriation of Clement is that the terminology the two evangelists employ is dissimilar — as we have seen, likely the result of a wide separation in culture and milieu. Yet we have shown that there are striking similarities that suggest some kind of dependence.

Even among those who have accepted that there exists a theological connection between Clement and Wesley, some remain skeptical that Wesley had actually read and assimilated for himself some of Clement's ideas. A few interpreters have suggested that Wesley was careless in citing Clement as a source, or that he had only a superficial and indirect acquaintance with the

---

[757] *Strom.* 7.10:59.7; *ANF* 2: 540. Italics mine.

Alexandrian's thought.[758] Neither of these conclusions is convincing, nor has either been substantiated. Rather, the textual evidence we have provided suggests Wesley had a fairly sophisticated grasp of the history of theological development and an ability to adapt classical sources to a contemporary setting. If we are correct in this assumption, then the background and formation of Wesley's theology has yet to be fully appreciated.

Most would agree that John Wesley's primary contribution to Christian thought has been in the area of soteriology.[759] His main task was to clarify the order and experience of salvation, along with its ethical outworking. In so doing, Wesley articulated an ecumenical soteriology that in some fashion accounts for the major branches of the church — Roman/Eastern, Lutheran/Reformed, and Anglican. It is our opinion that Clement of Alexandria was a primary source for Wesley, at least with regard to his notion of aspiring holiness. The evidence we

---

[758] David Bundy ("Christian Virtue: John Wesley and the Alexandrian Tradition," 142-43) suggests that an Alexandrian influence could have been mediated to Wesley through several avenues, including John Cassian, Psuedo-Dionysius or the Cambridge Platonists. Bundy proposes, however, that Anthony Horneck is a more likely suspect in the mediation of Alexandrian thought for Wesley. It is true that Wesley included Horneck's *The Happy Ascetic; or , The Best Exercise* in a much shortened and edited version in *A Christian Library*, 16:286-408. See the original edition by Anthony Horneck, *The Happy Ascketick: Or, The Best Exercise, To Which is Added, A Letter to a Person of Quality, Concerning the Holy Lives of the Primitive Christians* (London: T.N. for Henry Mortlock and Mark Pardoe, 1681). The prayers that conclude each of the fourteen exercises in Wesley's edition are not found in Horneck's original edition. Apparently, Wesley inserted them, or he may even have composed them. The fact that he considerably redacted and shortened Horneck's original suggests that he found the treatise useful, but not so much that it was worth reprinting in its entirety. While there is no question that Horneck had a credible grasp of patristic literature, it is a fact that there are only two allusions to Clement of Alexandria in the whole of *The Happy Ascketick*. These references appear in catena style in the original edition (pp. 104 05; 357). Would Wesley have found Horneck's two references to Clement and the content of *The Happy Ascketick* so compelling that he would stake his credibility on it by naming Clement as the inspiring source for *Character of a Methodist* in an open letter that he expected to be published (viz., "To the Editor of Lloyd's Evening Post," Ward and Heitzenrater, *Journal and Diaries*, V, 22: 72)? Based on all the available evidence we believe that it is far more likely Wesley read Clement for himself.

[759] This has been demonstrated in many places. For a recent treatment of Wesley's soteriology, see Kenneth J. Collins, *A Faithful Witness: John Wesley's Homiletical Theology* (Wilmore, KY: Wesley Heritage Press, 1993), 125-62.

have presented suggests that he read Clement, adapted the Alexandrian's perspective on key issues related to faith and character, and employed those insights in defending Methodism and articulating a distinctly Wesleyan soteriology. If this is so, then the question of how Wesley may have overcome the contextual differences (historical as well as philosophical) remains to be addressed. To assist in answering this question, we turn to a later Anglican for insight.

John Henry Newman (1801-90) was the acknowledged leader of a reform society known as the Oxford Movement, which flourished for over a decade between the years 1833 and 1845. Popularly known as Tractarianism (named for its publication *Tracts for the Times*), Newman and his colleagues sought to establish Anglicanism as the *via media* between Roman Catholicism and Protestantism. The means by which the Tractarians intended to accomplish this goal was by renewing the church's appeal to the church fathers and particularly, the doctrine of apostolic succession.[760]

One of Newman's more important contributions was to investigate how Christian doctrines develop over time and in various contexts, while maintaining fidelity to the teaching of Christ and the apostles. Newman set forth seven criteria for differentiating healthy doctrinal developments from harmful corruptions. These criteria are summarized as follows:

> 1. Is the type of the theological idea preserved despite variations in proportion and relationship between aspects or parts of the idea?

> 2. Does there exist continuity of the idea in spite of differences in the way it has been formulated as doctrine in various settings.

---

[760] *ODCC* s.v. "Newman, John Henry".

3. Has the theological idea demonstrated that it is vital and living through an ability to assimilate and incorporate other ideas without dissolution or disarrangement?

4. Can the developmental process of the theological idea can be traced logically over the course of time.

5. Does theological idea contain within itself a clear and definite anticipation of its future development.

6. Does the development of the theological idea proceed conservatively over time in ways that illustrate and corroborate the idea rather than obscure or modify it.

7. Is the theological idea marked by an enduring vitality throughout its development.[761]

Although Wesley preceded Newman by a full century, he anticipates at a practical level some of the methodological conceerns that Newman later attempted to resolve. We believe that Wesley not only recognized the perennial truth and relevance of Clement of Alexandria's ideas concerning salvation and its outward effects, but he borrowed some of those ideas, stripped them of their culturally bound language, and reunited them with biblical terminology — all for the purpose of providing a clear articulation and viable defense of Methodism.

Based upon the observations and discoveries made in chapter four and the evidence presented already in this chapter, and using Newman's criteria for judging legitimate developments in doctrine, we should be able to measure to some extent the efficacy of Clement's influence upon Wesley.

1. Preservation of Type

In both Clement and Wesley, there is a clear preservation of type or form among pertinent theological ideas. We have demonstrated that both writers agree

---

[761] John Henry Cardinal Newman, *An Essay on the Development of Christian Doctrine*, 6th ed. (Notre Dame: University of Notre Dame Press, 1989), 169-206.

on some vital nuances within the larger framework of Christian soteriology. For instance, both agree that saving faith cannot be separated on a practical and ethical level from regeneration and sanctification. Clement spends a great deal more effort on the epistemological foundations of faith than Wesley, who is largely content with the language of the Bible. This difference, however, does not obscure the fact that both writers closely associate faith with personal transformation and holy living.

2. Continuity of Principle

Doctrines are fundamentally different than principles, though they are vitally related. Newman explains:

> Principles are abstract and general, doctrines relate to facts; doctrines develop, and principles at first sight do not; doctrines grow and are enlarged, principles are permanent; doctrines are intellectual, and principles are more immediately ethical and practical.[762]

In evaluating the appropriateness of any observable development, one must distinguish between the doctrine itself and the principle that underlies it. If Newman's criterion is valid, we should be able to establish a continuity of principles in Wesley and Clement that, despite differences in the formulation of the doctrines, would nonetheless confirm Wesley's citing of Clement as one of his sources and substantiate a theological dependence.

For example, in our discussion of thematic similarities earlier in this chapter, we noted that both Wesley and Clement embrace the practical holiness of believers in Christ. Both believe that the divine economy provides for the attainment of a holy character and life on earth. Yet Clement's doctrine of *apatheia* has remained a sticking point for scholars trying to substantiate Wesley's dependence on Clement. In chapter three we cited Wesley's letter to *Lloyd's*

---

[762] Ibid., 178.

Evening Post published in 1767 in which he claims that *Character of a Methodist* was based upon the Alexandrian's portrait of Christian character and virtue.[763] Wesley's claim to have employed Clement as his source has been met with skepticism. It is obvious that Clement's ideal of Christian character as *apatheia* is at face value incompatible with Wesley's portrait of a Methodist.

In spite of these difficulties, our examination of the concept of *apatheia* in chapter four showed that the term is one of many used by Clement to reach his Greek audience with the gospel. Clement's method was to fill this originally Stoic term with biblical meaning, drawing an entirely appropriate connection between the passions and human sinfulness. *Apatheia*, as Clement uses it, is deliverance from the power of sinning in lieu of becoming morally like Christ. The soteriological analogue to *apatheia* is holiness — the actualization of righteousness in one's heart and life. Therefore in our opinion, Clement's doctrine of *apatheia* represents a legitimate development of the underlying principle.

In other historical and social contexts, *apatheia* was not a good term to describe the principle of holiness. Encumbered by its ancient philosophical connotations, *apatheia* did not effectively communicate Christian holiness for other writers of the same era located geographically in other places; otherwise, we would have evidence that it did. Wesley rightly rejected *apatheia* at face value as an inaccurate representation of Christian holiness. It is possible that Wesley did not fully recognize the altered shade of meaning that Clement had given it. Even so, this was not a major encumbrance since the context in which Clement uses it more often than not makes clear that he is talking about personal holiness. Clement spoke of Gnostic character in ways other than just *apatheia*. In any case, we know that Wesley was always drawn to biblical rather than abstract

---

[763] Recall Ward and Heitzenrater, *Journal and Diaries, V,* 22: 72: "Five or six and thirty years ago I much admired the character of a perfect Christian drawn by Clemens Alexandrinus. Five or six and twenty years ago, a thought came into my mind of drawing such a character myself, only in a more scriptural manner and mostly in the very words of Scripture."

theological language. Recall that in his *Letter to Lloyd's* Wesley said that he was inspired to write *Character of a Methodist* based on Clement's "character of a perfect Christian . . . only in a more scriptural manner and mostly in the very words of Scripture."[764]

If Newman's criterion is valid, then Wesley has contributed to the legitimate development of an ancient Alexandrian portrait of Christian character. Wesley's discarding *apatheia* in no way belies the claim Clement had influenced his thinking.

3. Assimilation without Corruption

An important characteristic of any truth statement is its ability to assimilate and incorporate other ideas without being corrupted or transmuted. Doctrines, unlike more abstract objects, are formed within the real world of Christian experience and therefore normally reflect to some degree their historical and cultural context.[765] To judge whether a doctrine is heretical, one must examine the theological idea underlying it and determine whether it reflects an assimilation of context and culture without corruption.

For example, if Clement of Alexandria's portrayal of the higher Christian life in terms of *gnosis* and *apatheia* does not prove to be a dogmatic reformulation of biblical ideas related to holiness and the purging of sin, then it should be regarded as a corruption of those essential ideas. However, if *gnosis* and *apatheia* as Clement used these terms, represent an assimilation of Greek terminology by biblical ideas, then they are legitimate doctrinal developments.

Wesley's statement that Clement's portrait of Christian character was a source for *Character of a Methodist* need not be dismissed out of hand. A close

---

[764] Ward and Heitzenrater, *Journals and Diaries, V,* 22: 72.

[765] See Newman, *Essay on the Development of Christian Doctrine,* 186.

examination of Clement's and Wesley's views, as we have undertaken in this study, reveals that both writers drew upon a common underlying principle — holiness of heart and life as the expected product of a living Christian faith. Whatever assimilation of contexts and language each writer may have made in order to communicate effectively does not ultimately obscure this underlying principle.

4. Logical Progression in Development

Newman's fourth criterion inquires whether the development of a theological idea can be traced logically over the course of time. He illustrates this by tracing how ideas develop in the mind:

> An idea under one or other of its aspects grows in the mind by remaining there; it becomes familiar and distinct, and is viewed in its relations; it leads to other aspects and these again to others, subtle, recondite, original, according to the character, intellectual and moral of the recipient; and thus a body of thought is gradually formed without his recognizing what is going on within him.[766]

Theological reflection takes place in a similar fashion. An idea arises within a school of thought, is explored and expanded by others, rediscovered in a later age, propagated, illustrated, and arranged systematically. The process of development the idea undergoes may be traced logically to see whether it has developed in an authentic way or been corrupted.[767]

In the case of Wesley and Clement, we have identified evidence of theological similarity if not outright dependence; however, we have also noted differences in emphasis, language, and style. The question is whether Wesley's development of these themes logically follows from Clement's thought. Again, we need not allow differences of historical and social location overturn Wesley's

---

[766] Ibid., 190.

[767] Ibid., 190-91.

claim of reliance on Clement's descriptions of Christian character and perfection. It was a logically sound theological development in Wesley's day for British evangelicals to employ the language of Scripture in formulating doctrine. From Wesley's eighteenth century location, it made no sense to retain particular philosophical terminology that was relevant only to a late second century Hellenistic audience. However, the principle of holy character was relevant in Wesley's day as well as Clement's. Both faced the challenge, as each era of preachers must, of making the gospel relevant to their generation. Scholars may look back and judge their effectiveness in meeting this challenge, but they must not diminish the difficulties posed by it.

In chapter four we attempted to demonstrate that Clement generally filled Greek philosophical terms and constructs with biblical content and meaning. As an apologist for the Christian faith writing for an ancient Alexandrian audience, the use of Greek terminology in service to the gospel was a logical and healthy development of the notion of holiness. Through the centuries, the church has regarded Clement's efforts as a beneficial enterprise. Wesley's use of Clement's ideas, recast in scriptural language for an English audience, was likewise a logical and healthy development of doctrine.

5. Anticipation of Future Development

Newman observes that living ideas carry within themselves anticipations of their future development, and that oftentimes an idea advanced in an earlier age becomes relevant at a much later time.[768] We have seen in detail how Clement conceives Christian salvation as a process that advances by stages from initial faith to perfection. It is well known that later writers in the Christian East held similar views, whil the Latin church as well as the Continental Reformers favored

---

[768] Ibid., 195-96. Though he does not say so here, Newman's remarks imply that God has providentially guided healthy developments in doctrinal theology over the centuries.

284

a more forensic description of Christian salvation. Wesley's use of Clement marked a recovery and further development of early Eastern soteriology. Clement's two stages of faith paradigm anticipates Wesley's recovery of a progressive model of salvation marked by the distinction between initial faith (justification, the new birth and regeneration) and Christian perfection (maturity, holiness, sanctification).

6. Conservative Development

For his sixth criterion Newman argues that legitimate developments in doctrine are by nature conservative; they illustrate and corroborate rather than obscure or correct the ideas on which they are based.[769] Recall that in chapter four we demonstrated that the substance of Clement's discussion of lower and higher stages of Christian existence, though employing philosophical terminology, is grounded in a careful reading of Old and New Testament passages. Some have argued that Clement overreached in his attempt to reconcile Christianity and philosophy.[770] However, we have seen that Clement's theologizing was for the most part a fairly conservative development of biblical doctrine.[771] Once one recognizes that Clement employed Greek philosophy to interpret Scripture, and that he regarded philosophical reasoning as subordinate to Scripture and not its equal, then the conviction of the larger church tradition concerning the value of his work is reaffirmed.

---

[769] Ibid., 200.

[770] Newman thinks he did. See ibid., 362: "Clement perhaps went too far in his accommodation to philosophy."

[771] Newman seems to contradict himself when he writes: "The cultivated minds of the Alexandrian Fathers, who are said to owe so much to Pagan science, certainly showed no gratitude or reverence towards their alleged instructors, but maintained the supremacy of Catholic Tradition. Clement [of Alexandria] speaks of heretical teachers as perverting Scripture, ..." Ibid., 349.

Among other things, this present study has attempted to demonstrate that Wesley's employment of St. Clement as a source was conservative in nature. As we have already noted, Wesley said that he admired Clement's portrait of character, which inspired him to produce one of his own, following more closely the language of Scripture. It is highly doubtful that Wesley would have named Clement as a source if he seriously thought that Clement had erred. And as we have seen, Wesley's whole purpose in writing *Character* was to argue that Methodism was nothing more than scriptural Christianity. It is impossible to trace the movement in Wesley's mind from his initial acquaintance with Clement's ideas of faith and holiness to the publication of *Character of a Methodist* in 1742. But we can say with confidence that the gestation of the ideas that eventually produced the treatise represents a conservative development that maintained fidelity to Scripture and the larger tradition.

7. Vitality over the Course of Development

The seventh and final criterion posed by Newman is whether a theological idea has been vital throughout its history of development. Vitality is a clear indication that corruption has not taken place. As Newman points out, corruptions in doctrine are relatively short-lived.[772]

Personal holiness is a biblical idea that has enjoyed perennial relevance and wide acceptance throughout the history of Christian thought. It was especially relevant for Clement, who lived in one of the more cosmopolitan and secular cities of the ancient world. His proscriptions of frivolous and often decadent Alexandrian society came alongside the evangelical call to Christian faith and holy living.[773] Clement was repulsed by the soul-deadening

---

[772] Ibid., 203-05.

[773] Note esp. *Paed.*, 2; *FC* 23: 93-198.

characteristics of an overly self-indulgent culture. He believed that the gospel would eventually improve society by liberating individuals from sin. so his call to virtue was practical in nature, not at all like Plato's contemplation of the virtues. Clement simply traded on the philosopher's terminology. In other words, he plundered the Egyptians.

Wesley, writing in a vastly different time and culture, also proscribed attitudes and practices that were deadening to the soul. He too believed that the gospel would create a better society through the redemption and transformation of individuals' lives. Having once sought holiness through ascetic piety, Wesley's post-Aldersgate evangelical call to holiness was issued on a practical level. He knew instinctively that formal theological language would not communicate the gospel well. Having studied formally, however, and having read the leading lights of theological reflection from centuries past, Wesley brought his learning to bear in the service of the gospel. He formulated his call to holy character in language that his audience could understand. Clothing his thoughts in the language of ordinary people, Wesley made an appeal that is more sophisticated than it appears on the surface, but one more vital than it would have been had he not sought to communicate it as he did.

If vitality is a suitable criterion for evaluating the development of an idea as it has been formulated doctrinally across time and cultural boundaries, Clement and Wesley both found the gospel idea of holiness sufficiently crucial to search out the best sources and means to communicate it in their respective historical contexts. Both were men of the people. They sought not to stand above the people, but to stand among them, showing them by teaching and example that the gospel demands personal holiness, and that divine grace is available toward that end.

Conclusion

The aim of this study has been threefold. First, we have attempted to establish as far as possible the plausibility of John Wesley's claim that Clemens Alexandrinus' portrait of Christian character had served as the inspiration for his 1742 treatise *Character of a Methodist.* Second, we have attempted to understand the extent to which Wesley's theology may have been more broadly influenced by Clement's soteriological perspectives, especially personal regeneration and progressive holiness. Third, having examined all the available evidence, we have sought to provide a plausible explanation for how an eighteenth century British evangelical might have adapted and employed a late second century Alexandrian model of Christian faith and piety.

While the two Charles Wesley hymns and the Edward Welchman connection might be regarded as peripherally significant to the accomplishment of our task, the testimony of Alexander Knox and the mentoring of the Wesleys by renowned Clemens Alexandrinus scholar John Potter cannot be dismissed. If John Wesley had not seriously read and engaged Clement's works, Knox was naively deluded and Potter was not as significant a mentor to John and Charles Wesley as the available evidence suggests.

The argument based on thematic similarities also may not stand alone; neither Wesley nor Clement had exclusive rights on a developmental model of

Christian holiness. It is well known that the Eastern fathers from the second century on held such views. But is this not precisely the point? These writers believed that their ideas reflected the purest form of the apostolic witness that had ultimately derived from Jesus Himself. That John Wesley should teach that faith normally increases by stages, or that his doctrine of holiness should presume that all righteousness is actual, or that his view of Christian perfection is essentially the proactive outworking of love — all these ideas *are* derived from Scripture. To this day, they remain traits that distinguish Wesley from the Continental Reformers, even as they distinguished Clement and his successors from Tertullian, Augustine and writers in the West. The fact that Wesley is theologically closer to the East and Clement than he is to the West and Augustine must not be overlooked in deciding the question of theological dependency.

The stylistic similarity between Wesley and Clement also must be considered. Clement's employment of the objective third person in describing the ideal Christian Gnostic is mirrored by Wesley's portrait of the ideal Methodist. Twenty-five years after *Character* first appeared Wesley wrote that his purpose had been to create a portrait of Christian character much like Clement's Christian Gnostic "only in a more scriptural manner and mostly in the very words of Scripture."[774] Indeed, Wesley's Methodist resembles Clement's Christian Gnostic with the philosophical terminology recast in the language of the English Bible.

Finally, any claim of theological dependence of John Wesley upon Clemens Alexandrinus must attempt to account for the disparities of history and culture. The theory of doctrinal development set forth by John Henry Newman does this. Wesley in some sense has anticipated Newman's common sense concerns. Newman accounts for the continuation and preservation of the apostolic witness through the ages. He shows how doctrinal orthodoxy was established and distinguished from heresy through the use of Scripture and

---

[774] Ward and Heitzenrater, *Journals and Diaries*, V, 22: 72.

tradition. Wesley argues in *Character of a Methodist* on the very same grounds. This much is clear: Wesley regarded the Alexandrian's work as significant and worthy of adaptation for his audience. In making that adaptation, he surely must have considered some of the issues addressed formally by Newman later. Given his keen interest in the ethical and experiential elements of the Christian life, Wesley would have read Clement for insight into these areas, making his own application in a way that was relevant to his Oxford Holy Club circle, and later the Methodist revival.

Appendix 1
The Unpublished Manuscripts

In these notes Wesley lists and affirms certain practices originally found in the canons of the ancient Eastern Church. Retaining the original marginal spacing, they are as follows:

I believe it a duty to observe, so far as I can (without breaking communion with my own church.)

1. To baptize by immersion.

2. To use Water, Oblation of Elements, Invocation, Alms, a Prothesis, in the Eucharist.

3. To pray for the faithful departed.

4. To observe Saturday and Sunday Pentecost as festival.

5. To abstain from blood, things strangled.

I think it prudent (our own church not considered) —

1. To observe the Stations.

2. Lent, especially the Holy Week.

292

    3. To turn to the East at the Creed.[775]

Urlin cites further notes from the manuscripts that deal primarily with the *Apostolic Canons.*[776] He was not so much concerned to prove anything about Wesley's understanding of the canons; rather, he wanted to fix the dating of the notes to around 1741 in order to show that Wesley's Aldersgate experience in 1738 had not caused him to abandon his reverence for the early church and primitive rituals, as some had charged.[777]

---

[775] Urlin, *John Wesley's Place in Church History,* 69-70. Cf. n. 1. Urlin observes that the words in parenthesis have been struck through.

[776] Ibid., 70-71, 73-74.

[777] Ibid., 76.

Appendix 2
John Wesley On Early Church Heresies

John Wesley was well acquainted with St. Augustine's writing, and on more than one occasion came out as a critic of the Bishop of Hippo. One of the best examples concerns Augustine's debate with Pelagius. Wesley in fact had serious reservations about Augustine's role in the condemnation of the British monk because of the implications it had in subsequent ages. He writes:

> Yea, I would not affirm that the arch-heretic [Pelagius] of the fifth century (as plentifully as he has been bespattered for many ages) was not one of the holiest men of that age, not excepting St. Augustine himself — a wonderful saint! as full of pride, passion, bitterness, censoriousness, and as foul-mouthed to all that contradicted him as George Fox himself. I verily believe the real heresy of Pelagius was neither more nor less than this, the holding that Christians may by the grace of God (not without it; that I take to be a mere slander) 'go on to perfection'; or, in other words, 'fulfil the law of Christ'. . . . St. Augustine was angry at Pelagius. Hence he slandered and abused him (as his manner was) without either fear or shame. And St. Augustine was then in the Christian world what Aristotle was afterwards. There needed no other proof of any assertion than *ipse dixit* — 'St. Augustine said it.'[778]

---

[778] "The Wisdom of God's Counsels," Outler, *Sermons, II*, 2: 555-56. See. esp. nn. 32, 33. See also "Letter to Mr. Alexander Coates," Jackson, *Works*, 12: 240

294

Wesley had given considerable attention to this controversy and had come to disagree with the tradition precisely because he had judged the evidence for himself. In spite of his contentious tone, one is forced to acknowledge that Wesley could not have drawn such a conclusion without having seriously engaged the texts of the arguments and the history of the controversy's interpretation. Furthermore, Wesley was aware that by rejecting so-called 'Pelagianism' the councils had not so much rejected the views held by Pelagius, but rather his younger contemporary, Celestius.[779] Modern scholarship tends to agree that Pelagius did not have as extreme a view of human autonomy as Augustine thought.[780]

Wesley viewed the heresy debates in the early church through his own unique lens. His primary concern, which in turn tended to govern all others, was the holiness of the church. In the sermon *Of the Church,* he writes:

> Does it not clearly appear . . . why, in the ancient Creed commonly called the Apostles', we term the universal or catholic church, 'the holy catholic church'? How many wonderful reasons have been found out for giving it this appellation! One learned man informs us, 'The church is called holy because Christ the head of it is holy.' Another eminent author affirms, 'It is so called because all its ordinance are designed to promote holiness;' and yet another, 'Because our Lord *intended* that all the members of the church should be holy.' Nay, the shortest and the plainest reason that can be given, and the only true one, is: the church is called 'holy' because it is holy; because every member thereof is holy, though in different degrees, as he that called them is holy.[781]

---

[779] "The Doctrine of Original Sin, Part IV," Jackson, *Works,* 9: 430. In his extract of a tract by Samuel Hebden, Celestius (Coelestius) is cited as the first Christian thinker to deny the doctrine of original sin.

[780] See John Ferguson, *Pelagius: A Historical and Theological Study* (Cambridge: W. Heffer & Sons Ltd., 1956), 172 ff.; also, Eugene TeSelle, *Augustine The Theologian* (New York: Herder and Herder, 1970), 278-94.

[781] "Of the Church," Outler, *Sermons, III,* 3: 55-56.

Though doctrinal orthodoxy was important for Wesley, it was not more important than the actual holiness of the church. Rhetorically, he asks:

> Can anything then be more absurd than for men to cry out, 'the Church! the Church!' and to pretend to be very zealous for it, and violent defenders of it; while they themselves have neither part nor lot therein, nor indeed know what the church is?[782]

Wesley believed that persons who truly belong to the church must demonstrate their membership by striving to live a holy life. He writes:

> [L]et all those who are real members of the church see that they walk holy and unblameable in all things.[783]

All holiness is actual holiness, as Wesley consistently argues.

It is also in this context that we must understand Wesley's supposed sympathy for Donatism, Novatianism, and Montanism. If anything, Wesley is guilty of alluding to these ancient debates without fully unpacking the history of them for his readers.[784] These sects shared in common a concern for the purity of the church, which as we have already seen, Wesley shared.

Wesley mentions the Novatianist controversy only once in a citation of a letter from John Gambold to his brother Charles.[785] He appears to agree with Gambold's criticism of the Roman priest Novatian (fl. 250 AD) who had acted with contempt for "poor sinners."

Wesley alludes to the Donatism controversy several times, but in only one instance does he come close to defending the Donatist position. In the open letter *An Answer to the Rev. Mr. Dodd,* he comments somewhat cynically:

---

[782] Ibid., 3: 56.

[783] Ibid.

[784] See the helpful annotations for "Of the Church," Outler, *Sermons, III,* 3: 55, n. 54 .

[785] Ward and Heitzenrater, *Journals and Diaries, I,* 18: 240.

> What the Donatists were, I do not know; but I suspect they were the
> real Christians of that age; and were therefore served by St.
> Augustine and his warm adherents, as the Methodists are now by
> their zealous adversaries.[786]

Wesley suggests that because the Donatists zealously guarded the holiness of the church they were not treated fairly at the hands of Augustine and his followers. Without lending approval to Donatism's principal arguments, Wesley observes that a similar state of affairs exists between Methodists and their opponents.

Wesley comments with greater candor on Montanus and the movement spawned by this early Christian figure. His critics' perennial misunderstanding led to the rather frequent charge that Methodism bore a strong resemblance to the second century heretical sect known as Montanism. Montanus, whose dates are uncertain, was active in the region of Phrygia. Montanism emerged ca. 156-57 AD and endured as a remnant until the close of the fourth century.[787] The prophetic movement Montanus founded was concerned primarily with ethical, not doctrinal issues.[788] Montanus believed that he had been given special authority by God to speak in the person of the Paraclete, the Holy Spirit. At first, Montanism was a revival movement that, though regarded with suspicion, was not distinguished from catholic Christianity. By 179 AD, however, Montanist prophets were openly condemned and their followers excluded from the catholic churches.

As he so often did when adversaries labeled his position, Wesley conceded the point in order to refute their argument. Wesley did in fact defend Montanus consistently; but he did so because of his larger concern for the holiness of the church. In 1750, Wesley read an interesting book by John Lacy (ca. 1664-1737)

---

[786] "An Answer to the Rev. Mr. Dodd," Jackson, *Works*, 11: 453.

[787] Phrygia was located in the southwestern portion of Asia Minor.

[788] Jaroslav Pelikan, *The Emergence of the Catholic Tradition (100-600)*, vol. 1, *The Christian Tradition: A History of the Development of Doctrine* (Chicago: University of Chicago Press, 1971), 100-101. Cf. *Catholic Encyclopedia*, s.v. "Montanists."

entitled *The General Delusion of Christians.* Lacy convinced Wesley of the merit of the Montanist cause.[789] As a result, he came to reconsider the events that led to the condemnation of Montanus. His conviction was strengthened that the loss of "faith and holiness" in the early church had brought about the loss of the "miraculous gifts."[790] Wesley was also aware, of course, that one of the most important writers of the Latin church, Tertullian (ca. 155-220), after producing many significant treatises defending the catholic church, joined the Montanist cause in 207 A.D.[791] As a result, Wesley wrote a brief defense of Montanus which he published in the *Arminian Magazine.*[792]

With the charge of Montanism being leveled so frequently, Wesley's partial acceptance of the label shows more his sagacity as a debater and apologist rather than a lapse in understanding.[793] Wesley, in fact, denied that he was a

---

[789] John Lacy, *The General Delusion of Christians, Touching the Ways of God's Revealing Himself, To, and By The Prophets, Evinc'd From Scripture and Primitive Antiquity* (London: Samuel Keimer, 1713). See especially pp. 242-358 in which Lacy ardently defends Montanus and his followers against the charge of heresy.

[790] Ward and Heitzenrater, *Journals and Diaries, III,* 20: 356-57, esp. n. 57.

[791] "The Mystery of Iniquity," Outler, *Sermons, II,* 2: 461. This is a particularly interesting sermon in that Wesley broadly criticizes the primitive church for moral and spiritual laxity. This criticism is couched in the larger theme of the universal corruption of humankind. Though Wesley was always optimistic about the regenerating power of divine grace to effect real holiness in the lives of individual believers, he never lost sight of the need for a fulfillment and completion of salvation at the coming of Christ. On Tertullian, see Quasten, *Patrology,* 2: 246-340, esp. p. 247: "Except for St. Augustine, Tertullian is the most important and original ecclesiastical author in Latin."

[792] "The Real Character of Montanus," Jackson, *Works,* 11: 485-86. The article appeared originally in the *Arminian Magazine* 8 (Jan. 1785): 35-36. Though the author's name is missing, Jackson apparently believed it belonged to Wesley and so included it. The writer contends that Montanus was not in the same league as other ancient heretics. He had been sound doctrinally on the important issues — e.g., the Incarnation and person of Christ, repentance and faith unto salvation, and the church. He also had been a man of exceptional character and personal holiness. The issue that eventually bought about his condemnation was his over-zealous attempt to reform the church.

[793] The Rector of St. Michael's in London, John Downes (not to be confused with one of Wesley's preachers by the same name) used the Montanist controversy to criticize Wesley and

298

Montanist. Josiah Tucker had compared Methodism to the Montanist sect in his *Brief History of the Principles of Methodism* (1742). Wesley responded the same year with *The Principles of a Methodist,* writing at one point:

> That I may say many things which have been said before, and perhaps by Calvin or Arminius, by Montanus or Barclay, or the Archbishop of Cambrai, is highly probable. But it cannot thence be inferred that I hold 'a *medley* of all their principles — Calvinism, Arminianism, Montanism, Quakerism, Quietism, all thrown together'. There might as well have been added Judaism, Mahometanism, paganism. It would have made the period rounder, and been full as easily *proved* — I mean *asserted*. For other proof is not yet produced.[794]

Montanus' apocalyptic visions and exaggerated notions concerning the Holy Spirit were rejected by the consensual church. Though Wesley taught that believers should expect the Holy Spirit to take an active role in their lives, he cannot accurately be termed a 'Montanist'.

As in the other cases, it was Montanus' character and his effort to renew the church, even though misguided, that Wesley defended. Though he acknowledged the miraculous and extraordinary work of the Holy Spirit in times past, Wesley did not teach that believers ought to seek such signs and wonders. Personal holiness of heart and life was his main concern, which he shared with many inside, and occasionally several who had stood outside, the ancient catholic tradition.

Methodism. Downes' tract, "Methodism Examined and Exposed" (1759) was the occasion of Wesley's "Letter to the Reverend Mr. Downes." Conyers Middleton's "Free Inquiry" (1749) was the occasion of Wesley's "Letter to The Reverend Dr. Conyers Middleton." Campbell notes in "John Wesley and Conyers Middleton on Divine Intervention in History," 40-41 that Middleton's polemic was primarily directed against Roman Catholic interests, but that it also took in groups he regarded as enthusiastic such as the Methodists.

[794]"The Principles of a Methodist," Davies, *The Methodist Societies,* 9: 65.

Appendix 3
"On Clemens Alexandrinus' Description
Of A Perfect Christian"

Here from afar the finish'd height
Of holiness is seen:
But, O! what heavy tracts of toil,
What deserts lie between?

Man for the simple life Divine
What will it cost to break;
Ere pleasure soft and wily pride
No more within him speak?

What lingering anguish must corrode
The root of nature's joy?
What secret shame and dire defeats
The pride of heart destroy?

Learn thou the whole of mortal state
In stillness to sustain;
Nor soothe with false delights of earth
Whom God has doom'd to pain.

Thy mind now multitude of thoughts,
Now stupor shall distress;

300

The venom of each latent vice
Wild images impress.

Yet darkly safe with God thy soul
His arm still onward bears,
Till through each tempest on her face
A peace beneath appears.

'Tis in that peace we see and act
By instincts from above;
With finer taste of wisdom fraught,
And mystic powers of love.

Yet ask not in mere ease and pomp
Of ghostly gifts to shine:
Till death the lownesses of man,
And decent griefs are thine.

Wesley published two versions of the poem, the difference being an alteration of the last line. The original version, which is reproduced above, was first included in a volume published by W. Strahan in 1739 entitled *Hymns and Sacred Poems*. A total of three editions of this volume were printed that year, all by Strahan.[795] A revised version of the poem appeared in Wesley's three volume *A Collection of Moral and Sacred Poems* published in 1744 by Farley.[796] For some unknown reason, Wesley decided to alter the last line in the 1739 version from "And decent griefs are thine," to "And Pitying Griefs are Thine" in the 1744 version.

Authorship of the poem has always been in question. G. Osborn is of the opinion that John Gambold is its author, even though it does not appear among

[795] Editions one and three are identical, the third being largely a resetting of the first. For additional bibliographic information see Baker, *A Union Catalogue of the Publications of John and Charles Wesley*, 28.

[796] *A Collection of Moral and Sacred Poems*, 3: 197.

Gambold's works. [797] Osborn bases his assumption primarily upon the fact that *On Clemens Alexandrinus' Description of a perfect Christian* appears among other works in the Farley edition of *A Collection of Moral and Sacred Poems*. The order of poems is:

> *The Mystery of Life*
> *Epitaph*
> *Upon Listening to the Vibrations of a Clock.*
> *On Clemens Alexandrinus's Description of a perfect Christian*
> *After Considering some of his Friends*
> *Religious Discourse*[798]

Of these, Wesley identifies only *The Mystery of Life* as having been authored by Gambold.[799] The Strahan edition contains all of the above poems, though they are not all grouped together. The following order appears:

> *The Mystery of Life*
> *Epitaph*
> *Virtue (from Herbert)*
> *Upon Listening to the Vibrations of a Clock*
> . . . .[Twenty additional poems]. . . . .
> *On Clemens Alexandrinus's Description of a perfect Christian*
> . . . .[Fifteen more poems]. . . . .
> *After Considering some of his Friends*
> *Religious Discourse*[800]

The poems' authors are not identified. Osborn's argument has merit however, for an examination of the collected works of John Gambold shows that he indeed had

---

[797] G. Osborn, ed., *The Poetical Works of John and Charles Wesley*, 13 vols. (London: Wesleyan-Methodist Conference Office, 1868-72), 1: 34-36. The editor makes his case in a brief footnote. For more on Gambold's relationship with the Wesleys and his eventual secession from the Church of England to join the Moravian Brethren, see Luke Tyerman, *The Oxford Methodists*, 155-200. Tyerman alludes to Gambold's early fascination with the Greek fathers on p. 162. See also John Gambold, *The Works of the Late Rev. John Gambold, A.M.* (Bath: S. Hazard, 1789).

[798] Gambold, *Works*, 3:193-205.

[799] Gambold, *Works*,3:193.

[800] *Hymns and Sacred Poems*, 7-63.

302

authored *Religious Discourse, The Mystery of Life, Upon Listening to the Vibrations of a Clock,* and *Epitaph.*[801] Still, the fact that the *Clemens Alexandrinus* poem does not appear in Gambold's works, nor is it identified by either Gambold or Wesley as to origin, suggests that its true author is still in doubt. Any member of the Oxford Holy Club could have written it, who had been in regular attendance during the years 1732-35 as the church fathers were read and discussed.

---

[801] Wesley shortened the title of Gambold's "Epitaph Upon Himself" to simply "Epitaph."

Bibliography

Allen, Diogenes. *Philosophy for Understanding Theology.* Atlanta, GA: John Knox Press, 1985.

Alston, Leonard. *Stoic and Christian in the Second Century.* London: Longmans, Green and Co., 1906.

Althaus, Paul. *The Theology of Martin Luther.* Translated by Robert C. Schultz. Philadelphia: Fortress Press, 1966.

Andrewes, Lancelot. *The Preces Privatae of Lancelot Andrewes.* Translated by F. E. Brightman. London: Methuen & Co., 1903.

_____. *The Works of Lancelot Andrewes.* 11 vols. Oxford: J. H. Parker, 1841-54.

Aristotle. *The Complete Works of Aristotle.* Edited by Jonathan Barnes. 2 vols. Princeton, NJ: Princeton University Press, 1984.

Baker, Frank. *John Wesley and the Church of England.* Nashville: Abingdon, 1970.

_____, ed. *A Union Catalogue of the Publications of John and Charles Wesley.* 2nd ed. Stone Mountain, GA: George Zimmerman, 1991.

_____. "A Wesley Bibliography: An Introduction to the Publications of John and Charles Wesley, 1981." TD [photocopy]. Vols. *32, 33 of The Bicentennial Edition of the Works of John Wesley.*

Barnard, Leslie W. *John Potter, An Eighteenth Century Archbishop.* Elms Court, G. B.: Arthur H. Stockwell Ltd., 1989.

Bennett, G. V. "Loyalist Oxford and the Revolution," In *The Eighteenth Century,* ed. L. S. Sutherland and L. G. Mitchell. Vol. 5, *The History of the University of Oxford,* ed. T. H. Ashton. Oxford: Clarendon Press, 1986.

Beveridge, William. *The Theological Works of William Beveridge, D.D.* 9 vols. Oxford: John Henry Parker, 1848.

Bigg, Charles. *The Christian Platonists of Alexandria: Eight Lectures Preached Before the University of Oxford in the Year 1866.* Oxford: Clarendon Press, 1886.

Bigger, Charles P. *Participation: A Platonic Inquiry.* Baton Rouge, LA: Louisiana State University Press, 1968

Bowmer, John C. *The Sacrament of the Lord's Supper in Early Methodism.* London: Dacre Press, 1951.

Bradley, D.J.M. "The Transformation of the Stoic Ethic in Clement." *Augustinian Review* 14 (1974): 41-66.

Bray, Gerald, ed. *Documents of the English reformation.* Minneapolis: Fortress Press, 1994.

Broadie, Sarah. *Ethics with Aristotle.* New York: Oxford University Press, 1991.

Bromiley, G. W. *Thomas Cranmer Theologian.* London: Lutterworth Press, 1956.

Brooks, Peter Newman. *Thomas Cranmer's Doctrine of the Eucharist.* 2nd ed. Houndmills, GB: Macmillan Academic and Professional, Ltd., 1965, 1981.

Bundy, David. "Christian Virtue: John Wesley and the Alexandrian Tradition." *Wesleyan Theological Journal* 26, no. 1 (Spring 1991): 139-163.

Calvin, John. *Institutes of the Christian Religion.* Edited by J. T. McNeill. Translated by F. L. Battles. Vols. 20, 21. *The Library of Christian Classics.* Philadelphia: Westminster Press, 1960.

Campbell, Ted A. "John Wesley's Conceptions and Uses of Christian Antiquity." Ph.D. diss., Southern Methodist University, 1984.

_____. *John Wesley and Christian Antiquity: Religious Vision and Cultural Change.* Nashville: Kingswood Books (Abingdon), 1991.

_____. "John Wesley and Conyers Middleton on Divine Intervention in History," *Church History* 55 (March 1986): 39-49.

Cave, William. *Primitive Christianity.* 1677; reprint, Oxford: J. Vincent, 1840.

Carroll, Thomas K., ed. *Selected Works/Jeremy Taylor.* The Classics of Western Spirituality Series. Mahwah, New Jersey: Paulist Press, 1990.

Chadwick, Henry. "Clement of Alexandria." In *The Cambridge History of Later Greek and Early Medieval Philosophy.* Edited by A. H. Armstrong. Cambridge: Cambridge University Press, 1967; reprint, Cambridge University Press, 1980.

_____. *Early Christian Thought and The Classical Tradition.* London: Oxford Clarendon, 1966.

Chemnitz, Martin. *Examination of the Council of Trent.* Translated by Fred Kramer. 2 vols. Springfield, IL: Concordia Seminary, 1964. Reprint. St. Louis: Concordia Publishing House, 1971.

Choufrine, Arkadi. *Gnosis, Theophany, Theosis: studies in Clement of Alexandria's Appropriation of His Background.* Patristic Studies. New York: Peter Lang Publishing, 2002.

Church of England. *Certain Sermons or Homilies Appointed to Be Read in The Time of Queen Elizabeth; and Reprinted By Authority From King James I., A.D. 1623.* 1822; reprint, Philadelphia: Edward C. Biddle, 1844.

Clark, Elizabeth A. *Clement's Use of Aristotle: The Aristotelian Contribution to Clement of Alexandria's Refutation of Gnosticism.* New York and Toronto: Edwin Mellen, 1977.

Clarkson, George E. *The Mysticism of William Law.* American University Studies, Series V Philosophy, vol. 124. New York: Peter Lang, 1992.

Clement of Alexandria. "Christ the Educator." Translated by Simon P. Wood. Vol. 23, *The Fathers of the Church.* New York: Fathers of the Church, 1954.

————. *Clement of Alexandria: Stromateis Books One to Three.* Translated by John Ferguson. Vol. 85, *The Fathers of the Church.* Washington, DC: Catholic University Press of America, 1991.

————. *Clementis Alexandrini opera quae extant, recognita et illustrata per Joannem Potterum.* 2 vols. Venetiis: A. Zatta, 1757.

————. *The Excerpta Ex Theodoto of Clement of Alexandria.* Translated by Robert P. Casey. London: Christophers, 1934.

————. *Exhortation to the Greeks.* Translated by G. W. Butterworth. *Loeb Classical Library Series.* Cambridge: Harvard University Press, 1919; reprint, 1982.

————. "Exhortation to the Heathen." Translated by W. Wilson. Vol. 2, *Ante-Nicene Fathers.* Eds. A. Roberts and J. Donaldson. Reprint. Grand Rapids: Eerdmans, 1989.

————. "Fragments." Translated by W. Wilson. Vol. 2 of *Ante-Nicene Fathers.* Edited by A. Roberts and J. Donaldson. Grand Rapids: Eerdmans, 1989.

————. "The Instructor." Translated by W. Wilson. Vol. 2, *Ante-Nicene Fathers.* Edited by A. Roberts and J. Donaldson. Grand Rapids: Eerdmans, 1989.

————. "The Stromata or Miscellanies." Translated by W. Wilson. Vol. 2, *Ante-Nicene Fathers.* Edited by A. Roberts and J. Donaldson. Grand Rapids: Eerdmans, 1989.

————. "Who is the Rich Man that Shall Be Saved?" Translated by W. Wilson. Vol. 2 of *Ante-Nicene Fathers.* Edited by A. Roberts and J. Donaldson. Grand Rapids: Eerdmans, 1989.

Collins, Kenneth, J. *A Faithful Witness: John Wesley's Homiletical Theology.*
Wilmore, KY: Wesley Heritage Press, 1993.

Cooper, John M. *Reason and Human Good in Aristotle.* Cambridge, MA:
Harvard University Press, 1975.

Coppleston, Frederick. *A History of Philosophy.* Vols. 1-3. Westminster, MD:
The Newman Press, 1962, 1963; reprint, New York: Image Books, 1985.

Council of Trent. *Canons and Decrees of the Council of Trent.* Translated by H. J.
Schroeder. St. Louis: B. Herder Book Co., 1941.

Cranmer, Thomas (1489-1556). *Miscellaneous Writings and Letters of Thomas
Cranmer.* Edited by John Cox. 2 vols. Cambridge: The University Press,
1846

Cross, F. L. and Livingston, E. A., eds., *The Oxford Dictionary of the Christian
Church.* Third edition. Oxford: Oxford University Press, 1997.

Dale, James. "Charles Wesley, The 'Odyssey,' and Clement of Alexandria."
Proceedings of the Wesley Historical Society. 48 (May, 1992): 150-52.

Davies, Horton. *Worship and Theology in England.* 5 vols. Princeton: Princeton
University Press, 1965-70.

Davis, Leo Donald. *The First Seven Ecumenical Councils.* Theology and Life
Series No. 21. Collegeville, MN: The Liturgical Press, 1983.

De Faye, Eugéne. *Clement d'Alexandrie.* 2nd ed. Paris: Ernest Leroux, 1906.

Dickens, A. G. *The English reformation.* 2nd ed. London: B. T. Batsford, Ltd.,
1989.

Eusebius of Caesarea. *Eusebius: The History of the Church from Christ to
Constantine.* Translated by G.A. Williamson. Baltimore: Penguin Books
Inc., 1965; reprint, Minneapolis: Augsburg Publishing House, 1975.

Flew, R. Newton. *The Idea of Perfection in Christian Theology.* London: H.
Milford, Oxford University Press, 1934; reprint, New York: Humanities
Press, 1968.

Ferguson, John. *Clement of Alexandria.* New York: Twayne, 1974.

Ford, David C. "Saint Makarios of Egypt and John Wesley: Variations on the
Theme of Sanctification." *Greek Orthodox Theological Review* 33, no. 3
(1988): 285-312.

Forster, Charles, ed. *Thirty Years Correspondence between John Jebb and Alexander
Knox.* Second edition. 2 vols. London: Duncan and Cochran, 1836.

Fraser, P. M. *Ptolemaic Alexandria.* 2 vols. London: Oxford University Press,
1972.

Gambold, John. *The Works of the Late Rev. John Gambold, A.M.* Bath: S. Hazard, 1789.

Greenslade, S. L. *The English reformation and the Fathers of the Church.* Oxford: Clarendon, 1960.

Green, V. H. H. *The Young Mr. Wesley.* London: E. Arnold, 1961; reprint, London: Wyvern, 1963.

Haaugaard, William P. "From the reformation to the Eighteenth Century." *The Study of Anglicanism.* Edited by Stephen Sykes and John Booty. London: SPCK, 1988.

_____. "Renaissance Patristic Scholarship and Theology in Sixteenth-Century England." *Sixteenth Century Journal* 10 (1979): 37-60.

Hefele, K. J., *A History of the Christian Councils,* Translated by W. Clark, H. Oxenham, E. H. Plumptre. 4 vols. Edinburgh: T&T Clark, 1872-95.

Herbermann, C. G. *et al.,* eds. *The Catholic Encyclopedia.* New York: Robert Appleton Co., 1907-1912.

Heitzenrater, Richard P., ed. *Diary of an Oxford Methodist, Benjamin Ingham.* Durham, NC: Duke University Press, 1985.

_____. *The Elusive Mr. Wesley: John Wesley His Own Biographer.* 2 vols. Nashville: Abingdon, 1984.

_____. "John Wesley and the Oxford Methodists, 1725-35." Ph.D. diss., Duke University, 1972.

Hill, W. Speed, ed. *Studies in Richard Hooker: Essays Preliminary to An Edition of His Works.* Cleveland: The Press of Case Western Reserve University, 1972.

Hooker, Richard. *The Works of that Learned and Judicious Divine Mr. Richard Hooker: With An Account of His Life and Death by Isaac Walton.* Edited by John Keble. Oxford: University Press, 1836.

Horneck, Anthony. *The Happy Ascketick: Or, The Best Exercise, To Which is Added, A Letter to a Person of Quality, Concerning the Holy Lives of the Primitive Christians.* London: T. N. for Henry Mortlock and Mark Pardoe, 1681.

Hort, F. J A. and Mayor, Joseph B. *Clement of Alexandria: Miscellanies Book VII, The Greek Text with Introduction, Translation, Notes, Dissertations and Indices.* London: Macmillan, 1902.

Hughes, H. Trevor. *The Piety of Jeremy Taylor.* New York: Macmillan & Co. Ltd., 1960.

Hunter, Frederick. *John Wesley and the Coming Comprehensive Church.* London: Epworth Press, 1968.

Hutchinson, D. S. *The Virtues of Aristotle.* London: Routledge & Kegan Paul, 1986.

Jaeger, Werner. *Two Rediscovered Works of Ancient Christian Literature: Gregory of Nyssa and Macarius.* Leiden: E.J. Brill, 1954.

Jarboe, Betty M. *John and Charles Wesley: A Bibliography.* ATLA Bibliography Series, No. 22. Metuchen, NJ: American Theological Library Association and Scarecrow Press, 1987.

Jewel, John. *The Works of John Jewel, Bishop of Salisbury.* Edited by John Ayre. 4 vols. Cambridge: The University Press, 1845.

Johnson, Elizabeth. *An Account of Mrs. Elizabeth Johnson.* London: W. Pine and Son, [1799].

Jones, J., trans. *A Discourse Concerning The Salvation of Rich Men.* London: Phillip Guillim, 1711.

Kaye, John. *Some Account of the Writings and Opinions of Clement of Alexandria.* London: Rivington, 1835.

Knox, Alexander. *Remains of Alexander Knox, Esq.* 3rd ed. 4 vols. London: Duncan and Malcolm, 1844.

Lacy, John. *The General Delusion of Christians, Touching the Ways of God's Revealing Himself, To, and By The Prophets, Evinc'd From Scripture and Primitive Antiquity.* London: Samuel Keimer, 1713.

Lathbury, Thomas. *A History of the Nonjurors: Their Controversies and Writings.* London: W. Pickering, 1845.

Law, William. *The Works of the Reverend William Law, M.A.* Brockenhurst, Hampshire: G. Moreton, 1892-93.

Liddell, Henry George. *A Lexicon Abridged from Liddell and Scott's Greek-English Lexicon* 1871; reprint, Oxford: Clarendon Press, 1983.

Lilla, Salvatore R. C. *Clement of Alexandria.* Oxford Theological Monographs. London: Oxford, 1971.

Lindström, Harald. *Wesley and Sanctification.* London: Epworth, 1946.

Lodge, Rupert C. *Plato's Theory of Ethics.* New York: Harcourt, Brace and Co., 1928.

Lonergan, Bernard. *Method in Theology.* Toronto: University of Toronto Press, 1971.

Lossky, Nicholas. *Lancelot Andrewes The Preacher (1555-1626): The Origins of the Mystical Theology of the Church of England.* Translated by Andrew Louth. Oxford: Clarendon Press, 1991.

Maddox, Randy. "John Wesley and Eastern Orthodoxy: Influences, Convergences, and Differences." *Asbury Theological Journal,* 45, no. 2 (Fall 1990): 29-53.

Mandelbaum, Maurice. *The Problem of Historical Knowledge.* New York: Liveright, 1938.

McAdoo, H. R. *The Eucharistic Theology of Jeremy Taylor Today.* Norwich: The Canterbury Press Norwich, 1988

_____. *The Spirit of Anglicanism.* New York: Charles Scriber's Sons, 1965.

McIntosh, Lawrence D. "The Nature and Design of Christianity in John Wesley's Early Theology: A Study in the Relationship of Love and Faith." Ph.D. diss., Drew University, 1966.

Merritt, John G. "Dialogue Within a Tradition: John Wesley and Gregory of Nyssa Discuss Christian Perfection." *Wesleyan Theological Journal* 22, no. 2 (Fall 1987): 92-116.

Migne, J. P. *Patrologiae cursus completus. . . Series Graeca.* 161 vols. Paris: Migne, 1857-66.

Molland, Einar. *The Conception of the Gospel in The Alexandrian Theology.* Oslo: I Kommissjon Hos Jacob Dybwad, 1938.

Newman, John Henry. *Essay on the Development of Christian Doctrine.* 1878; reprint, Notre Dame: Notre Dame Press, 1989.

Osborn, E. F. *The Philosophy of Clement of Alexandria.* London: Cambridge University Press, 1957.

Osborn, G., ed. *The Poetical Works of John and Charles Wesley.* 13 vols. London, Wesleyan-Methodist Conference Office, 1868-72.

Outler, Albert C., ed. *John Wesley.* New York: Oxford, 1964.

_____. *Theology in the Wesleyan Spirit.* Nashville: Discipleship Resources, 1975.

_____. *The Wesleyan Theological Heritage.* Edited by Thomas C. Oden and Leicester R. Longden. Grand Rapids: Zondervan, 1991.

Owen, Trevor A. *Lancelot Andrewes.* Volume 325, *Twayne English Authors Series.* Boston: Twayne Publishers, 1981

310

Patrick, John. *The Troall Lecture for 1899-1900: Clement of Alexandria.* Edinburgh and London: William Blackwood, 1914.

Pearson, John. *An Exposition of the Creed.* 1659; reprint, London: J.F. Dove, 1832.

————. *The Minor Theological Works of John Pearson, D.D.* 2 vols. Oxford: The University Press, 1844.

Piette, Maxim. *John Wesley in the Evolution of Protestantism.* Translated by J. B. Howard. New York: Sheed & Ward, 1937.

Potter, John. *The Theological Works of the Most Reverend Dr. John Potter, Late Lord Archbishop of Canterbury, Containing His Sermons, Charges, Discourse of Church Government and Divinity Lectures.* 3. vols. Oxford: Printed at the Theatre, 1753, 54.

Procter, Everett. *Christian Controversy in Alexandria: Clement's Polemic Against the Basilideans and Valentinians.* American University Studies. Series VII, Theology and Religion. Vol. 172. New York: Peter Lang Publishing, Inc., 1995.

Quarrie, P. "The Christ Church Collections Books." In *The Eighteenth Century,* ed. L. S. Sutherland and L. G. Mitchell. Vol. 5, *The History of the University of Oxford,* ed. T. H. Ashton. Oxford: Clarendon Press, 1986.

Quasten, Johannes. *Patrology.* 4 vols. Westminster, MD: Christian Classics, 1950, 86.

Rack, Henry D. *Reasonable Enthusiast.* Philadelphia: Trinity Press International, 1989.

Reidy, Maurice F. *Bishop Lancelot Andrewes Jacobean Court Preacher.* Chicago: Loyola University Press, 1955.

Ridley, Jasper *Thomas Cranmer.* Oxford: Clarendon Press, 1962.

Rowe, Kenneth E., ed. *The Place of Wesley in the Christian Tradition: Essays Delivered at Drew University in Celebration of the Commencement of the Publication of the Oxford Edition of the Works of John Wesley.* Metuchen, NJ: Scarecrow Press, 1976.

Rudolph, Kurt. *Gnosis: The Nature and History of Gnosticism.* Translated by P. W. Coxon and K. H. Kuhn. Edited by R. M. Wilson. San Francisco: Harper Collins, 1983, 1987.

Rupp, Gordon. *Religion in England 1688-1791.* Oxford: Clarendon, 1986.

————. *Studies in the Making of The English Protestant Tradition.* London: Cambridge University Press, 1966.

Sayre, Kenneth M. *Plato's Late Ontology: A Riddle Resolved*. Princeton, NJ: Princeton University Press, 1983.

Schaff, Philip, ed. *A Select Library of Nicene and Post-Nicene Fathers*. First Series. Buffalo: n.p., 1886-90; reprint, Grand Rapids: Eerdmans, 1952, 1989.

Schroeder, H.J., trans. *Canons and Decrees of The Council of Trent*. St. Louis, MO: B. Herder, 1941. Reprint, Rockford, IL: Tan Books, 1978.

Seeburg, Reinhold. *Text-Book of the History of Doctrines*. Translated by Charles E. Hay. 2 volumes. Grand Rapids: Baker Book House, 1958.

Sherman, Nancy. *The Fabric of Character: Aristotle's Theory of Virtue*. Oxford, Clarendon, 1989.

Simon, John S. *John Wesley and the Religious Societies*. London: Epworth, 1921.

Simonetti, Manlio. *Biblical Interpretation in the Early Church*. Translated by J. A. Hughes. Edited by A Berquist and M. Bockmuehl. Edinburgh: T&T Clark, 1994.

Smith, Nigel. *Perfection Proclaimed: Language and Literature in English Radical Religion, 1640-1660*. Oxford: Clarendon, 1989.

Smyth, C. H. *Cranmer and the reformation Under Edward VI*. London: SPCK, 1973.

Sommerville, C. John. *Popular Religion in Restoration England*. Gainesville: University Presses of Florida, 1977.

Southey, Robert. *The Life of Wesley and the Rise and Progress of Methodism*. Edited by M. Fitzgerald. 2 vols. London: Longman, Brown, Green, and Longmans, 1846; reprint, London: Oxford University Press, H. Milford, 1925.

Stählin, Otto. *Clemens Alexandrinus erter Band: Protrepicus und Paedagogus*. 3rd ed. Vol. 12, *Die Griechischen Christlichen Schriftstellar der Ersten Drei Jahrhunderte*. Berlin: Akademie-Verlag, 1972.

_____. *Clemens Alexandrinus zweiter Band: Stromata Buch I-VI*. 4th ed. Vol. 15, *Die Griechischen Christlichen Schriftstellar der Ersten Drei Jahrhunderte*. Berlin: Akademie-Verlag, 1985.

_____. *Clements Alexandrinus dritter Band: Stromata Buch VII und VIII: Excerpta ex Theodoto; Eclogue Propheticae; Quis dives salvetur; Frangmente*. 2nd ed. Vol. 17, *Die Griechischen Christlichen Schriftstellar der Ersten Drei Jahrhunderte*. Berlin: Akademie-Verlag, 1970.

Stanwood, P. G., ed. *Jeremy Taylor: Holy Living and Holy Dying*. 2 vols. Oxford: Clarendon, 1989.

Stephen, L. and Lee, S. *The Dictionary of National Biography.* 66 vols. London: Oxford University Press, 1917.

Stewart, J. A. *Plato's Doctrine of Ideas.* New York: Russell & Russell, Inc., 1964.

Sykes, Stephen and Booty, John, eds. *The Study of Anglicanism.* London: SPCK, 1988.

Taylor, Jeremy. *The Whole Works of the Right Rev. Jeremy Taylor, D.D.* Edited by Reginald Heber. 15 vols. London: C. and J. Rivington *et al.*, 1828

Todd, John M. *John Wesley and the Catholic Church.* London: Hodder and Stoughton, 1958.

Tollington, R. B. *Clement of Alexandria: A Study in Christian Liberalism.* 2 vols. London: Williams and Norgate, 1914.

Tripp, David. "Clement of Alexandria and the Wesley Brothers." *Proceedings of the Wesley Historical Society.* 49 (Feb. 1994): 113-16.

Turner, C. H. "A Primitive Edition of the Apostolic Constitutions and Canons: An Early List of Apostles and Disciples." *Journal of Theological Studies.* 15 (1914): 53-65.

_____. "Notes on the Apostolic Constitutions." *Journal of Theological Studies.* 16 (1915): 54-61

_____. "Notes on the Apostolic Constitutions," *Journal of Theological Studies.* 21 (1920): 160-68;

_____. "Notes on the Apostolic Constitutions," *Journal of Theological Studies.* 31 (1930): 128-41.

Tyerman, Luke. *Life and Times of the Rev. John Wesley, Founder of the Methodists.* 3 vols. London: Hodder and Stoughton, 1871.

_____. *Life and Times of the Rev. Samuel Wesley, M.A., Rector of Epworth, and Father of the Revs. John and Charles Wesley, the Founders of the Methodists.* London: Simpkin, 1866.

_____. *The Oxford Methodists.* New York: Harper & Brothers, Publishers, 1873.

Urlin, R. Denny. *The Churchman's Life of Wesley.* London: S.P.C.K., 1880.

_____. *Father Reeece: The Old Methodist Minister, Twice President of the Conference.* London: Elliot Stock, 1901.

_____. *John Wesley's Place in Church History.* London: Rivington, 1870.

Van den Hoek, Annewies. *Clement of Alexandria and His Use of Philo in the Stromateis.* Leiden: E. J. Brill, 1988.

Wagner, Walter H. *After the Apostles: Christianity in the Second Century.* Minneapolis, MN: Fortress Press, 1994.

_____. "The Paideia Motif in the Theology of Clement of Alexandria." Ph.D. diss., Drew University, 1968.

Wakefield, Gordon S. "La littérature du Désert chez John Wesley." *Irenikon* 51, no. 2 (1978): 155-70.

Weidner, H. D. Introduction to *The Via Media of the Anglican Church,* by John Henry Newman. Oxford: Clarendon Press, 1990.

Welchman, Edward. *Articuli Eccesiae Anglicanae Textibus Sacrae Scripturae et Patrum Primaevorum Testimoniis Confirmati, Brevibusque Notis Illustrati.* 1713; reprint, London: F. C. & J. Rivington and G. & W. B. Whittaker, 1819.

_____. *The Thirty-Nine Articles of the Church of England Illustrated with Notes, and Confirmed by Texts of The Holy Scripture and Testimonies of the Primitive Fathers.* 8th edition. 1713 reprint, London: J. F. and C. Rivington, 1790.

Welsby, Paul A. *Lancelot Andrewes 1555-1626.* London: SPCK, 1958.

Wesley, John. *The Bicentennial Edition of the Works of John Wesley.* Edited by Frank Baker. Nashville: Abingdon, 1984 ff.

_____. *A Christian Library.* 30 vols. Bristol: Farley, 1749-55; reprint, London: T. Blanshard, 1819.

_____. *A Collection of Moral and Sacred Poems from the Most Celebrated English Authors.* 3. vols. Bristol: Farley, 1744.

_____. *The Doctrine of Salvation, Faith, and Good Works.* 4th ed. London: W. Strahan, 1741.

_____. *Explanatory Notes Upon the New Testament.* 1755; reprint, Grand Rapids: Baker, 1981.

_____. *Explanatory Notes Upon the Old Testament.* 1765; reprint, Salem, OH: Schmul, 1975.

_____. *Hymns and Sacred Poems.* 3rd. ed. London: W. Strahan, 1739.

_____. *The Journal of the Rev. John Wesley, A.M.* Edited by Nehemiah Curnock. 8 vols. London: Epworth, 1938.

_____. *The Letters of the Rev. John Wesley.* Edited by John Telford. 8 vols. London: Epworth, 1931.

_____. *The Works of John Wesley*. Edited by Thomas Jackson. 3rd edition. 14 vols. 1829-31; reprint, Grand Rapids: Baker, 1986.

Wesley, John and Charles. *Hymns and Sacred Poems*. London: W. Strahan, 1739.

Winter, Friedrich Julius. *Die Ethik Des Clemens von Alexandrien*. Leipzig: Dörffling und Franke, 1882.

Wolfson, Harry Austryn. *Faith, Trinity, Incarnation*. Vol. 1, *The Philosophy of the Church Fathers*. Cambridge, MA: Harvard University Press, 1970.

Wyrwa, Dietmar. _Die Christlicke Platonaneignung in den Stromateis des Clemens von Alexandrien. Berlin: Walter de Gruyter, 1983.

Index

318

Newman, John Henry, 1, 2, 8, 27, 103, 140, 288, 289, 290, 291, 292, 293, 294, 295, 296, 297, 300, 301, 317, 319, 323, 326

Nicaea (Council of, Creed of), 3, 51, 117, 196

Nonjurors, 63

Notes on Justification. See Cranmer, Thomas

Novatian, 308

Novatianism, 68, 307

On Clemems Alexandrinus' Description of a Perfect Christian, 72

Origen, 11, 14, 15, 51, 54, 56, 109, 111, 118

Outler, Albert, 45, 64, 65, 66, 67, 110

Paedagogos, 130

Pantaenus, 119, 122

pathos, 179, 181, 182, 184, 190, 191, 205

Patrick, Simon,, 4, 75

Pawson, John, 61

Pearse, Edward, 74

Pearson, John, 2, 33, 35, 56, 57

Pelagius, Pelagianism, 68, 305, 306

Penn, William, 75

perfection, v, 57, 64, 66, 71, 75, 76, 77, 79, 80, 82, 87, 88, 92, 96, 97, 98, 99, 100, 101, 102, 103, 104, 105, 106, 112, 114, 115, 136, 137, 141, 144, 145, 146, 147, 149, 163, 164, 165, 166, 167, 171, 176, 185, 187, 200, 201, 205, 206, 209, 213, 222, 225, 245, 253, 255, 256, 257, 258, 260, 261, 262, 263, 264, 265, 266, 268, 269, 270, 273, 274, 275, 276, 294, 295, 300, 305, 320, 322, 324

Peripatetics, 126

Philo, 124

phobos, 202

pistis, 148, 157

Plato, 88, 89, 124, 125, 126, 169, 170, 192, 193, 195, 196, 207, 209, 210, 260, 280, 281, 322, 324, 325

pneumatikoi, 145

Polycarp, 44, 45

Potter, John, 37, 38, 226, 227, 228, 229, 230, 231, 299

Preces Privatae, 24, 25, 316

primitive church, 1, 4, 6, 14, 15, 32, 36, 44, 50, 52, 61, 64, 67, 68, 99, 111, 309

prolepsis, 142, 144, 146, 148

Protrepticos, 129, 130

psychikoi, 145

Ptolemies, 120

　　Euergetes, 121

　　Philadelphus, 121

Quis Dives Salvetur?, 137

Radical Reformers, 90

Reece, Rev. Richard, 61

regeneration, v, 152, 155, 225, 255, 258, 269, 270, 271, 272, 273, 274, 275, 276, 290, 295, 299

Roman Christianity/Church, 2, 4, 7, 10, 11, 13, 16, 20, 26, 30, 35, 37, 42, 44, 65, 67, 74, 108, 123, 225, 257, 273, 288, 308

sanctification, 55, 57, 64, 66, 67, 72, 76, 77, 78, 80, 89, 91, 93, 102, 156, 160, 162, 172, 175, 182, 185, 187, 200, 202, 211, 237, 256, 265, 270, 271, 273, 274, 276, 290, 296

TEXTS AND STUDIES IN RELIGION

88a. William of Tyre, **A Middle English Chronicle of the First Crusade: The Caxton** *Eracles*: **Volume I**: edited and with an Introduction by Dana Cushing

88b. William of Tyre, **A Middle English Chronicle of the First Crusade: The Caxton** *Eracles*: **Volume II**: edited and with an Introduction by Dana Cushing

89. Peter Russell Jones, **The Epistle of Jude as Expounded by the Fathers–Clement of Alexandria, Didymus of Alexandria, the** *Scholia* **of Cramer's Catena, Pseudo-Oecumenius, and Bede**

90. Viola Coloman and Frederick Van Fleteren (eds.), **Saint Anselm–A Thinker for Yesterday and Today: Anselm's Thought Viewed by Our Contemporaries: Proceedings of the International Anselm Conference Centre National de Recherche Scientifique Paris: Under Haut Patronage of Henri Cardinal de Lubac**

91. John R. Fortin (ed.), **Saint Anselm–His Origins and Influence**

92. Brian Møller Jensen, **Tropes and Sequences in the Liturgy of the Church in Piacenza in the Twelfth Century: An Analysis and an Edition of the Texts**

93. Richard Kyle, **The Ministry of John Knox–Pastor, Preacher, and Prophet**

94. Theodor Damian, **Theological and Spiritual Dimensions of Icons According to St. Theodore of Studion**

95a. Masudul Alam Choudhury, **Explaining the Qur'an–A Socio-Scientific Inquiry, Book 1**

95b. Masudul Alam Choudhury, **Explaining the Qur'an–A Socio-Scientific Inquiry, Book 1**

96. Samuel J. Rogal, **An Analysis of Various Versions of A.M. Toplady's** *Rock of Ages, Cleft for Me* **(1774-2001)**

97. Kåre Fuglseth, **A Comparison of Greek Words in Philo and the New Testament**

98. Mark F. Rooker, **Studies in Hebrew Language, Intertextuality, and Theology**

99. Caroline J. Nolan, **A Critical Appraisal of the Origin and Nature of the Institution of the Monarchy in Israel in the Light of Eric Voegelin's Theory of Symbolic Forms**

100. C. George Fry and Joel R. Kurz, **Berthold von Schenk (1895-1974)–Pioneer of Lutheran Liturgical Renewal**

101. LindaSue Francisca Schlee, **A Meditative Study of the Mysticism of the Waters in** *El castillo interior* **of Santa Teresa de Jesús and** *El cántico espiritual* **of San Juan de la Cruz**

102. Neil D. Anderson, **A Definitive Study of Evidence Concerning John Wesley's Appropriation of the Thought of Clement of Alexandria**

103. David B. Griffiths, **Buddhist Discursive Formations–Keywords, Emotions, Ethics**

104. Paul Berry, **The Latin Language and Christianity**

105. **A Translation of Abbot Leontios' Life of Saint Gregory, Bishop of Agrigento**, commentary and translation by John R.C. Martyn

106. Michael Parsons, **Luther and Calvin on Old Testament Narratives: Reformation Thought and Narrative Text**

107. Daniel G. Di Domizio, **Religion in Secularized Culture–The Czech Experience**